PRENTICE HALL

PRODUCT TESTING ACTIVITIES by *Consumer Reports*

TEACHING GUIDE

Charlotte Baecher
Director
Consumers Union Education Division

Anita Holmes
Editor
Consumers Union Education Division

Geoffrey Martin, Ph.D.
Project Leader
Consumers Union Technical Department

Consumers Union, publisher of *Consumer Reports* and *Zillions*, is a nonprofit organization established in 1936 to provide consumers with information and advice on goods, services, health, and personal finance; and it initiates and cooperates with individual and group efforts to maintain and enhance the quality of life for consumers.

Prentice Hall
Product Testing Activities
by Consumer Reports

Teaching Guide

ISBN 0-13-988122-0

10 9 8 7 6 5 4 3   96 95 94 93

Prentice Hall
A Division of Simon & Schuster
Englewood Cliffs, New Jersey

TABLE OF CONTENTS

Your students are surrounded by science and math whenever they use a product, see an ad, or step into a store. This program helps you make those lessons come alive in the classroom.

Consumers Union is a nonprofit organization that has been testing products and publishing *Consumer Reports* for more than 50 years. Over the last decade, it has asked youngsters to help test products for *Zillions, Consumer Reports for Kids.* The product testing activities in this program have grown from a desire to help youngsters develop a healthy skepticism about the commercial world of consumer goods and to use product testing as a doorway to the remarkable world of technology and science.

HOW TO APPROACH THIS PROGRAM

Product testing is exploratory. There are no "right answers" for students to arrive at. What's important is sound scientific *process*. The introduction in the Student Databook emphasizes this, giving students this message: "Nobody knows which product is best *before* it's tested. Don't think about right answers — think about the *right way to test*."

Product testing also involves hands-on encounters with many science concepts. Testing antacids (or shampoos or yogurt) teaches about acids and bases. Testing sports drinks makes ions, salts, even the body's digestive and metabolic processes, a little clearer. Test bubble gum and you teach solubility.

In this program, science concepts are clues to help conduct tests, not words to memorize. The first page of each unit teaching guide identifies the concepts the unit's testing activities help develop.

A key to successful classroom use of these testing activities is emphasizing their practical application in students' lives. Sharing test findings can help family members and friends choose the best product, get the most for their money, or have a better understanding of how everyday products work. You're also encouraged to send test results to *Consumer Reports* (a form is provided on the last page of each unit in this guide). Your class's data may contribute to ratings of products in *Zillions.*

HOW TO USE THIS PROGRAM

1. Select test samples of interest.

A typical unit requires three or four samples of a product for testing. In some units, especially paper goods and foods, new test samples are required. In others, used or partially used samples may be brought from home (jeans, food wraps, glues, nail enamel, shampoo, etc.).

A unit's success may depend on how familiar the test samples are. Time taken to poll students' brand preferences will probably pay off in heightened student interest. Where possible, include advertised brands (are their claims true?) and store brands (how do they measure up?).

2. Code the test samples yourself.

Students should do "blind" tests — they shouldn't know the brand names of the test samples until the testing is completed. (This helps reduce the impact brand-name biases could have on testers' judgments of the products.) If you assign codes for the class (rather than having each group assign its own codes), all small groups will test identically coded products. That will make compilation of class data much easier.

3. Divide the class into small groups.

Product testing is a cooperative process. At *Consumer Reports,* several technicians work together to test products, under the direction of a project

leader. The Student Databooks are designed for up to four students to use together (although some teachers may prefer to have each person in the group fill in his or her own Databook). Each group might also choose a "leader" to coordinate the testing and recording of data. Cooperative learning is at the heart of these activities — testers need to discuss their observations and hypotheses, solve problems, and make plans together.

4. Prepare students to use a number-line scoring system.

The introduction to the Student Databook takes students through the product testing process, including use of number lines for scoring. Review that section and cover these points:

- *Number lines help convert data to numerical scores.* Number lines, followed immediately by a scoring bar (see below), appear in many of the testing activities. In some cases, students will fill in one (or both) ends of the number line with data from their test (e.g., longest and shortest length).

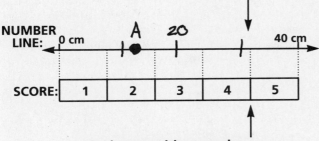

1. Plot test data here.

NUMBER LINE: 0 cm   A   20   40 cm

SCORE: | 1 | 2 | 3 | 4 | 5 |

2. Line up with scores here.
(If A were 12 cm, its score would be 2, for example)

- *The better the product, the higher its score should be.* Scoring for Databook activities is based on a scale of **1** (poor or worst) to **5** (excellent or best). Caution students against confusing rank-order numbers with scores — giving the top-performing products a score of 1 (instead of 5) would throw off the ratings.

5. Discuss the idea of "weighting" scores.

Scores for more important tests should count for more (just like final exams, which count for more than a quiz). When testing is done, students have to decide which tests were more important, give tests an Importance Factor, then multiply scores by those factors to determine weighted scores. Students may be amazed at how weighting scores affects product rankings. Science is more than data: A scientist looks at the whole picture and uses good judgment, too!

6. Choose testing activities to fit into your curriculum.

The testing activities in this program are a good introduction to data collection and analysis, experimental controls, variables, and general scientific method. As such they would be useful when laboratory methods are being taught, with the whole class doing the same testing activities or different groups doing different ones.

Various units also illustrate and deepen a variety of topics in the science textbook (e.g., *Testing Food Wraps* with phase changes and evaporation). The Science Concept Index on page 151 correlates each product testing activity with the concepts it helps teach.

7. Encourage independent testing by the small groups.

The Databooks are designed to be used by up to four students working on their own. Even at the risk of making errors, students should be encouraged to puzzle through and work things out for themselves. This will help them gain confidence in their ability to reason on their own and encourage them to learn from one another. A brief class discussion before each test can enhance this process.

8. Follow each activity's testing sequence.

Each activity in the Student Databooks starts out with step-by-step tests and ends up with tests that

CARTOON BALLOONS LIKE THIS APPEAR THROUGHOUT THE STUDENT DATABOOKS TO ENCOURAGE OPEN-ENDED THINKING. WHAT DO YOU THINK IS MORE IMPORTANT — WHETHER STUDENTS' RESPONSES ARE WHAT YOU EXPECT, OR HOW THEY ARRIVED AT THEIR ANSWER? WRITE YOUR HYPOTHESIS HERE.

_____

_____

_____

students design. Earlier tests help students better understand the product and the testing process. Students may have difficulty with later tests if they skip the earlier ones. (Pre-tests illustrate a product's properties but don't lead to comparative evaluations.)

9. Focus on students' data.

The teaching guide describes possible testing outcomes to aid planning and discussion. But these aren't "right answers" that students should arrive at. Focus on what students learned and whether their testing process was sound. Treating students' data as the central focus enhances learning and communicates respect for and confidence in their work.

10. Take advantage of home-extension opportunities.

The very nature of these testing activities invites active family participation. Several student-designed tests can be done as home assignments. In addition, families can be polled to help determine everything from test sample selection to weighting tests. Test conclusions can be presented as flyers, checklists, etc. for use by family members.

11. Treat data interpretation as an exploration.

The problem-solving, "no-right-answer" nature of science really comes to life when small groups compare their data, discover that every group didn't get the exact same data, and learn that no one is "right" or "wrong." Use this to initiate a problem-solving process to uncover reasons for variation and ways to combine class data to arrive at meaningful conclusions. Data interpretation activities are a hands-on way of teaching basic statistics. Variation, sampling, measurement error, means and medians are all part of the process of deciding how to interpret test data.

TROUBLE-SHOOTING TIPS

Not enough time? Class-time estimates are given for each product test. Generally, a unit will take 5 to 8 class periods. Since each unit is designed to develop incrementally, the units are best cut from the end if time is short. Other options:

- Do just the first one or two tests in class, and assign the others as homework. (Form small groups on the basis of who'll have the opportunity to work together after school.)
- Eliminate the student-designed tests in the later pages of each Databook.
- Carry out the first two or three tests as an introduction to the topic, and have students express conclusions in writing.
- Team-teach. Some testing activities may integrate with other courses (like mathematics, language arts), and those teachers may cover parts of the activities during their class time.

Not enough sets of equipment for the whole class? Tests require a minimal amount of equipment, so even classes that aren't equipped with labs can do the tests. But some equipment may be hard to get in quantity for several small groups (e.g., a pan balance or thermometers). Here are some alternatives:

- Split scheduling. Assemble the materials for all the chosen units at the beginning of the term and schedule one group at a time on each unit. This spreads out the load on equipment and test samples.
- Diversify: Do the first one or two tests of a unit as a class, then divide the class into small groups, with each group assigned to do one of the remaining tests.

A FINAL WORD

We hope these activities give you and your students a taste of the excitement and satisfaction that we experience in our product testing labs here at Consumers Union. We're looking forward to hearing from you!

PRENTICE HALL

PRODUCT TESTING ACTIVITIES by Consumer Reports

TESTING ANTACIDS

Students are not asked to taste, chew, or swallow any antacids during this test.

Testing Antacids helps students discover the science and technology governing the performance of antacids: why tablets are chewed (**reaction rates**); how they work (**acids and bases, pH indicators**); why acid is continually added during testing (**how the stomach works, titration**); how antacids keep the acid level steady (**buffers**); and how they "use up" acid (**neutralization, equivalence point**). Students will also learn about test design, controlling variables, and recording and analyzing data. Collecting, analyzing, and interpreting data help teach time calculations, rates of change, graphing, and statistics.

Tests are designed for groups of four. Students work together to conduct and plan tests, analyze data, solve problems, and develop a scientific rating of antacids. The chart below links the tests students will perform with the science skills and concepts those testing activities will help teach.

CURRICULUM SKILLS AND CONCEPTS

Test and Student Databook Page	Highlighted Skills	Science Concepts
Getting Started p. 1	Controlling Variables, Blind Testing	Principles of Testing
To Chew or Not to Chew, p. 2	Observation, Measuring pH	Acids and Bases, Reaction Rates
The Speediest Antacid, p. 3	Measuring pH, Timed Experiments, Controlling Variables	pH Indicators, Digestion
The Steady-pH Test p. 4	Measuring pH, Recording Data, Graphing, Titrating	Digestive System, Bases, Buffers
Total Acid Neutralized, p. 6	Data Analysis, Number Lines	Neutralization, Equivalence Point
Baking Soda Test p. 7	Designing a Test, Comparing Data	Test Design, Buffers, Reaction Rates
Interpret Your Test Data, p. 8	Critical Thinking, Forming Conclusions	Weighted Scores, Statistics

MATERIALS NEEDED for each small group:

❑ **Test samples:** 3 antacids, all the same strength (regular or extra strength), and baking soda. It's easier if just tablets are tested, but liquids could be substituted. (5 tablets/teaspoons of each sample should suffice for each small group.)

❑ **For pre-planned tests:** Safety goggles for each tester, 750 mL of 0.1 N HCl solution, 100-mL graduated cylinder, stirring rods, timer, spoon, two 250-mL beakers, pH paper, colored pencils.

CLASS-TIME REQUIREMENTS:

❑ To prepare for testing: 1 class period
❑ For Pre-test and Test 1: 1 class period
❑ For Tests 2 and 3: 20 minutes per test sample (3 antacids should be tested simultaneously)
❑ For Test 4: 1 class period
❑ For data interpretation: 1 class period

GETTING STARTED

1. Prepare test samples in advance.
Antacid tablets should be kept in covered plastic containers coded A to C for students to take as needed. Save the packages and labels for examination by students after testing is concluded.

2. Distribute Student Databooks, one to each group.

DISCUSS:

1. One thing that will vary in these tests is the antacids. But other things (like how finely they're crushed and how vigorously they're stirred) shouldn't vary. Why not? *(Because differences in test results could be due to the uncontrolled variables instead of the antacids.)*

2. Discuss responses to the balloon. Can ads affect judgments subconsciously? Does blind-coding test samples control this variable? What other variables should be controlled?

HAVE YOU SEEN ANTACID COMMERCIALS? COULD THEY AFFECT THE WAY YOU JUDGE THESE TESTS? IF SO, HOW COULD YOU CONTROL THIS VARIABLE?
Ad claims can affect your opinion of a product without your being aware of it. Identifying test samples by code rather than brand name can keep ads from affecting your judgments about the products.

3. The goal of testing is to come up with *reliable* results (results that would probably be gotten again if the tests were repeated) and *valid* results (results that reflect actual differences among the products). How does controlling variables help you do that? What else should you pay attention to? *(Collect data carefully and keep good records, check data, follow procedures carefully.)*

TESTS ALREADY DESIGNED FOR STUDENTS

The following tests describe the testing procedures students should follow. Allow student groups to work independently and solve problems among themselves. Wait until they've completed their testing before discussing or reviewing the tests. The goal is to encourage independent thinking, creative problem-solving, and increased confidence in their scientific abilities.

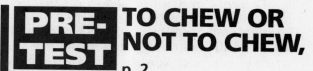

PRE-TEST
TO CHEW OR NOT TO CHEW, p. 2

QUESTION: Do antacids work faster whole or crushed?

WHAT STUDENTS WILL DO:
Students will add HCl to a crushed and a whole antacid tablet and stir both until one dissolves. They'll compare dissolving speed and pH of the solutions.

MATERIALS FOR EACH GROUP:
2 identical antacid tablets, safety goggles, 0.1N HCl solution (100 mL), graduated cylinder, 2 stirring rods, timer, spoon, 2 beakers or glasses (250 mL), pH paper.

OBJECTIVES:
To distinguish between acids and bases; to compare solubility rates; to develop skills needed for later tests (how to work with acids, pH indicators, controlling variables).

CONCEPTS:
Acids and bases: Acids are hydrogen compounds eager to give up a hydrogen ion (+ charge). Bases (alkalis) are compounds with hydroxide ions (- charge), eager to link up with a hydrogen ion.

Neutralization: What happens when acids and bases react with each other. The pH of the resulting solution will be somewhere between the pH values of the starting reactants (acid and base).

pH is a measure of the hydrogen-ion concentration of a solution. The more hydrogen ions there are, the more acidic the solution is: pH from 0 (most hydrogen ions, most acidic) to 7 (neutral) indicates

(continued)

decreasing acidity; pH from 7 to 14 indicates increasing alkalinity. (The pH numbers come from negative exponents of 10, so the lower the number the more hydrogen ions there are.)

Rate of reaction varies directly with the surface area of solid reactants. So a crushed tablet will react more rapidly than a whole tablet. By chewing an antacid tablet, the user is effectively increasing its surface area.

DISCUSS:

1. What does it mean when a solution's pH is under 7? *(The presence of acid [more hydrogen ions].)* What does it mean when it's over 7? *(The presence of a base.)* What does it mean when it's about 7? As an acid is being neutralized, how does its pH change? What chemical changes take place? *(Hydrogen ions from an acid are neutralized by hydroxide ions from a base to form water and a salt and are removed from the solution.)*

2. Discuss responses to the balloon: Is there a link between how many pieces an antacid is in and how much acid it neutralizes? Did the pH rise faster with the crushed tablet or the whole tablet? In which form would the base come into contact with the acid most rapidly? *(Explore relationship between reaction rate and the surface area of reactants.)*

IS THERE A LINK BETWEEN HOW QUICKLY A TABLET REMOVES ACID AND WHETHER IT'S IN PIECES? EXPLAIN.
Yes. When pulverized, most of the antacid's base comes into contact with the acid right away. When left whole, just the outside layer does, so it reacts at the slower rate.

1. THE SPEEDIEST ANTACID, p.3

QUESTION: Which antacid works the fastest?

WHAT STUDENTS WILL DO:
After crushing an antacid, students will add 50 mL HCl solution, watch the pH indicator, and time how long it takes to bring the solution to a pH of 4.

MATERIALS FOR EACH GROUP:
3 coded antacid tablets (1 of each), safety goggles, 0.1N HCl solution (150 mL), graduated cylinder, stirring rod, timer, spoon, beaker or glass (250 mL), pH paper.

OBJECTIVES:
To compare antacid performance; to develop skill at using pH indicators and performing timed experiments; to perform time computations and use number lines.

CONCEPTS:
pH indicators: pH paper changes color depending on the hydrogen ion concentration (acid or base) of the solution.

Indigestion: Gastric juices can cause the stomach to become too acidic. Discomfort can be relieved by taking a mild base (antacid) to reduce the acidity.

DISCUSS:

1. Was any antacid *much* faster or slower than the others? Why don't antacids use *stronger* (more alkali) bases in order to work faster? *(They could harm the tissues of the throat and mouth. Also, strong bases can't be buffered so they wouldn't be able to maintain a constant pH.)*

2. Which variables could have a big impact on reaction rates? *(How finely the antacids are crushed, stirring rate)* How did you control these variables? *(Discuss the balloon.)*

HOW FINELY A TABLET IS CRUSHED AND HOW MUCH YOU STIR ARE VARIABLES. HOW CAN YOU CONTROL THEM IN THIS TEST?
Crush tablets to the same fineness, count the number of stirs for each, etc.

2. THE STEADY-pH TEST, p. 4

QUESTION: Which antacid keeps the acid level even for the longest time?

WHAT STUDENTS WILL DO:

Students will simulate the working of a real stomach, which may continue to produce acid after an antacid is taken. They will add acid (HCl) to a crushed tablet, test pH, test and add more acid every 3 minutes for 18 minutes, and graph data to see which antacid maintained a pH between 3 and 5 the longest.

MATERIALS FOR EACH GROUP:

Same as for Test 1, but 3 sets of everything, more 0.1 N HCl solution (330 mL), and different-colored pencils.

OBJECTIVES:

To introduce the concepts of buffers and the acidic nature of stomach fluids; to understand and perform simple titrations; and to develop skill at graphing data.

CONCEPTS:

Stomach, digestion, and the role of acids: Hydrochloric acid (HCl), produced in the stomach, keeps the pH of gastric juices between 1.2 and 3. The digestive enzyme pepsin needs low pH to break down proteins. (It slows down but keeps working up to pH 5.) The pH of the 0.1 N HCl used in this experiment is 1.1.

Buffers are substances that maintain the acidity (or basicity) of a solution because they can neutralize both acids and bases. A buffer will partially neutralize an acid and will keep the solution's pH from changing when small amounts of acid or base are added. Good antacids' buffers can keep the pH stable as acid is continually added.

Titration is a method of measuring how much of a substance (antacid base) is present in a solution by gradually adding a reactant (acid) and seeing how much of that reactant is needed to "use up" that substance.

DISCUSS:

1. How does the procedure you followed imitate the way the stomach works? *(The stomach may continue to produce acid, even after someone has taken an antacid. So an antacid needs to balance pH over time.)*

2. Why was it important for an antacid to keep the pH between 3 and 5? What does it mean if the solution falls below 3? *(The antacid has stopped neutralizing the acid.)* What does it mean if it goes over 5? *(It's not leaving the gastric juices acidic enough to work; pepsin stops working at pH 5. Discuss the answers to the balloon on page 6.)*

3. What variables did you control during this test? *(Why was it important to clean the beaker between tests? Why was it important for the HCl measurements to be exact?)*

4. What does your graph show about antacids: Did they neutralize the acid all at once, or did they keep the pH at a steady acidic pH? How did they do that—why didn't all of the antacid's base link up with the acid all at once? *(Explore the concept of buffers.)*

5. Is there a relationship between how *fast* antacids work and how *steady* they keep the pH? Compare the two tests' scores. Which do you think is more important, how fast an antacid works (Speediest Antacid Test) or how steady it keeps the pH (Steady-pH Test)? Why?

3. TOTAL ACID NEUTRALIZED, p. 6

QUESTION: Which antacid neutralized the most acid?

WHAT STUDENTS WILL DO:

Students will find the total milliliters of HCl each antacid neutralized before its pH fell below 3.

MATERIALS FOR EACH GROUP:

Data from The Steady-pH Test (Box 2, page 4).

OBJECTIVES:

To understand neutralization; to reinforce concepts of acids, bases, buffers, and pH.

CONCEPTS:

Neutralization: What happens when acids and bases react with each other: The pH of the resulting solution will be somewhere between the pH values of the starting reactants (acid and base).

Equivalence point: The end point of neutralization, where equal numbers of acid and base molecules have reacted. Its pH is not necessarily pH 7. If the products of the neutralization reaction are buffers, as is the case with antacids, the pH of the neutralized solution will not be 7. Students can estimate the equivalence point as the point on their graphs where the pH drops sharply below the steady level it was keeping.

DISCUSS:

1. What does it mean to say an acid is "neutralized"? What happened to the acid you kept pouring in: Why didn't it make the pH go down (become more acidic)? *(Explore the concept of neutralization.)*

2. What do you think would happen if all fluid in the stomach were totally neutralized (to pH 7)? *(Digestive juices would stop working.)*

3. Why didn't the pH in this test ever rise to pH 7? What kept the acid from reacting with all of the base in the antacid right away and raising the pH to 7? *(Explore the concept of buffers. Or demonstrate the concept: See the activity on the following page.)*

WHAT DO YOU THINK HAS HAPPENED TO THE ANTACID WHEN THE pH DROPS BELOW 3? WHY DOES THAT SIGNAL THE END OF THE TEST?

When its pH drops below 3, the solution is becoming more acidic because the antacid has been "used up" and has just about stopped neutralizing the acid.

A TEST STUDENTS WILL DESIGN THEMSELVES

Testing procedures for the next test are not provided. Each small group must devise its own plan and procedures. The goal is to encourage hands-on, common-sense creativity and problem solving by students. There is no one answer or one "right way" to do this test.

4. THE BAKING SODA TEST, p. 7

QUESTION: Does baking soda perform as well as antacid products?

POSSIBLE PROCEDURE:
Students could imitate procedures for the Steady pH Test: See how much acid baking soda will neutralize and how steady it will hold the pH, then compare with results of antacid tests. *(Baking soda's solution will reach a higher pH than the antacids' solutions, but its pH will fall each time acid is added. It's too strong a base and its neutralization reaction doesn't form a good buffer.)*

OBJECTIVES:
To reinforce the concepts and skills developed during the antacid tests.

CONCEPT:
Test design: Tests should be planned to collect measurable and comparable data and to control variables that could skew data. In this instance, the test should be designed like the preceding antacid tests so data will be comparable (and so students will be able to discover how baking soda and commercial antacid products compare).

DISCUSS:

1. What testing procedure did you follow? What happened? What were your conclusions — how does baking soda compare with antacid products?

HOW CAN I FIND OUT HOW MUCH BAKING SODA TO USE? WRITE YOUR IDEA HERE. *Read the baking soda label. Or read labels of antacid products that contain sodium bicarbonate and see how much of it they contain.*

BRAND X BAKING SODA

2. Discuss responses to the balloon. How did you determine a "dose size" of baking soda? If the dose were too big or too small, would that prevent your test data from being comparable to the other antacids? Why or why not? (*Yes, it could affect how high the pH goes and the pattern of decreasing in pH instead of staying steady.*)

ACTIVITY:

Test a "buffered" baking soda: Add 1/4 teaspoon of baking soda to 50 mL of orange juice. Citric acid forms a buffer with baking soda. Add the 0.1 N HCl and measure pH, as was done in the Steady-pH test. The "buffered" baking soda's performance will be very similar to the commercial antacids you tested.

EXTRA ACTIVITY: INTERPRET LABELS

An important step in evaluating over-the-counter medications is reading about their contraindications (when they shouldn't be used), possible side effects, and dosage recommendations and cautions.

QUESTION: What else should you know about these medications?

WHAT STUDENTS WILL DO: Each person in the group should examine one antacid label and record information on contraindications, side effects, and dosage on a chart (an enlarged version of the chart below). When the chart is completed, discuss what was learned from the labels.

MATERIALS FOR EACH GROUP: Package inserts or bottles from each of the antacids tested containing ingredient, dosage, and warning information.

LABEL INFO...

	A	B	C
Active Ingredients			
Contra-indications			
Possible Side Effects			
Dosage Information			

DISCUSS:

1. What dosage recommendations are given on the antacid labels? How important do you think it is to read and follow these recommendations? (*An acid-stomach could be symptomatic of a more serious problem that requires medical attention; continual ingestion of antacids could affect the pH of your stomach; antacids could lead to other problems like constipation.*)

2. Who should *not* take the antacids, according to the label warnings? Do you think these warnings are prominent enough for people to notice them?

INTERPRET YOUR TEST DATA, p. 8

Students have gathered data and assigned raw scores for all antacid tests. Now they have to figure out what it all means.

Data alone can't say which antacid is best. Like all facts, data have to be thought about, evaluated, and interpreted in a useful and meaningful way. If misinterpreted, data can mislead consumers, instead of guiding them. There's no one right way to deal with data.

WHAT STUDENTS WILL DO:

After transcribing scores for the antacids from their Databook, students will decide which test is most important, "weight" scores by adding in the important test's scores twice, then rank antacids from best to worst.

OBJECTIVE:

To understand the concepts of weighting scores and ranking.

CONCEPT:

Weighting: Some tests measure more important qualities than other tests do. How antacids score in important tests should count for more (have a greater impact on the antacid's overall score).

DISCUSS:

Discuss responses to the balloon. What are the pros and cons of weighting scores—of making important tests' scores count for more? Did weighting the scores change the antacids' rankings? *(Have students add raw scores and rank antacids, then compare that with their weighted-score rankings. Which is more meaningful? Why?)*

IF ONE TEST IS MORE IMPORTANT THAN THE OTHERS, SHOULD ITS SCORES COUNT FOR MORE? WHY OR WHY NOT?
Yes — otherwise less important tests could skew results.

EXTRA ACTIVITY: PUT TOGETHER THE CLASS'S TEST DATA

CONCEPTS:

Variation: Data can vary as a result of differences within a brand, making it advisable to test multiple samples. Variation can also arise from uncontrolled variables or changes in testing conditions.

Measurement error: Measurements recorded during testing are subject to variation due either to measurement inaccuracy (like how accurately pH colors are read or how precisely HCl is measured) or to differences in test conditions. A reliable measurement is closely repeatable from one test run to another.

ACTIVITY:

Make an enlarged copy of the chart on the following page. Have all groups write their raw scores in the appropriate box. (Each box will have as many numbers as there are groups.) Then decide on Importance Factors for each test and determine weighted scores.

DISCUSS:

1. Did everyone who did these tests come up with the same raw scores for the test antacids? Why not? Is it possible every antacid A wasn't exactly the same? Can performance vary within a brand? Is it possible measurement errors were made? *(Perhaps in titration measurements, pH interpretations, or timing accuracy.)*

2. How can we determine which measurements are most reliable (most likely to happen again if the tests were repeated)? What if we performed each test several times instead of once? What if we based the antacids' ratings on the whole class's raw scores combined, instead of just one group's?

3. Examine the class's raw data (on the chart). Which antacid's scores varied very little? Which antacid's performance could you predict with more confidence? *(The one with the least variation in scores.)*

SEND YOUR RATINGS OF ANTACIDS
TO *CONSUMER REPORTS*

The class should fill in this chart and answer all questions about the antacids. Attach a written summary of the class's conclusions. Then mail to the address below.

WHICH ANTACID IS BEST?

"RAW" SCORES

Write the class's combined scores for each test in the boxes below.
Are these ❏ mean scores or ❏ median scores? (Check *one*.)

TEST	A	B	C
1. Speediest Antacid			
2. Steady-pH			
3. Total Acid Neutralized			
TOTALS			

(Raw-Score Totals)

"WEIGHTED" SCORES

1. Assign Importance Factors to the tests. (3=*most* important, 1=*least* important)

2. Multiply the class's combined raw scores by the Importance Factors.

IMPORTANCE FACTOR:	A	B	C
1.			
2.			
3.			
TOTALS			

(Weighted-Score Totals)

(1) **Code**   **Brand**   **Tablet or liquid?**

A _____ _____

B _____ _____

C _____ _____

(2) How many small groups tested the antacids? _____

(3) Date _____

(4) Person to contact (name and address):

_____

_____

_____

_____

(5) **Mail To:**

**Consumer Reports
Education Division
101 Truman Avenue
Yonkers, New York 10703-1057**

PRENTICE HALL — PRODUCT TESTING ACTIVITIES by Consumer Reports

TESTING BANDAGES

Testing Bandages helps students discover the science and technology behind bandages: Why some bandages stick better **(adhesion, flexiblility, characteristics of skin)**; whether they trap moisture **(perspiration, evaporation, vapor permeability)**; whether they let air pass through **(gas permeability, blood clotting)**; how well they stretch and flex **(tensile strength)**; and whether they loosen in water. It builds scientific inquiry and testing skills by having students form hypotheses and control variables throughout and by challenging them to design testing procedures themselves. Tests are open-ended:

There is no one answer, no desired conclusion. Collecting, analyzing, and interpreting the data also involve number lines, adding, averaging, and statistics (variation, sampling, weighting).

Tests encourage cooperative learning. They are designed for groups of four. Students will work together to conduct and plan tests, analyze data, solve problems, interpret results, and develop a scientific rating of the test bandages. The chart below links the tests students will perform with the science skills and concepts those testing activities will help teach.

CURRICULUM SKILLS AND CONCEPTS

Test and Student Databook Page	Highlighted Skills	Science Concepts
Getting Started p. 1	Controlling Variables, Blind Testing	Principles of Testing
The Stick Test p. 2	Controlling Variables, Number Lines	Adhesion, Paired Comparison Testing
The Soggy-Skin Test p. 3	Observation, Forming Hypotheses	Skin, Evaporation, Vapor Permeability
The Breathing Test p. 4	Using Experimental Controls, Observation	Oxygen, Healing, Gas Permeability
The Sweaty, Oily Stick Test p. 5	Designing a Test, Collecting Data	Skin Secretions, Adhesive Solvents
The Wash-Off Test p. 6	Designing a Test, Controlling Variables	Adhesion, Solubility
The Knuckle Test p. 6	Measuring Angles, Designing a Test	Tensile Strength, Geometry
Ouch! The Peel-Off Test, p. 7	Designing a Test, Controlling Variables	Pain, Hair, Sensory Testing
Interpret Your Test Data p. 8	Rank Ordering, Forming Conclusions	Weighted Scores, Variation

MATERIALS NEEDED for each small group:

❏ **Test samples:**
4 brands of bandages (all the same size), two with plastic strips and two with cloth or mesh strips. Include a store or generic brand. Each group will need 7 samples of each brand.

AVOID bandages with medicated pads.

❏ **For pre-planned tests:**
Construction paper (dark color), sponge, paper towel, tape, water, fan, apple, knife.

CLASS-TIME REQUIREMENTS:

❏ To prepare for testing: 1 class period
❏ To conduct Tests 1 to 3: 2 class periods
❏ To conduct Tests 4 to 7: 2 to 3 class periods (can be assigned as homework)
❏ For data analysis and interpretation: 1 class period

GETTING STARTED

1. Code test samples.

Students should do "blind tests" of the bandages by testing *coded* samples: They should not know the test samples' brand names until the tests are completed.

Prepare test samples in advance: Use a marker pen to black out all brand name identification on wrappers and to code them A through D. Have black marker pens by the test bandages so students can remove wrappings and mark code letters directly on the bandages as they take them.

2. Distribute Student Databooks, one to each small group.

DISCUSS:

1. The goal of testing is to come up with reliable results — results that would probably be gotten again if the tests were repeated. How does controlling variables help you do that? What else should you pay attention to? *(Keep good records, check data, etc.)*

> BANDAGES HAVE TROUBLE STICKING ON WET SKIN AND ON JOINTS THAT BEND A LOT. HOW COULD YOU CONTROL THESE VARIABLES?
> *Make sure skin is dry, apply bandages to the same joint, apply both bandages going up and down or both going sideways.*

2. Discuss responses to the balloon. How would you control these variables? Why did we black out brand names and identify bandages by code letters instead? *(Explore how testers' biases might affect their judgments without them even being aware of it.)*

3. Bandage tests could be done by *one* person in your group or by *every* person. Which do you think is better? Why? *(The more data collected, the less of an impact any variation will have on the results. But that would require lots more time and bandages. The Databook has bandage tests done by one person per group.)*

TESTS ALREADY DESIGNED FOR STUDENTS

The first three tests describe testing procedures for students to follow. Allow student groups to work independently and solve problems among themselves. Wait until they've completed their testing before discussing or reviewing the tests. The goal is to encourage independent thinking, creative problem-solving, and increased confidence in their scientific abilities.

1. THE STICK TEST, p. 2

QUESTION: Which bandage sticks best?

WHAT STUDENTS WILL DO:
Students will stick two test bandages at a time on a joint and count the number of bends each bandage takes before loosening.

MATERIALS FOR EACH GROUP:
4 coded bandages (1 of each).

OBJECTIVES:
To introduce the concepts of adhesion and flexibility; to reinforce the importance of controlling variables.

CONCEPTS:

Adhesion: A tendency of one substance to stick to another. Most synthetic glues consist of *polymers*—huge molecules (made up of many simpler molecules) that are strong, flexible, and very attracted to other substances. Bandages use a pressure-sensitive type of adhesive.

Paired comparisons: Testing products by comparing pairs makes controlling variables easier. Comparing two bandages on the same joint controls such variables as skin moisture and force of bends.

DISCUSS:

1. Have small groups compare data *(Box 1)*. Did all groups get the same number of bends for each bandage? Why might data vary? *(Differences in skin type, skin moisture, bending strength, variation among samples.)* Would lots of data (repeating the test several times) make test results more reliable? *(It would reduce the impact of variation or error on the results.)*

2. What makes a bandage stick? *(Explore pressure-sensitive adhesives.)* Why does bending a joint loosen the bandage?

HOW FAR YOU BEND YOUR JOINT IS A VARIABLE. WHAT OTHER VARIABLES SHOULD BE CONTROLLED?

Skin moisture, location of bandages, how well they're pressed on, how tightly they're applied, whether the joint is bent when the bandages are applied.

3. Discuss responses to the balloon. What did you do in the test? Why?

2. THE SOGGY-SKIN TEST, p. 3

QUESTION: Will any bandages make skin soggy?

WHAT STUDENTS WILL DO:

Students will apply the test bandages to construction paper, dampen the back of the paper, tape it around the edges to a window, and fan it for 15 minutes to speed drying. If the paper under a bandage is still moist, the bandage will probably make skin soggy.

OBJECTIVES:

To understand that skin gives off moisture; to discover vapor permeability; to make observations and form hypotheses.

MATERIALS FOR EACH GROUP:

4 coded bandages, construction paper (dark color, 10-cm-by-20-cm), sponge, paper towel, tape, water, fan.

CONCEPTS:

Skin: Like any living tissue, skin is continually "breathing"—giving off gaseous by-products of respiration. Skin also helps cool the body by releasing sweat.

Evaporation: This phase change from liquid water to gas occurs when moisture comes into contact with drier air. When water molecules have enough energy (heat), they vaporize. As sweat vaporizes, it takes heat from the body and cools it.

Vapor permeability: Due to their physical and molecular structure, some materials allow the passage of vapor molecules.

SOMETHING THAT'S POROUS (HAS TINY HOLES) WILL LET MOISTURE PASS THROUGH. SHOULD ADHESIVE STRIPS ON BANDAGES BE POROUS? WRITE YOUR HYPOTHESIS HERE.

If adhesive strips on bandages aren't porous, they'll trap the skin's moisture and make the skin soft and soggy.

DISCUSS:

1. Discuss responses to the first balloon. Which bandages look like they have the most vapor-permeable adhesive strips? Did they do best in this test? Why or why not? *(Although fabric bandages are porous, they may absorb water and thus impede drying.)*

WHERE DOES THE WATER GO AS THE PAPER DRIES? WRITE YOUR HYPOTHESIS HERE.

The water changes to vapor – it evaporates into the air. If the adhesive strip is vapor permeable, it will let the water underneath evaporate like the water on the rest of the paper.

2. Discuss responses to the second balloon. *(Explore the concept of evaporation.)*

3. Why did the test have you tape the dampened, bandaged paper *around the edges* and *to a window or wall*, which is *non-porous*? *(So all evaporation would occur up through the bandages, not directly into the air.)*

3. THE BREATHING TEST, p. 4

QUESTION: How well do bandage pads let air in?

WHAT STUDENTS WILL DO:
Students will bandage fresh-cut apples and check under the bandage pads the next day. The browner that part of the apple is, the more oxygen-permeable the bandage pad is.

MATERIALS PER GROUP:
4 coded bandages, ripe apple (not bruised), knife for slicing.

OBJECTIVES:
To understand oxygen's role in healing; to introduce the concepts of gas permeability and experimental controls.

> **CONCEPT:**
> **Oxygen and the healing process:** Platelets in the blood huddle together (clot) when in contact with the air. If a bandage blocks too much air, clotting and healing are slowed.

DISCUSS:

1. Discuss responses to the first balloon. Why is it important for air to reach wounds? (*For clotting.*)

> WILL THE PART OF THE APPLE <u>UNDER</u> THE BANDAGE PAD TURN AS BROWN AS THE PART UNDER THE ADHESIVE STRIPS? WHY?
> *Probably not. The strip will block out some air. The gauze pad (which is covered by the strip, too) will block out more air.*

2. Why is it better in this test for the apple part under the bandage to be brown? (*It means air got in. Discuss responses to the second balloon.*)

> WHICH IS THE SIGN OF A <u>BETTER</u> BANDAGE—LETTING THE APPLE UNDERNEATH TURN BROWN OR KEEPING IT WHITE? WHY?
> *Letting air in (having the apple underneath turn brown) is a sign of a better bandage because air promotes healing.*

TESTS STUDENTS WILL DESIGN THEMSELVES

Testing procedures are not provided for the following tests. Each small group must devise its own plans and procedures. The goal is to encourage hands-on, common-sense creativity and problem-solving by students. *There are several possible answers. There's no one "right way" to do these tests.*

4. THE SWEATY, OILY STICK TEST, p. 5

QUESTION: Which bandage sticks best to sweaty, oily skin?

POSSIBLE PROCEDURES:
Students could adapt Test 1 (The Stick Test) by applying water or oil to the skin. Or they could test by applying pairs of test samples, doing strenuous activities, and seeing which bandage sticks longer. (This test could be a homework activity.)

OBJECTIVES:
To design a controlled test; to understand how water and oil loosen an adhesive's grip.

> **CONCEPTS:**
> **Skin:** Skin protects the body from germs, plays a role in cooling the body off, and lubricates itself to keep from drying out. It is continually secreting oils and releasing moisture.
>
> **Adhesive solvents:** Water and/or oil may loosen an adhesive's grip by dissolving or deactivating the adhesives. These solvents can also interfere with adhesion by coating the skin and preventing pressure-sensitive adhesives from contacting a surface they can stick to.

DISCUSS:

1. Why does the skin release oils and moisture? (*See skin concept above.*) What effect do oil and sweat have on a bandage's stick? Why? (*See adhesive solvents above.*)

2. Compare results of this test and Test 1. Is there a relationship between bandages that stick when dry and when wet? What can you infer from this?

IN REAL LIFE, WHEN DO SWEAT AND SKIN OIL CAUSE THE MOST PROBLEMS — BEFORE OR AFTER A BANDAGE IS PUT ON? HOW CAN YOUR TEST IMITATE THIS? *Since skin should be washed and dried off before a bandage is applied, sweating and secreting oil after the bandage is applied are more likely to cause problems.*

3. Discuss responses to the balloon. What was your hypothesis? *(Explore how skin secretes oil and water.)* Did your hypothesis influence how you designed your test?

5. THE WASH-OFF TEST, p. 6

QUESTION: Which bandage stays on best under water?

POSSIBLE PROCEDURE:
This could be a "use-test" homework project: Students could apply bandage pairs before washing dishes or taking a shower to see which sticks longer. They might gather more data if they can enlist other testers (parents, siblings), but that would require more bandages.

OBJECTIVES:
To design a controlled test; to deepen understanding of adhesion and the forces that can work against it.

DISCUSS:
1. Why are bandages more likely to come off if you're swimming than if you're just standing around in water? *(Stress pulls them off; moving water gets between the adhesive and the skin.)*

2. What variables did you control? How did you control them? *(Pressure when applying bandages; where on the body bandages were placed; temperature of water; type of soap used; movement in the water; definition of "loosening.")*

3. Do the results of this test correlate with Test 1 (The Stick Test) results? Do they correlate with Test 4 (The Sweaty, Oily Stick Test) results? What can you infer about the test bandages' adhesives?

6. THE KNUCKLE TEST, p. 6

QUESTION: Which bandage lets you bend your finger the easiest?

POSSIBLE PROCEDURES:
Students could wrap bandages firmly around a knuckle, try to bend the finger, and observe tears or fraying, how far the finger bent, and how comfortable the bandage felt. Or they could use a protractor to measure how far the fingers would bend the first time they tried, then after a fixed number of tries.

OBJECTIVES:
To discover the selective nature of adhesives; to understand the concept of tensile strength; to measure angles.

CONCEPTS:
Tensile strength: A measure of the greatest tension a material can bear without tearing.

Geometry: How far bandaged fingers bend can be measured by measuring the angle formed.

DISCUSS:
1. Did the bandages tend to stick better to your skin or to themselves (when overlapped on a finger)? *(They'll stick better to themselves.)* Why are bandages' adhesive strips a better adhesive surface than your skin? *(Explore which has less moisture, oil, interfering particles like hair, etc.)*

2. Were some bandage strips harder to bend than others? What might make a bandage hard to bend? *(Its material's tensile strength? Its lack of flexibility?)*

3. What variables did you control? *(How tightly you applied the bandage? Location? Strength of flex?)*

4. Did small groups' results agree? If not, were any variables not controlled the same way by all groups?

7. OUCH! THE PEEL-OFF TEST, p. 7

QUESTION: Which bandage hurts the least when you peel it off?

POSSIBLE PROCEDURE:

Using paired samples, students may apply and pull off bandages, noting which hurts less. Or they can judge each bandage separately.

OBJECTIVES:

To deepen understanding of the skin; to discover how hair differs from living tissue; to design a controlled sensory test.

CONCEPTS:

Pain: Skin houses nerve endings, which relay information from outside the body to the brain. Most pain felt when removing bandages is due to adhesives pulling on hairs that are associated with nerve endings.

Nature of hair: Unlike skin, hair isn't living and it doesn't secrete oils or moisture, so it's a better adhesive surface.

DISCUSS:

1. It usually hurts when bandages are pulled off. What do you think causes the pain? Does the bandage stick better to skin or to hair on the skin? *(To hair.)* Why does it stick better to hair? *(Explore the nature of hair.)*

2. Is it hard to get scientific measurements of something as personal as "pain"? What did you do? Why?

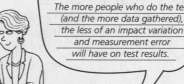

WHICH WOULD BE BETTER, HAVING SEVERAL PEOPLE TEST FOR PAIN AND COMBINE THEIR RANKINGS OR DOING IT ALL BY YOURSELF? WHY? *The more people who do the test (and the more data gathered), the less of an impact variation and measurement error will have on test results.*

3. Discuss responses to the balloon. Why does getting lots of data make test results more reliable? *(It reduces the impact of error on the results. Like in an exam, the more questions there are, the less of an impact each one has on the final grade.)*

DEALING WITH DATA

Students have gathered data and assigned raw scores for all seven bandage tests. Now they have to figure out what it all means!

Data alone can't say which bandage is best. Like all facts, data have to be thought about, evaluated, and interpreted in a useful and meaningful way. If misinterpreted, data can mislead consumers instead of guiding them. There's no one right way to deal with data.

- While "dealing with data," students will be using basic mathematics skills as well as learning statistics in a hands-on way. They will be saying "what it all means"—expressing in simple written sentences what their tests revealed about bandages. Data are seen as a means to an end, rather than an end in themselves.

- The Databooks have students analyze and interpret the data their small group collected. Much can be learned by having small groups compare their results and combine their data to come up with class results.

INTERPRET YOUR TEST DATA, p. 8

WHAT STUDENTS WILL DO:

After transcribing test scores onto the chart, students will "weight" the scores by deleting the least important test and adding the most important test's scores twice. They'll rank bandages from best to worst, compute unit costs, and fill in a ratings chart.

OBJECTIVES:

To understand the concept of "weighting" scores so important qualities count for more; to build analytic and inference skills by ranking bandages and forming conclusions.

MATERIALS:

Original bandage packages (with brand name, price, and number of bandages).

DISCUSS:

1. Is there a relationship between bandages' scores in adhesion tests and how painful they are to remove? Introduce the concept of "weighting" (assigning importance to) different product qualities: Is it more important for a bandage to stay on or to peel off painlessly after use?

2. How does crossing out some test scores and doubling other test scores "weight" the overall total scores? Would the bandages have ranked differently if their scores were not weighted? Should ratings be based on weighted or unweighted scores? Why?

3. Which bandage is least expensive? Should price affect the bandages' ranking or be dealt with separately? Compare rank orders and prices: Are there any "good buys"?

4. Share and discuss students' written conclusions. Do the tests indicate that one type of bandage would be better than the others for a certain application (e.g., swimming)?

EXTRA ACTIVITY: PUT TOGETHER THE CLASS'S TEST DATA

CONCEPT:

Variation: Data can vary as a result of differences in product samples, testing methods, and testers' perceptions and interpretations, so it's advisable to repeat tests a number of times.

ACTIVITY:

Post an enlarged copy of the chart on the next page of this guide. Have all groups write their raw scores in the appropriate boxes. (Each box will have several scores.) Analyze the raw data using questions 1 through 4 below, then assign Importance Factors and compute weighted scores.

DISCUSS:

1. Did everyone who tested come up with the same scores? Why not? Is it possible every bandage A wasn't exactly the same? Can performance vary within a brand? Can measurement errors be made?

2. How can we determine which measurements are most *reliable* (most likely to happen again if the test were repeated)? *(Explore performing each test several times; basing ratings on the class's data.)*

3. Examine the class's data on the chart. Which bandage, if any, has very little *variation* in its data (the small groups' test scores are similar)? Which bandage has wide variation in its scores? Which bandage's performance could you predict with more confidence? *(The one with the least variation in scores.)*

4. What's the better way to tally the small groups' raw scores — figure out means or medians? *(Have some students do it one way and others the other way. Are scores different? Which is more appropriate?)*

SEND YOUR RATINGS OF BANDAGES TO *CONSUMER REPORTS*

The class should fill in this chart and answer all questions about the bandages. Attach a written summary of the class's conclusions. Then mail to the address below.

WHICH BANDAGE IS BEST?

"RAW" SCORES

Write the class's combined scores for each test in the boxes below.
Are these ❏ mean scores or ❏ median scores? (Check *one*.)

TEST	A	B	C	D
1. Stick				
2. Soggy-Skin				
3. Breath-ing				
4. Sweaty, Stick				
5. Wash-Off				
6. Knuckle				
7. Ouch!				
TOTALS				

(Raw-Score Totals)

"WEIGHTED" SCORES

1. Assign Importance Factors to the tests. (3= *most* important 1 = *least* important)
2. Multiply the class's combined raw scores by the Importance Factors.

IMPORTANCE FACTOR:	A	B	C	D
1.				
2.				
3.				
4.				
5.				
6.				
7.				
TOTALS				

(Weighted-Score Totals)

(1) **Code   Brand   Type**

A _____ _____

B _____ _____

C _____ _____

D _____ _____

(2) How many small groups tested the bandages?_____

(3) Date_____

(4) Person to contact (name and address):

_____

_____

_____

_____

(5) **Mail To:**

**Consumer Reports
Education Division
101 Truman Avenue
Yonkers, New York 10703-1057**

PRENTICE HALL — **PRODUCT TESTING ACTIVITIES** by *Consumer Reports*

TESTING BOTTLED WATER

Testing Bottled Water helps students discover what's really in bottled water and how bottled waters compare. Students will discover which sparkling water contains the most bubbles (**carbonation, gas solubility**); which bottled waters are preferred by most people (**blind testing, sensory analysis, representative random samples**); which ones have offtastes (**solubility of solids, trace substances, sensory analysis**); what solid substances, such as mineral salts, are dissolved in bottled water (**evaporation, physical and chemical properties of water, geometry of crystals**); and which waters are bottled in recyclable containers (**solid waste, environmental impact**).

Testing Bottled Water builds scientific inquiry and testing skills by challenging students to evaluate different brands and types of bottled water, thereby empowering students to form their own conclusions independent of advertising claims. *There is no one "right" answer, no desired conclusion, no one right way to test.*

Tests are designed for groups of four. Students will work together planning tests, double-checking data, solving problems, and developing an understanding of the differences among bottled waters. The chart below links tests students will perform with the science skills and concepts those activities help teach.

CURRICULUM SKILLS AND CONCEPTS

Test and Student Databook Page	Highlighted Skills	Science Concepts
Getting Started p. 1	Controlling Variables, Blind Testing	Principles of Testing
Bubbles-Breakdown Test, p. 2	Manipulation, Measuring, Ratios	Carbonation, Gas Solubility
The Taste-Preference Test, p. 3	Paired Comparisons, Blind Testing	Sensory Analysis, Representative Random Sampling
Offtaste Test p. 4	Making Sensory Judgments	Solubility of Solids, Sensory Analysis
The Packaging Test p. 5	Designing a Test, Researching	Environmental Impact, Solid Waste
Solid-Stuff Analysis p. 6	Manipulation, Observation	Properties of Water, Geometry of Crystals
Cost Analysis p. 8	Calculating Ratio	Unit Price
Interpret Your Test Data, p. 8	Analyzing Data	Test Conclusions

MATERIALS NEEDED
for each small group:

❑ **Test samples:** 2 unopened, same-sized bottles of each of the following: 3 sparkling waters (unflavored seltzer, club soda, and sparkling mineral water) and 2 still waters (spring and distilled). 1-liter bottles are preferred. Also include tap water (in a bottle).

❑ **For pre-planned tests:** Balance, timer, paper cups, pencils and paper, graduated cylinder, 6 250-mL beakers, magnifying glass or a binocular microscope, tracing paper, spatula, marker, calculator, vinegar and medicine dropper (optional).

CLASS-TIME REQUIREMENTS:

❑ To prepare for testing: 1 class period
❑ To conduct Tests 1 through 6: 2 class periods
❑ For data analysis and interpretation: 1 class period

GETTING STARTED

1. Distribute Student Databooks, one to each group.

DISCUSS:

1. Do you drink bottled water? Which one? Why?

2. Discuss students' responses to the balloon.

WHY DO SOME PEOPLE DRINK BOTTLED WATER RATHER THAN TAP WATER? ARE THESE *GOOD* REASONS? EXPLAIN.
People may not like the taste of their local tap water; may be looking for carbonation; may have health reasons (as a substitute for sugared or alcoholic drinks or because local water isn't pure); or may think it's trendy.

3. The goal of testing is to come up with reliable results (results that would probably be found again if the test were repeated) and valid results (results that reflect actual differences among the products). How does controlling variables help you do that? What else should you pay attention to? *(Collect data carefully and keep good records.)*

4. Why should each water be assigned a code letter? *(Discuss blind testing and how coding test samples can reduce bias in scientific tests.)*

2. Code test samples.

Students should test the bottled waters "blind"— they should not know the brand names or prices of the waters they test. Prepare test samples ahead of time: Carbonated water must not be opened. Leave it in its original bottle, but cover price tags and brand name identification. Put the still waters in three identical containers (so the tap water isn't identifiable). Code the sparkling waters A through C; the still waters D through F. (Make tap water F to accommodate Tests 4 and 6's instructions.)

TESTS ALREADY DESIGNED FOR STUDENTS

The following tests describe the testing procedures students should follow. Allow student groups to work independently and solve problems among themselves. Wait until they've completed their testing before discussing or reviewing the tests. The goal is to encourage independent thinking, creative problem-solving, and increased confidence in their scientific abilities.

1. BUBBLES-BREAK-DOWN TEST, p. 2

QUESTION: Which sparkling water has the most CO_2?

WHAT STUDENTS WILL DO:
Students will open and close each sparkling water three times over 20 minutes, weigh each bottle to determine how much gas has escaped, then leave all bottles open for 24 hours to let all the gas escape. The next day they will compare total weight losses to determine which water had the most CO_2.

CONCEPTS:

Carbonation is carbon dioxide gas (CO_2) dissolved in water. The gas dissolves in water under pressure. As long as a bottle of carbonated water is capped, carbonation remains. When the cap is removed, pressure decreases and allows some gas to escape. The escape of a gas from a liquid solution is called **effervescence**.

Solubility of CO_2 depends on both pressure and temperature. At room temperature under 1 atmosphere of pressure, about 750 mL of CO_2 will dissolve in a liter of water. Greater solubility (carbonation) can be achieved by increasing pressure and decreasing temperature.

Volume and weight of gas: Carbon dioxide weighs about 1.9 grams per liter. Under moderate pressure, several liters of CO_2 can be dissolved in a liter of water (Box 1 test data). The volume of dissolved CO_2 can be calculated by solving for χ:

$$\frac{1.9 \text{ g } CO_2}{1 \text{ L}} = \frac{\text{g } CO_2}{\chi \text{ L}}$$

MATERIALS FOR EACH GROUP:

1-liter bottle of each sparkling water (coded and unopened), balance, timer.

OBJECTIVES:

To determine the amount of dissolved carbon dioxide in each liter of water; to understand factors that affect the solubility of CO_2 in water; to discover relationships between the amount of dissolved CO_2 and pressure; to make measurements and perform calculations.

DISCUSS:

1. What is carbonation? How do bottlers carbonate waters?

2. Why do you think some people prefer their water carbonated?

3. Why does a carbonated drink bubble over when it is opened? *(Pressure is released and the dissolved CO_2 turns into gas and expands in volume.)* How can you keep this from happening? *(Open the bottle slowly in stages to let the gas escape gradually.)*

4. Discuss responses to the balloon.

CARBON DIOXIDE GAS WEIGHS ABOUT 1.9 GRAMS PER LITER. FROM YOUR DATA, CALCULATE HOW MANY LITERS OF CO_2 WERE PLACED INTO EACH BOTTLE. *Answers will vary: May range from 2 to 4 liters of CO_2 in a 1-liter bottle.*

ACTIVITIES:

• **Graph the weight of the bottles over time.** Create line graphs showing how many grams were lost during each time period. Discuss when the waters lost CO_2 most rapidly and why.

• **Make seltzer:** Demonstrate how water can be carbonated. Use a seltzer bottle and CO_2 cartridge.

• **Make carbon dioxide:** Demonstrate the physical properties of carbon dioxide:

1) Stretch a large balloon by blowing it up and letting the air out a few times. Be sure it fits over the flask opening.

2) Put 75 mL of vinegar in a 250-mL flask.

3) Weigh out 4 grams of baking soda and wrap it tightly in a piece of paper.

4) Drop the baking soda packet into the flask and quickly stretch the balloon over the neck of the flask. Observe what happens in the flask and to the balloon. Discuss: What is filling up the balloon? *(CO_2)* Where is the gas coming from? *(Baking soda, a solid form of CO_2, reacts with the acid in vinegar and CO_2 gas is released.)*

5) Swirl the mixture until foaming stops.

6) Hold the neck of the balloon around the flask tightly and carefully twist the balloon once or twice.

7) Affix a twist-tie tightly around the twisted balloon neck.

8) Remove the balloon from the flask and measure its diameter. Estimate the volume of gas inside and then its weight. (One liter, [1,000 cm^3] of CO_2 weighs 1.9 grams.)

2. THE TASTE-PREFERENCE TEST, p. 3

QUESTIONS: Which sparkling water do people prefer? Which still water do they prefer?

WHAT STUDENTS WILL DO:

Students will taste pairs of still waters (including a tap water) and choose the preferred one until all possible combinations of waters have been compared. They'll do the same for sparkling waters. The still and sparkling water selected the most times wins.

MATERIALS FOR EACH GROUP:

6 coded test waters, cooled to the same temperature, 3 paper cups for each tester, paper and pencils.

OBJECTIVES:

To understand the concepts of sampling and paired-comparison testing; to make judgments by paired comparisons; to develop sensory testing skills.

DISCUSS:

1. Why is it important to have every water cooled to the same temperature? *(Temperature affects taste.)* What other variables should you control? *(Open bottles at same time; use unopened bottles; leave open for the same length of time; etc.)*

2. The more tasters the better. Why? *(The more paired comparisons that are done, the less influence one person will have and the more reliable the data will be.)* If all tasters are students' peers, what might the results be? all adults? What differences other than age might make a difference in tasters' responses? Do you think that the winner in your tests is the water that's preferred by the most people in your school? in your community? Who did your tasters represent? *(Discuss the representative random sampling concept below.)*

3. What makes paired comparisons an effective way of evaluating test samples? What difficulties might you encounter if you tried to test all the waters simultaneously?

4. Does order of testing matter? How could you control this variable? *(Have some tasters compare A vs. B first, others start with B vs. C, and still others, C vs. A.)*

5. Water should quench thirst and be refreshing. Did all the test waters meet these criteria? What other uses are sparkling waters good for?

CONCEPTS:

Representative random sampling: The number of tasters and who they are will affect the results of a taste-preference test. Thus tasters should be representative of the people who use the product. The more people who do the test, the less impact one person's opinion will have on the results.

Paired-comparisons testing: The process of comparing all combinations of test samples and choosing the preferred one makes it easier to control variables. This method is particularly useful in sensory testing where standards of reference (for scoring flavor and freshness) may be particularly difficult to define. In this test all sparkling waters will be compared with each other. All still waters will be compared separately.

ACTIVITIES:

- **Combine groups' scores.** Combine the scores of each group to get a bigger sampling. (To get even more data, students can perform this test at home on family members.)
- **Test local waters.** Students might test samples of tap water from different neighborhoods to determine whether tap waters differ from location to location.

---

3. OFFTASTE TEST, p. 4

QUESTION: What offtastes can you detect in the waters?

WHAT STUDENTS WILL DO:
Students will taste each water, attempt to detect any offtastes identified in the chart on page 4, then check any offtastes they find.

MATERIALS FOR EACH GROUP:
6 coded test waters at room temperature, 6 paper cups for each tester.

OBJECTIVES:
To detect offtastes present in bottled water; to use descriptive vocabulary to identify tastes in water; to recognize how dissolved solids and trace substances can affect the taste of bottled water; to reinforce the value of blind testing.

CONCEPTS:

Trace substances are substances that are present in very small amounts but can still be detected. Trace substances might enter tap or bottled water from the source, pipes, intentional chlorination, etc.

Sensory analysis (taste): The mouth and nose are a sensory system that can be trained to discriminate tastes and flavors. Like vision and touch, the sense of taste can become a scientist's tool.

DISCUSS:

1. What variables might affect this test? *(Temperature of water, kind of cups used, environmental conditions, order of tasting, whether or not a person has a cold, etc.)*

2. Do the bubbles get in the way of sensing and analyzing carbonated water? *(Carbonation might mask unpleasant tastes and make a beverage more appealing to drink.)* How might you control this variable? *("Flatten" a water by removing its CO_2.)*

3. Why is it difficult to apply descriptive terms to water? *(Different people may use the words differently.)* Does trying to associate the tastes with past experiences help (e.g., chlorinated water tastes like swimming pool water)? What other ways might one taste test waters? *(Try to develop standards of reference for the different offtastes.)* Might a water that tastes metallic to one person taste fine to another? Would it help if you tasted metal first to define "metallic"?

4. What other words can you use to describe the way water tastes? *(Bitter, tangy, flat, fruity, rusty.)*

5. What substances dissolved in water might cause offtastes? *(Dissolved minerals and salts, organic materials, etc.)* Do you think these substances are harmful, helpful, or neither? *(In most communities in the U.S. drinking water is safe to drink. Nevertheless, in some communities the local water is contaminated. Dangerous solvents, organic chemicals, heavy metals, bacteria, algae are among the common pollutants.)* How could we find out about the water quality in our community? *(Contact your nearest EPA office.)*

A TEST STUDENTS WILL DESIGN THEMSELVES

Testing procedures are not provided for the following test. Each small group must devise its own plan and procedures. The goal is to encourage hands-on, common-sense creativity and problem-solving by students. There's no one "right way" to do this test.

4. THE PACKAGING TEST, p. 5

QUESTION: Which waters come in containers that can be reused, recycled, or returned for deposit?

OBJECTIVES:
To develop skill at analyzing a problem and creating a way to test it; to understand what is involved in designing a test; to collect and analyze data; to determine which properties make a package environmentally desirable; to gather information using community resources.

POSSIBLE PROCEDURE:
Students could first examine containers to find out what they're made of and check labels to determine whether the containers are returnable and recyclable. (There's a code on all plastic containers.) Students could then survey stores, the sanitation department, and recycling centers to find out about local recycling options.

MATERIALS STUDENTS MAY NEED:
Original containers of the 5 bottled waters.

CONCEPTS:
Solid waste includes garbage, trash, and other non-liquid wastes. Most is disposed of at sanitary landfills where it may pile up and take years or decades to decompose. Some is recycled; some is burned as fuel.

Recycling, which not only gets rid of wastes but also creates useful materials, is considered the solid waste solution of the future by many environmentalists. Whether a bottled water container is recyclable depends not only on the type of material it is made from, but also on what types of materials a community recycles. Community recycling policies and practices vary a great deal.

DISCUSS:

1. What are some environmental consequences of using disposable plastic and glass containers? Is disposing vs. recycling the only concern? Or does it matter what resources are used to make a container? *(Discuss the solid waste problem. Explore the fact that most plastics are made from petroleum, so any environmental problems associated with this industry should be considered. Also consider the fact that petroleum is a non-renewable resource. Glass requires a lot of energy to produce but uses an almost limitless resource — sand.)*

2. Discuss students' responses to the balloon.

WHAT KINDS OF CONTAINERS DOES YOUR COMMUNITY RECYCLE? WILL THAT AFFECT HOW YOU SCORE THE CONTAINERS? HOW? *Some communities don't recycle at all. Others recycle only certain plastics, bottles, and cartons. Check with a local sanitation department or a local environmental group.*

3. How do the test waters compare? Is any type of packaging significantly more earth-friendly than another? How do bottled waters compare with tap?

4. Do you think plastic or glass makes a better drink container? Why? *(Sparkling water will lose carbonation faster in plastic bottles than in glass bottles. Plastic doesn't break.)*

ACTIVITIES:

• **Visit a landfill operation.** Find out how solid waste is handled.

• **Start a recycling program.** Investigate local recycling options and set up a recycling program for the school or community.

5. SOLID-STUFF ANALYSIS, p. 6

QUESTION: Which waters contain dissolved solids?

WHAT STUDENTS WILL DO:

Students will let water samples evaporate to dryness and examine and measure any powdery or crystalline residue left behind to determine the amount of dissolved solids in each water. They will also describe the residues and form hypotheses about what each might contain. With a microscope students may discover organic residue such as algae and diatoms, especially in tap water.

(Distilled water will leave no residue; most seltzers will leave hardly any; club soda, some sparkling mineral waters, and many tap waters may leave detectable amounts, since they most likely contain salts and minerals. Calcium, magnesium, sodium, potassium, and iron salts are often present in tap waters; sodium and potassium salts are common in club sodas.)

MATERIALS FOR EACH GROUP:

100 mL each of the 6 test waters; graduated cylinder; 6 250-mL beakers; magnifying glass, tracing paper, spatula, marker that writes on glass, vinegar (optional), medicine dropper (optional).

OBJECTIVES:

To determine which bottled waters contain dissolved solids; to describe these solids physical properties.

DISCUSS:

1. Where did the water go? *(Evaporated into the air.)* Why didn't the dissolved solids evaporate with the water? *(Because they have extremely high boiling points and do not volatilize [vaporize into gas].)*

2. If you condensed the water vapor, would it have dissolved solids? *(No.)* What do we call water captured in this way? *(Distilled.)*

3. Does the presence of dissolved solids mean the water is polluted? *(Not necessarily. The presence of dissolved minerals and salts in water is normal.)* Note: Federal guidelines for "total dissolved solids" (TDS) and "maximum contaminant level" (MCL) in tap water are 500 mg per liter. A proposed MCL for bottled mineral waters would be the same.

4. Which water had the most solids in parts per million (ppm)? What minerals might have been dissolved in the waters? What data support your hypotheses?

5. If a sediment bubbles or fizzes in vinegar, what does that mean? Discuss students' responses to the balloon.

CALCIUM CARBONATE, SODIUM CARBONATE, AND OTHER CARBONATES CONTAIN CO_2. THUS THEY WILL BUBBLE WHEN MIXED WITH VINEGAR (ACID). WHAT TEST WOULD TELL IF ANY OF THE WATERS CONTAIN A CARBONATE? *To test the hypothesis, students should add a drop of vinegar to the sediment they suspect of containing calcium carbonate or sodium carbonate.*

ACTIVITIES:

- **Water Quality.** Invite a local water supplier or EPA officer to visit the class and discuss water quality in your community.
- **Testing pH.** The Federal government has set guidelines for pH in bottled waters. It suggests (but does not require) that bottled still water have a pH between 6.5 and 8.5. Have students use pH strips to test the pH of each test water.
- **Make distilled water** using the traditional Erlenmeyer flask, one-holed rubber stopper, and tubing method, or simply boil water and collect water vapor on a lid.

COST ANALYSIS, p. 8

QUESTION: After tap water, which test water is least expensive?

WHAT STUDENTS WILL DO:
Students will read labels to determine volume and price per container. They will then figure out number of servings and price per serving.

MATERIALS PER GROUP:
Labels from the 5 bottled waters, calculator.

OBJECTIVES:
To compare prices on a unit basis and judge value; to build skills in ratio calculations and label reading.

CONCEPT:
Unit price: In order to compare the price of similar products (which often come in different-sized containers), one has to compare price on a unit basis. Units may be calculated in terms of weight, volume, or "servings."

DISCUSS:
Why is price particularly important with a product that's likely to be used in great quantities (like a bottled water)?

ACTIVITY:
Figure long-term costs: Have students determine how much water they drink per day and then figure what it would cost per week, per month, and per year if they drank only their preferred bottled water.

DEALING WITH DATA

Of the tests performed on bottled water, only three were given numerical scores. Therefore, the data collected must be analyzed and interpreted qualitatively rather than quantitatively.

Data alone can't say which water is best. Like all facts, data have to be thought about, evaluated, and interpreted in a useful and meaningful way. If misinterpreted, data can mislead consumers instead of guiding them.

INTERPRET YOUR TEST DATA, p. 8

OBJECTIVES:
To express a view concerning what the public ought to know about bottled (and tap) water. To reach conclusions about which water to drink and to express those conclusions in writing.

DISCUSS:

1. What were your conclusions about the waters? What data support your conclusions? How did the tap water compare to the bottled water? What personal judgments were involved?

2. When would you choose a bottled water? When wouldn't you? Why?

ACTIVITY:
Compile the class data on bottled water: Complete the information asked for on the following page. (Note that page 8 calls for drawing *horizontal* bar graphs of data. If students are not familiar with graphing horizontally, review that first.)

COMPILE THE CLASS'S DATA ON BOTTLED WATER

STEP 1
Bar graph the amount of CO$_2$ in each sparkling water.

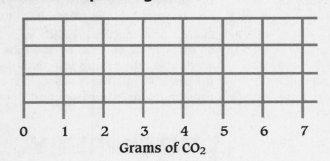

Water

A

B

C

0 1 2 3 4 5 6 7

Grams of CO$_2$

STEP 4

Rank the test waters in order of taste.

Sparkling Waters

Best-tasting: _____

2nd place: _____

3rd place: _____

Still Waters

Best-tasting: _____

2nd place: _____

3rd place: _____

STEP 2
Identify test samples and bar graph the number of offtastes in each bottled water.

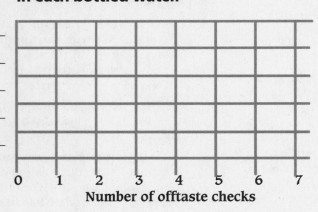

Water Brand

A _____

B _____

C _____

D _____

E _____

0 1 2 3 4 5 6 7

Number of offtaste checks

STEP 5

Which bottled water does the class recommend? Why? How does tap water compare?

_____

_____

_____

_____

_____

_____

STEP 3
Bar graph the price per serving of each bottled water.

Water

A

B

C

D

E

$.0 .20 .40 .60 .80 1.00 1.10 1.20

Price per serving

CONSUMER REPORTS wants to see what you've done. Mail your report to: *Consumer Reports* **Education Division 101 Truman Avenue Yonkers, New York 10703-1057**

Name: _____

School: _____

Address: _____

_____

PRENTICE HALL

PRODUCT TESTING ACTIVITIES by Consumer Reports

TESTING BUBBLE GUM

Testing Bubble Gum helps students discover the science and technology governing the performance of bubble gum: the physical properties of its gum base **(elasticity, plasticity)** and sweeteners **(solubility, food chemistry)**; physical changes resulting from chewing **(saliva, solubility rates, exponential decay curves)**; and sensory attributes **(flavor intensity).** In the process, students develop skill at graphing, controlling variables, and geometry **(measuring diameter).**

Collecting, analyzing, and interpreting the data also involve weight and time calculations, rates of change, and basic statistics (variation, sampling, measurement error). Tests are designed for groups of four. Students work together to conduct and plan tests, analyze data, solve problems, and develop a scientific rating of bubble gums. The chart below links the tests students will perform with the science skills and concepts those testing activities will help teach.

CURRICULUM SKILLS AND CONCEPTS

Test and Student Databook Page	Highlighted Skills	Science Concepts
Getting Started p. 1	Controlling Variables, Blind Testing	Principles of Testing
The Chewing Test p. 2	Observations, Timed Experiments, Graphing	Elasticity, Soluble Flavorings, Taste
The Gum-Base Test p. 5	Rates of Change, Inferring	Solubility, Exponential Decay Curves
The Bubble-ability Test p. 6	Designing a Test, Measuring Spheres	Polymers, Elasticity
The Taste-Preference Test p. 7	Designing a Test, Controlling Variables	Preference Testing, Sampling
Interpret Your Test Data p. 8	Critical Thinking, Rank Ordering	Weighted Scores, Health

MATERIALS NEEDED for each small group:

❑ **Test samples:** 4 different bubble gums: 2 regular, 2 sugar-free (but all the same flavor).

❑ **For pre-planned tests:** Wax paper, timer, colored pencils, balance, water, paper cups.

❑ **Note:** If you don't have enough balances or timers for the whole class, have each group do the tests in a different sequence. That way they can share the equipment.

CLASS-TIME REQUIREMENTS:

❑ To prepare for testing: 1 class period
❑ To conduct Tests 1 through 3: 2 class periods (Data analysis will take additional time and can be assigned as homework.)
❑ To conduct Tests 4 and 5: 1 to 2 class periods
❑ For data analysis and interpretation: 1 class period

GETTING STARTED

1. Prepare test samples in advance.

Gum wrappers should be covered with masking tape (to hide brand identifications) and gums should be placed in bowls coded A through D for students to take from. Save outer packages for analysis after testing is concluded. Have someone who will not be doing these tests prepare the gums. (*Assign this to students who wear braces, or are on sugar-restricted diets, or for other reasons can't chew the gums.*)

2. Distribute Student Databooks, one to each student group.

DISCUSS:

1. Discuss responses to the balloon. Would covering brand names and coding the gums control this variable? (*Yes and no: Some testers might still recognize gums by their shape.*)

IF YOU HAVE A FAVORITE BUBBLE GUM, COULD THAT AFFECT THE WAY YOU JUDGE THESE TESTS?

HOW CAN YOU CONTROL THIS VARIABLE? *Covering brand-name identification on all test gums and coding them helps control this variable.*

2. One thing that will vary in these tests is the bubble gums. But other things (like how long they're left unwrapped and the temperature where they're stored) shouldn't vary. Why not? (*Differences among the gums could be due to uncontrolled variables.*)

3. The goal of testing is to come up with *reliable* results (results that would probably be gotten again if the tests were repeated) and *valid* results (results that reflect actual differences among the products). What helps you do this? (*Controlling variables, collecting and recording data carefully.*)

TESTS ALREADY DESIGNED FOR STUDENTS

The following tests describe the testing procedures students should follow. Allow student groups to work independently and solve problems among themselves. Wait until they've completed their testing before discussing or reviewing the tests. The goal is to encourage independent thinking, creative problem-solving, and increased confidence.

1,2 THE CHEWING TEST, p. 2

QUESTION: Which gum's flavor and chewability lasts the longest?

WHAT STUDENTS WILL DO:
Each student will chew each gum and evaluate its flavor and chewability over six minutes. Students will then calculate average scores for the group, graph them, and decide how to interpret the graphs and rank the gums.

MATERIALS:
4 coded gums, wax paper, timer, different-colored pencils, water, paper cups.

OBJECTIVES:
To develop sensory discrimination skills; to control variables; to build graphing skills.

CONCEPTS:
Soluble flavorings: The amount and kinds of flavoring a gum has affect how intense (strong and long-lasting) its flavor is. Since flavorings dissolve in saliva, they will be swallowed. As that happens, flavor intensity will diminish and the gum will lose weight.

Tongue and taste: Sweeteners are detected by taste buds on the tip of the tongue.

Elasticity is the tendency of polymers with long molecular chains (like gum) to return to their original shape and size after being stretched and manipulated.

DISCUSS

1. What variables were controlled in the Chewing Test? (*Chewing time, tester bias, etc.*) What variables were *not* controlled? (*Rate of chewing, size of the gum piece.*) Could these affect results?

2. Discuss responses to the first balloon. If gum D were always chewed last, might its chewability scores suffer? (*Yes.*) Check your data: Did the gums get lower chewability scores when they were chewed last?

BY THE TIME YOU POP THE LAST PIECE OF GUM IN YOUR MOUTH, YOU'LL HAVE BEEN CHEWING FOR 18 MINUTES. IF THAT LAST GUM SEEMS TOUGH, IT MAY BE THAT YOUR JAWS ARE TIRED!

IF EACH TESTER STARTS WITH A DIFFERENT GUM AND CHEWS GUM IN A DIFFERENT ORDER, WOULD THAT CONTROL THIS VARIABLE? *Yes. Consumer Reports "randomizes" the order in which test samples are tried to control factors like "jaw fatigue."*

3. Examine the individual scores each tester wrote in Boxes 1 and 2 (on page 3 of the Databook). Did testers' scores agree, or were there big differences? What might account for that? (*Uncontrolled variables, different definitions of chewability and flavor, etc.*)

4. What do you think makes a gum less flavorful and harder to chew over time—what does the gum lose? (*As it's chewed, the gum loses its sweeteners, flavorings,*

and softeners, which are all soluble. Large amounts of sweeteners, which are present initially, affect the texture of the gum. Likewise, losing softeners makes gum harder and tougher to chew.*)

5. Why do you think some solids pulverize into tiny pieces when chewed, but others stay in one elastic-like piece? (*Explore polymers: long molecule chains stick to each other and allow the solid gum to stretch.*)

WHICH IS MOST IMPORTANT – HOW FLAVORFUL AND CHEWABLE GUMS WERE AT THE <u>START</u>, IN THE <u>MIDDLE</u>, OR AT THE <u>END</u>? WHY? *Answers will vary. Students could poll others to find out how long they chew gum and how long they expect the flavor to last.*

6. Which should count for more, the gums' scores at the beginning, the middle, or the end of the 6 minutes? What did your group base its scores on? Why? (*Discuss responses to the second balloon.*)

7. Is there a relationship between a gum's chewability-loss and its flavor-loss? (*Compare graphs. Both should diminish over time, since gum flavorings and softeners are soluble.*)

WERE THE GUMS' FLAVOR LINES CLOSE TOGETHER OR FAR APART? SHOULD THEIR SCORES BE CLOSE TOGETHER OR FAR APART? EXPLAIN.

If the gums' flavor lines stay close together, scores should be close. If some are close, but others far away, scores should reflect that.

8. How did you decide whether the gums' scores should be close together or far apart? (*Discuss responses to the third balloon.*)

ACTIVITY:

Control the size-of-gum variable. Most gum pieces will be different sizes. Weigh each one, then cut the larger pieces so they equal the smaller ones. (Or double the amount of smaller-sized gums used in the test.) Repeat the flavor and chewability tests. Do scores change?

3. THE GUM-BASE TEST, p. 5

QUESTION: Which gum has the most gum base?

WHAT STUDENTS WILL DO:

First one student will chew a piece of gum until it stops losing weight to see how long it takes for sweeteners and flavoring to dissolve (about 8 to 12 minutes). Then each student will chew one test gum that amount of time and weigh the remaining gum base. (This way, all four gums can be tested at once.)

MATERIALS:

4 coded gums, wax paper, timer, balance.

OBJECTIVES:

To understand solubility and the physical composition of gum; to develop skill at calculating and interpreting rates.

CONCEPTS:

Solubility: Some ingredients (sweeteners and flavorings) are soluble in saliva, but some (gum base) aren't. Chewing, therefore, lets you measure soluble and insoluble components of gum. The weight a piece of gum loses when chewed is the weight of the sweeteners and flavorings it contained.

Exponential decay curves: A gum's weight-loss curve will be similar to the "half-life" curve of a radioactive substance.

DISCUSS:

1. Do you think the amount of gum base a gum has is important? Why or why not? (*Explore possible links between amount of gum base and how big a bubble you can blow, how many pieces you chew at once, etc.*)

2. Why did the test gums lose weight when you chewed them? (*Sweeteners and flavorings dissolved and were swallowed.*) Why did the weight loss slow down and stop after several minutes? (*Flavorings dissolve from the gum at a constant percent rate. When more flavor is present [at the start], the weight loss is greater. When less is present [at the end], weight loss is less.*)

THE SWEETENERS USED IN SUGARLESS GUMS WEIGH A LOT LESS THAN SUGAR. JUDGING FROM THE GUMS' WEIGHT LOSS, CAN YOU GUESS WHICH GUMS ARE SUGARLESS? *Sugar-free gums have less weight to lose when their sweeteners dissolve. So gums that lost the least weight are most likely the sugar-free ones.*

3. Discuss responses to the balloon. Can you infer which gums were sugarless and which weren't based solely on their weight loss? Explain. (*Sugar-free gums contain sweeteners that weigh much less than sugar. So they have less weight to lose when their sweeteners dissolve.*)

ACTIVITIES:

- **Calculate percent of weight comprised of gum base.** Do gum pieces that start out bigger end up having more gum base? Using their Gum-base test data, students can compute the percent of each gum's weight comprised of gum base. (*Divide weight of gum base by pre-chewed weight and multiply by 100.*)

- **Graph a gum's weight loss over 12 minutes.** Using the data collected when determining chewing time for this test, students can graph the 2-minute weight readings. The graph will look like an exponential decay curve. (See below.)

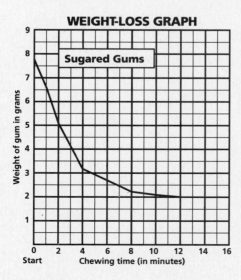

WEIGHT-LOSS GRAPH

Sugared Gums

Weight of gum in grams

Chewing time (in minutes)

Start

TESTS STUDENTS WILL DESIGN THEMSELVES

Testing procedures are not provided for the following two tests. Each small group must devise its own plan and procedures. The goal is to encourage hands-on, common sense creativity and problem solving by students. There's no one "right way" to do these tests.

4. THE BUBBLE-ABILITY TEST, p. 6

QUESTION: Which gum is best for blowing bubbles?

POSSIBLE PROCEDURES:
Students could use homemade calipers (hinged, scissors-like pieces of cardboard) to measure how big the bubble gets before popping, then use a ruler to see how far apart the caliper opening is. Or they could compare pairs of gums: Blow bubbles with two gums and note which is bigger. The winning gum is continually compared with other winning gums until there's one clear winner.

OBJECTIVES:
To understand how to design a controlled test; to observe the physical properties of polymers and discover why some gums make bigger bubbles than others; to discover ways to measure a sphere; to understand the concept of variation.

CONCEPTS:

Elasticity: The tendency of polymers with long molecular chains (like gum) to return to their original shape and size after being stretched and manipulated.

DISCUSS:

1. How important is bubble-ability in a bubble gum? Why? What do you think makes one gum a better bubble-blower than another gum? (*Differences in composition of the gum base. Explore the concept of elasticity: Some gums' polymers are more flexible and cohesive.*)

CAN YOU MEASURE BUBBLES WITH A RULER? PROBABLY NOT. A BETTER METHOD OF MEASURING WOULD BE TO: *Use calipers to measure (see how wide they open to fit around the bubble). Or judge bubbles against a scale drawing. Or do paired comparisons.*

2. What method of measuring bubbles did you think of? Did it work? Why or why not? How many bubbles were blown? By whom? In what order? Who judged size? Do you think these things matter? (*Yes: They are all variables to be controlled.*)

HOW MANY TIMES WILL YOU BLOW BUBBLES WITH EACH GUM? HOW WILL YOU SCORE A GUM IF ITS BUBBLE SIZES ARE ALWAYS VERY DIFFERENT? *The more bubble size varies, the less reliable your data are and the more times you should repeat the test. Compute mean or median size from your data, and use that for scoring.*

3. What variables did you control? (*Bubble-blowing skills? How much gum was used? How long it was chewed? How objectively size was judged? Lip fatigue?*) How did you control them?

4. Is there a relationship between amount of gum base and bubble-ability? Between chewability and bubble-ability?

5. THE TASTE-PREFER-ENCE TEST, p. 7

QUESTION: Which gum tastes best?

POSSIBLE PROCEDURES:

Students may conduct a blind test where they (and perhaps others) taste the gums and indicate preferences. Doing paired comparisons (pairing A to B, A to C, etc. and choosing the better of the two, then "facing off" winners) will provide reliable data. Rating all four together by assigning preference scores to each is also possible.

OBJECTIVES:

To develop skill at designing controlled tests; to understand the concepts of preference testing and sampling; to make predictions.

DISCUSS:

1. How did you conduct this test? What data did you collect? What variables did you control? (*Tester bias? Length of time testers chewed? Number of pieces of gum? The order in which gums were tasted?*)

HOW CAN YOU FIND OUT WHICH GUM WILL BE LIKED BY MOST GUM-CHEWERS? DOES IT MATTER HOW MANY TASTE-TESTERS YOU USE? DOES IT MATTER WHO THEY ARE? *Having more people rate gums will make results more reliable (more likely to predict what others will like). Testers should be representative of people who chew gum.*

2. If you repeated your taste-preference test with other testers, do you think results would be the same? Would it matter if the other testers were completely different from you? Why? (*People of different ages with different backgrounds may have different likes and dislikes. Preference panels should be representative of gum-chewers.*)

3. Have small groups compare their taste-preference scores. Are the gums' ranking orders the same or different? If different, what might have caused the differences? (*Different testing methods, different sampling, different controls.*)

INTERPRET YOUR TEST DATA, p. 8

Students have gathered data and assigned raw scores for all five bubble gum tests. Now they have to figure out what it all means. Data alone can't say which gum is best. Like all facts, data have to be thought about, evaluated, and interpreted in a useful and meaningful way. If misinterpreted, data can mislead consumers instead of guiding them.

WHAT STUDENTS WILL DO:

Students will decide how important tests are, assign them Importance Factors, multiply raw scores by those factors to determine weighted scores, then rank gums from best to worst.

OBJECTIVES:

To understand the concepts of weighting and rank-ordering; to consider health questions.

CONCEPTS:

Weighting: Some tests measure more important qualities than other tests. How gums score in important tests should count for more.

Health questions: Sugars (*sucrose, fructose, glucose*) and slowly metabolizing sugar-like compounds (*sorbitol, mannitol*) are empty calories that provide energy but no other nutrients. They can contribute to weight gain; the sugars also contribute to tooth decay. Some sugar substitutes carry health warnings.

DISCUSS:

1. What are the most important things a gum should do? Which tests got an Importance Factor of 3 (most important)? Why?

2. What are the pros and cons of weighting scores—of making important tests' scores count for more? (*Have each group add raw scores and rank-order gums, then compare that with their weighted-score rankings. Which is more meaningful? Why?*)

3. Discuss responses to the balloon. Is the sugar content of gum a concern? Why do some "sugarless" gum labels say "not low calorie"? (*Technically they don't contain sugar; but they do contain slowly metabolized sugar-like compounds that have the same caloric value as sugar.*) What health rating did you give the test gums? Why?

EXTRA ACTIVITY: PUT TOGETHER THE CLASS'S TEST DATA

CONCEPTS:

- **Sampling:** The samples selected for testing can affect results.

- **Variation:** Data can vary as a result of differences within a brand, making it advisable to test multiple samples. Variation can also arise from uncontrolled variables or changes in testing conditions.

- **Measurement error:** Measurements recorded during testing are subject to variation due to measurement inaccuracy or differences in test conditions. A reliable measurement is closely repeatable from one test run to another.

ACTIVITY:

Make an enlarged copy of the chart on the following page. Have all groups write their raw scores in the appropriate boxes. (Each box will have as many numbers as there are groups.) Assign Importance Factors and determine weighted scores.

DISCUSS:

1. Did everyone who tested come up with the same raw scores for the test gums? Why not? Is it possible every gum A wasn't exactly the same? Can performance vary within a brand? Is it possible measurement errors were made? (*Explore rounding, different interpretations and scoring by testers.*)

2. How can we determine which measurements are most reliable (most likely to happen again if the tests were repeated)? What if we performed each test several times instead of once? What if we based the gums' ratings on the whole class's raw scores combined, instead of just one group's?

3. Examine the class's raw data (on the chart). Which gum (if any) has very little variation in its test scores? Which gum's performance could you predict with more confidence? (*The one with the least variation in scores.*)

SEND YOUR RATINGS OF BUBBLE GUM TO *CONSUMER REPORTS*

The class should fill in this chart and answer all questions about the gums. Attach a written summary of the class's conclusions. Then mail to the address below.

WHICH BUBBLE GUM IS BEST?

"RAW" SCORES

Write the class's combined scores for each test in the boxes below.
Are these ❑ mean scores or ❑ median scores? (Check *one*.)

TEST	A	B	C	D
1. Flavor				
2. Chew-ability				
3. Gum-Base				
4. Bubble-ability				
5. Taste-Preference				
TOTALS				

(Raw-Score Totals)

"WEIGHTED" SCORES

1. Assign Importance Factors to the tests. (3=*most* important, 1=*least* important)

2. Multiply the class's combined raw scores by the Importance Factors.

IMPORTANCE FACTOR:	A	B	C	D
1.				
2.				
3.				
4.				
5.				
TOTALS				

(Weighted-Score Totals)

(1) **Code** **Brand** **Type**
(sugarless or not?)

A _____ _____

B _____ _____

C _____ _____

D _____ _____

(2) How many small groups tested the gums?_____

(3) Date_____

(4) Person to contact (name and address):

_____

_____

_____

_____

(5) **Mail To:**

Consumer Reports
Education Division
101 Truman Avenue
Yonkers, New York 10703-1057

PRENTICE HALL

PRODUCT TESTING ACTIVITIES by Consumer Reports

TESTING CEREALS

Testing Cereals integrates science and nutrition: the four basic grains **(blind testing, sensory analysis, types of grains)**; taste **(sweetness and flavor)**; nutrition **(carbohydrates, fats, sodium, label reading)**; serving size **(measuring, collecting and interpreting data, label reading)**; crispy-crunch evaluation **(designing experiments, food texture)**; cost analysis **(unit price)**. Students also learn how to articulate hypotheses, design scientifically valid tests, and identify and control variables. They discover that in evaluating foods, subjective criteria play an important role and provide significant data if an appropriate ranking system is applied.

Tests are designed for groups of four students to do together. The chart below links tests students will perform with the science skills and concepts they will learn.

CURRICULUM SKILLS AND CONCEPTS

Test and Student Databook Page	Highlighted Skills	Science Concepts
Getting Started p. 1	Controlling Variables, Blind Testing	Principles of Testing
The Four Basic Grains p. 2	Sensory Analysis	Maintaining Objectivity
The Taste Test p. 3	Sensory Analysis (Taste)	Sweeteners, Flavor Intensity
The Nutrition Test p. 4	Counting Calories, Graphing, Reading Labels	Balanced Diet, Carbohydrates
The Serving-Size Test p. 6	Measuring, Calculating	Serving Sizes, Ratios
The Crispy-Crunch Test, p. 7	Designing Experiments, Variables	Porosity of Solids
Cost Analysis p. 8	Calculating Ratios	Unit Price
Interpret Your Test Data, p. 8	Drawing Conclusions, Making Recommendations	Rank Orders

MATERIALS NEEDED
for each small group:

❏ **Test samples:**
For the pre-test: 4 single-grain, low-sugar cereals (oat, wheat, corn, rice), as similar in shape and/or density as possible.
For the tests: 4 different types of cereal (sugar-coated; granola or with nuts and fruit; low-sugar flake or square; and low-sugar, low-sodium).

❏ **For pre-planned tests:**
Paper cups, spoons, milk, water, cereal box labels, cereal bowl, colored pencils, calculator, balance, measuring cup.

❏ **Note:**
To curtail costs, students can bring samples for the pre-test from home, as only small quantities will be needed.

CLASS-TIME REQUIREMENTS:

❏ To prepare and do the Pre-Test: 1 class period
❏ For Tests 1 and 2: 1 class period.
❏ For Tests 3 and 4: 1 or 2 class periods
❏ For data interpretation and discussion: 1 class period

GETTING STARTED

1. Code test samples.

Although students should test the cereals "blind," it won't be possible to disguise brands: Cereals' shapes will identify them. In several tests students will be using packages for label reading. Despite this, sound procedure requires that cereals be identified by codes rather than brand names.

Prepare test samples in advance: Tape over (or black out) brand names on the test cereal boxes. Transfer cereals to covered containers. Code the 4 pre-test cereals W, X, Y, and Z. Code the 4 test cereals A, B, C, and D.

2. Distribute Student Databooks, one to each group.

DISCUSS:

1. What kinds of dry cereal do you prefer? What particular quality, or qualities, do you look for when choosing a cereal?

2. What is a well-balanced diet? Should cereals be part of a person's diet? (*Explore the importance of cereals as sources of carbohydrates and energy.*)

3. Discuss responses to the balloon.

WHAT ARE THE MAIN INGREDIENTS OF CEREALS? ARE SOME INGREDIENTS BETTER FOR YOU THAN OTHERS? WRITE YOUR HYPOTHESES HERE. *Grains are the main ingredients. Many cereals also contain sweeteners, salt, dried fruits, raisins, flavorings, etc. Fortified cereals have added vitamins and minerals. All these ingredients have a place in our diets; sugars and fats should be consumed in moderation.*

4. Discuss the product testing process described on page 1. What are variables? Why is it important to control them? What are data? Why is keeping records important?

TESTS ALREADY DESIGNED FOR STUDENTS

The following tests describe the testing procedures students should follow. Allow student groups to work independently and solve problems among themselves. Wait until they've completed their testing before discussing or reviewing the tests. The goal is to encourage independent thinking, creative problem-solving, and increased confidence in their scientific abilities.

PRE-TEST THE FOUR BASIC GRAINS, p. 2

QUESTION: How do the four main cereal grains differ in flavor?

WHAT STUDENTS WILL DO:

Students will sample each cereal dry, check off tastes and flavors of each cereal, sample the cereals with milk to determine whether milk enhances any flavors or tastes, then attempt to identify the grain in each cereal.

MATERIALS FOR EACH TESTER:

4 single-grain, low-sugar cereals (oat, wheat, corn, rice), coded W, X, Y, and Z, paper cups, spoon, milk, water.

Note: Very few dry cereals are composed of only a single grain. Most combine two or three. Here are some single-grain cereals that also have low-sugar content and few added flavors:

GRAIN	CEREAL
Wheat	Shredded Wheat, Puffed Wheat
Corn	Corn Flakes, Corn Chex
Rice	Puffed Rice, Rice Chex, Rice Crispies
Oats	Cheerios, Oat Flakes

OBJECTIVES:

To identify four cereal grain flavors; to use descriptive vocabulary to identify tastes and flavors in cereals.

CONCEPTS:

Kinds of cereals: Cereals are edible grains (wheat, oats, corn, rice) or a food prepared from such grains. The main ingredient in most breakfast cereals is grain, but many also contain nuts, dried fruits, malts, flavorings, sweeteners, etc.

(continued)

Tastes and flavors: All foods contain substances that stimulate the senses of taste and smell. Tastes, sensed by specialized cells in the tongue, include sensations for saltiness, sweetness, bitterness, and sourness. Flavors, sensed by specialized cells in the nose, include toasty, nutty, fruity, and a host of other stimuli such as aromas of all kinds. Sensory evaluations of foods are based primarily on taste, flavor, and aroma and to some extent on texture and appearance.

DISCUSS:

1. Were you able to accurately distinguish the different grain flavors? How else might you learn to distinguish these flavors? *(Possibly sample the whole grains.)*

2. Which cereal had the most flavor? the least? Did flavor intensity come from the grain or some other ingredient? How could you find out? *(Possibly read the cereal box label.)*

3. Did milk affect the taste of the cereals? Why? *(Chemicals that produce tastes might dissolve in milk and stimulate more taste cells in the tongue. The milk's taste might mask or bring out tastes of the cereal.)*

4. Did you prefer one grain over another? Explain. *(Discuss responses to the balloon.)*

WHICH GRAIN FLAVOR DID YOU LIKE BEST? WHY? WOULD OTHER PEOPLE AGREE WITH YOU? TEST YOUR HYPOTHESIS. *Answers will vary. To test their hypothesis, students could conduct a preference taste test involving a range of people.*

5. Why did we code the cereals before doing this test? *(To control the variable of tester bias.)* Would using a blindfold be a better way to control this variable? What other variables did we control? *(Followed same procedure for each cereal, used the same cups, cleaned mouth with water between tastings, etc.)*

ACTIVITY:

• **Make a taste map of the tongue.** Certain tastes are sensed by different parts of the tongue. Obtain cotton swabs and solutions of salt water (salty), sugar water (sweet), flat tonic water (bitter), and lemon juice or diluted vinegar (sour). Dip a swab into each solution and touch it to the tip, front sides, back sides, and back middle of the tongue. Where is the taste strongest? Based on your observations, make a taste map of your tongue. *(Tip, salty and sweet; front sides, salty and sour; back middle, bitter; back sides, sour.)*

1. THE TASTE TEST, p. 3

QUESTION: Which test cereals have the right amount of sweetness and plenty of grain flavor?

WHAT STUDENTS WILL DO:
Students will taste the cereals twice, first to rate them for sweetness, then to rate them for intensity of grain flavor.

MATERIALS FOR EACH TESTER:
4 test cereals (coded A, B, C, and D), 5 paper cups, spoon, water, milk (optional).

OBJECTIVES:
To rank cereals for sweetness and grain flavor intensity; to develop sensory discrimination skills.

CONCEPTS:

Sweeteners: The sweet tastes in cereals are produced by various carbohydrates and occasionally by sugar substitutes. Table sugar (sucrose) is only one source of sweetness. Honey, corn syrup, malt syrup, and certain fruit juices contain sugars other than sucrose and are used to impart sweetness to dry cereals. Some cereals are sweetened with a synthetic sweetener, aspartame, which isn't a carbohydrate.

Flavor intensity is the amount of flavor a food has. An intense flavor can be either pleasant or unpleasant. The opposite of flavorful is bland. Many cereal grains are toasted, which enhances their otherwise bland flavor.

DISCUSS:

1. Did any of the cereals have lots of grain flavor but not enough sweetness? How could you correct this? *(Explore the idea of sweetening a cereal yourself with sugar.)* Some people prefer to buy an unsweetened cereal and sweeten it themselves. Do you think this is a good idea? Why or why not? *(Doing so lets you control the amount of sugar ingested. It also ensures that the cereal you're buying is mostly grain. Heavily pre-sweetened cereals can be half sugar.)*

2. In addition to a grain flavor, what other flavors should a cereal have? Where do you think the flavors come from? *(Help students determine the different kinds of flavorings added to cereals.)*

3. Discuss students' responses to the balloon.

WOULD ADDING MILK TO THE CEREALS CHANGE THE RESULTS OF THIS TEST? TEST YOUR HYPOTHESIS. *Milk is likely to enhance the flavors in a cereal. (See question 3, page 3 of this guide.)*

ACTIVITIES:

• **Determine the ingredients in cereals.** Read ingredients labels on the test cereals and on cereal boxes at home to determine the wide variety of ingredients found in cereals.

• **Measure sweetness.** To quantify sweetness, have students add sugar to an unsweetened cereal, a half-teaspoon at a time. How much sugar is just right?

---

2. THE NUTRITION TEST, p. 4

QUESTION: How much fat, sugar, sodium, and complex carbohydrates are in a serving of each cereal?

WHAT STUDENTS WILL DO:

In part A, students will read nutrition labels on the test cereals; record amounts of fat, sugar, and sodium per serving; rank cereals based on how much of those nutrients they contain, then determine overall ranking by averaging ranks. In part B, students will record and bar graph amounts of sugar and complex carbohydrates and judge sugar and carbohydrates ratios.

MATERIALS:

Labels from coded test cereals A, B, C, and D, calculator, different-colored pencils.

OBJECTIVES:

To compare the per-serving amount of fat, sugar, sodium, and complex carbohydrates in the test cereals; to distinguish simple from complex carbohydrates; to build graphing skills.

CONCEPTS:

Nutrients are necessary for energy, growth, and maintenance of the body. Nutrients are found in the foods we eat and include proteins, carbohydrates (sugars and starches), and fats.

To maintain health, people need a well-balanced diet that derives 55 to 70 percent of its calories from carbohydrates, 20 to 30 percent from fats, and 10 to 15 percent from proteins. Grains are a good source of complex carbohydrates and also contain fiber, proteins, vitamins, and minerals.

DISCUSS:

1. What is a balanced diet? What positive roles do fats, sugars, and sodium play in the body? *(Fats help make certain vital chemicals and provide a source of stored energy. Sugars are a more immediate source of energy. Sodium plays a role in processes like transmitting nerve impulses.)*

2. What negative effects might excessive amounts of fats, sugars, and sodium have on the body? *(Too much fat and sugar can increase body weight above normal. Some fats contribute to the clogging of arteries over time, leading to heart problems. Too* *much sodium is linked with increased blood pressure in some people.)*

3. What is the major source of calories in all of the cereals? *(Carbohydrates.)* Which cereals have a high ratio of complex carbohydrates (starches) to simple carbohydrates (sugars)? *(Discuss students' bar graphs.)*

4. Discuss students' responses to the balloon.

> MOST CEREALS GIVE NUTRITION INFORMATION WITH AND WITHOUT MILK. WOULD FACTORING IN MILK CHANGE THIS NUTRITION PROFILE? HOW?
> *Yes. Milk is high in protein and also contains fats, sodium and carbohydrates. Whether milk is whole, lowfat, or skim will make a big difference in the calories and fat it adds.*

ACTIVITIES:

- **Create a cereal.** Students can create their own breakfast cereals. Their formulations can consist of some of the pre-test cereals, other whole grain cereals, fresh or dried fruits, unsalted nuts, and other foods. In preparing their formulations, students should make an "ingredients label" like that found on commercial cereal boxes, listing ingredients in order of predominance by weight. Students can bring their formulations to school for taste testing by classmates.

- **Compare RDA's.** Have students study the nutrition-label panel on the cereal boxes to determine the U. S. Recommended Daily Allowance (U.S. RDA) for vitamins and minerals. Students may find that some manufacturers fortify cereals by adding vitamins and minerals to give them unusually high RDA's. Which cereals seem to be fortified? *(Can cereals that are nearly half sugar provide many vitamins and minerals without being fortified?)*

3. THE SERVING-SIZE TEST, p. 6

QUESTION: How do actual serving sizes compare with those given on cereal labels?

WHAT STUDENTS WILL DO:
Students will pour what they consider to be a serving of each cereal into a bowl, weigh that amount of cereal, and compare with the serving size stated on the label. They will hypothesize how a larger or smaller serving than the one listed on the cereal label would affect the nutrition information given there.

MATERIALS FOR EACH GROUP:
4 test cereals coded A, B, C and D, labels from those cereals, cereal bowl, balance (0.1g), calculator, measuring cup.

OBJECTIVES:
To determine whether actual serving sizes are equivalent to serving sizes stated on the label; to make weight measurements.

CONCEPT:
Serving sizes: The concept of what constitutes a single serving is arbitrary rather than scientific. Obviously, one person's single serving will vary from that of another, although to some extent they will be similar due to the somewhat uniform size of cereal bowls. Nutrition information on the label should be adjusted to reflect the actual amount of cereal eaten.

DISCUSS:

1. Of what value is this serving-size analysis? *(It can help you figure out how many calories and how many nutrients you're getting from a serving of cereal.)*

2. Why do you think serving sizes differ? *(Different cereals have different weights and volumes.)* When estimating nutrients per serving, which is easier to use — serving size based on weight or volume? Why?

3. How could you come up with a standard serving size that was realistic? *(Have many people pour out a single serving. Average the amounts poured.)* Might the size of the bowl influence the cereal-pourers? *(Possibly. People might put more cereal in a large bowl than in a small one.)* How could you correct this? *(Give each person a range of bowls to choose from.)*

4. Discuss students' responses to the balloon.

SUPPOSE THE SERVING SIZE YOU POUR OUT IS LARGER OR SMALLER THAN THE SERVING SIZE ON THE CEREAL BOX. HOW WOULD THIS AFFECT CALORIE AND NUTRIENT DATA? *If your serving size is smaller, number of calories and amount of nutrients will be smaller; if serving size is larger, the opposite will be true.*

ACTIVITIES:

- **Serving size ratios.** Students will determine the ratio between an actual serving size and the serving size on the label (actual size divided by label-size). Students could use these actual-to-label-size ratios to compute nutrition information for actual serving sizes.

- **Conduct a survey.** As a follow-up to question 3, students might survey population segments (children and adults of all ages and weights, or people in specific weight or age categories). All subjects should be given a box of the same cereal and a selection of cereal bowls and asked to pour out what they consider to be one serving. Data should be averaged to arrive at a serving size. Results for different population segments could be compared.

A TEST STUDENTS WILL DESIGN THEMSELVES

Testing procedures are not provided for the next test. Each small group must devise its own procedures and identify the materials needed and the variables to be controlled. The goal is to encourage hands-on, common-sense creativity and problem solving.

4. THE CRISPY-CRUNCH TEST, p. 7

QUESTION: Do some cereals stay crispier in milk than others?

POSSIBLE PROCEDURES:
Students might chew the cereals dry to determine their starting crispiness. They could then measure out a serving of one cereal into a bowl, add enough milk to cover, then taste the cereals again at short time intervals to determine levels of crispiness. The cereals could be ranked according to the length of time it took to lose their original crispiness.

OBJECTIVES:
To determine which cereal remains crispy in milk the longest; to understand how to design a controlled test; to develop sensory testing skills.

CONCEPT:
Porosity of solids: The extent to which a solid becomes soggy when immersed in milk is due to a number of factors including its shape and porosity. Porosity refers to the property of having pores, which are tiny channels or spaces. When the pores of a cereal flake fill up with milk, the previously solid and crispy flake becomes wet and soggy.

DISCUSS:
1. What variables did you control? (*Soaking time in milk, intervals between tastings, size of bowl, amount of milk used.*)

2. Is this an objective or subjective test? Why? (*Probably subjective; crispiness* values determined by chewing a cereal or otherwise feeling it in your mouth or hands will vary from person to person and thus be subjective.) How could you make it more objective? *(Use an instrument that can measure the moisture level of the cereals.)*

3. What properties of cereals might make the cereals become soggy in milk? *(Cereals that are porous absorb milk easily and will become soggy quickly.)* What might slow or prevent this process? *(Not removing natural waterproof coats from the cereal grains during processing would keep cereals from becoming soggy quickly. Coating cereals whose natural waterproof coats were removed during processing with a hardened sugar glaze.)*

4. Discuss responses to the balloon.

IS THERE A RELATIONSHIP BETWEEN HOW SWEET A CEREAL IS AND HOW WELL IT KEEPS ITS CRUNCH? DOES IT MATTER WHETHER THE SWEETNESS COATS THE OUTSIDE OF A CEREAL OR IS BAKED INSIDE? *Sugar dissolves more quickly in liquids than flour does, so the sweeter cereals might lose their crunch first unless they're coated. A hardened sugar glaze could prohibit liquid absorption. Could test by setting up a controlled test with lots of samples*

DEALING WITH DATA

Students have collected a great deal of data in the process of performing the various tests on cereals. The data include subjective determinations (flavor and taste, texture), objective measurements and derived values (nutrient amounts), and assignment of ranking and other scores. Now it is time for students to make some sense of the data to arrive at overall conclusions.

On page 8 (Interpret Your Test Data), students have been asked to factor in cost data by determining price per serving.

COST ANALYSIS AND INTERPRET YOUR TEST DATA, p. 8

WHAT STUDENTS WILL DO:

Students will calculate the unit price of the cereals, then review test results, decide what's most important when choosing a cereal, and make recommendations.

OBJECTIVES:

To figure and compare unit costs; to perform calculations; to analyze test data; to devise a method of interpreting data to arrive at a significant conclusion.

DISCUSS:

1. Which tests were subjective? Which were objective?

2. Based on the data, are processed dry cereals generally healthful products? *(Some are more so than others.)*

3. How did each group rank the cereal characteristics on page 8? Why?

4. Have small groups share the conclusions they wrote in response to the questions on page 8 of the Student Databook. Did the small groups arrive at the same or different conclusions? Why? Do their data differ, or just their opinions? Explore.

COMPILE THE CLASS'S DATA ON CEREALS

STEP 1
Graph the crispness scores for each cereal. (Average the class's data.)

Cereal   Brand

A   _____

B   _____

C   _____

D   _____

1   2   3   4   5

STEP 2
Graph the actual serving sizes the class poured in Test 3. (Average the class data.)

A

B

C

D

10   15   20   25   30   35   40   45 g
Weight of actual serving

STEP 3
Graph the cost of an actual serving of each cereal. (Average the class data.)

A

B

C

D

$.10   .20   .30   .40   .50   .60   .70   .80

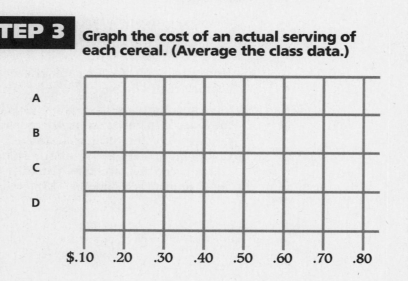

STEP 4
Rank the cereals in order of grain flavor.

Best: _____

2nd place: _____

3rd place: _____

4th place: _____

5th place: _____

_____

STEP 5
Which cereal does the class recommend? Why?

_____

_____

_____

_____

_____

_____

CONSUMER REPORTS wants to see what you've done.
Mail your report to:
Consumer Reports **Education Divison 101 Truman Avenue Yonkers, New York 10703-1057**

Name:_____

School:_____

Address:_____

_____

PRENTICE HALL
PRODUCT TESTING ACTIVITIES
by Consumer Reports

TESTING DISPOSABLE CUPS

Testing Disposable Cups helps students discover how well different types of cups keep drinks hot or cold and perform other cup tasks. Rather than comparing brands, students will compare three types of disposable cups and a nondisposable ceramic cup. Students will discover how cups lose (and gain) heat (**heat transfer, insulation, measuring, graphing temperature change**); why cups tip over (**geometry**); which cups feel most comfortable (**predicting, designing use tests**); and which cups pose environmental problems (**volume of solids**).

Students will also design tests themselves (**problem solving, planning, controlling variables**). These, as well as data analysis and graphing activities, could be homework assignments.

Tests are designed for groups of four. Students work together to conduct and plan tests, analyze data, solve problems, and develop a scientific rating of the test cups. The chart below links the tests students will perform with the science skills and concepts those testing activities help teach.

CURRICULUM SKILLS AND CONCEPTS

Test and Student Databook Page	Highlighted Skills	Science Concepts
Getting Started p. 1	Controlling Variables, Blind Testing	Principles of Testing
The Heat-Loss Test p. 2	Measuring and Graphing, Temperature Change	Heat Transfer, Heat Capacity
Cool-Touch Test p. 4	Forming Hypotheses, Observation	Conduction, Insulation
The Heat-Gain Test p. 4	Making and Interpreting Graphs, Inferring	Heat Transfer, Insulation
The Tip-Over Test p. 6	Designing a Test, Measuring Shapes	Geometry
Comfort Test p. 7	Designing a Test, Evaluating Data	Representative Samples
Trash Test p. 7	Measuring Volume, Estimating	Degradability
Interpret Your Test Data p. 8	Ranking, Critical Thinking, Forming Conclusions	Weighted Scores, Statistics

MATERIALS NEEDED
for each small group:

❑ **Test samples:** Three types of disposable cups (waxed paper for cold drinks, foam polystyrene, and plastic-coated paper for hot drinks) and a ceramic nondisposable cup. Cups should be the same size (since surface area is a variable to control). (5 of each type of disposable cup should suffice.)

❑ **For pre-planned tests:** Aluminum foil, 4 thermometers, measuring cup, timer, rubber bands, sharp pencil, hot water (60 to 65°C), ice water (0 to 5°C), and different-colored pencils for the graphing activities.

CLASS-TIME REQUIREMENTS:
❑ To prepare for testing: 1 class period
❑ For Tests 1 and 2: 1 class period (plus 30 min for data analysis)
❑ For Test 3: 1 class period (plus 30 min for data analysis)
❑ For Tests 4 to 6: 1 or 2 class periods
❑ For data interpretation: 1 class period

GETTING STARTED

1. Code test samples.

This test is designed to test cup types, not brands. Although students will notice which cups are paper, polystyrene, plastic, etc., the cups still should be identified by code letter to simplify data collection.

Prepare test samples in advance: Remove packaging. Code the test cups A, B, C, and D. (Write codes on packaging.)

2. Distribute Student Databooks, one to each student group.

DISCUSS:

1. Describe the disposable cups you've used at home, in school, at fast-food chains, and at parties. Might a different type of cup be suitable for each of those uses? What qualities do good cups (and bad cups) have? What are the pros and cons of using disposable cups instead of reusable ones? What might testing cups reveal?

2. Discuss the product-testing process described on page 1. Why is it important that others be able to get the same results if they repeated the tests? What can you do to make your test results repeatable? (*Explore controlling variables, taking measurements, recording data carefully, using explicit criteria.*)

3. Why would the temperature of the place you put the hot-drink cups affect how quickly they cooled off? (*Heat transfer is proportional to the difference in temperature between the cups' contents and their surroundings. Cups in cool places will cool off faster than cups in warm places.*) How can you control this variable?

THE TEMPERATURE OF THE PLACE WHERE YOU PUT CUPS OF HOT WATER WILL AFFECT HOW QUICKLY THEY COOL OFF. HOW COULD YOU CONTROL THIS VARIABLE? *Put all cups in the same place during the test; check to make sure none are in a draft or direct sunlight, etc.*

TESTS ALREADY DESIGNED FOR STUDENTS

The first three tests describe testing procedures for students to follow. Allow students to work independently. Each group should solve problems among themselves. Wait until groups have completed testing before discussing or reviewing tests. The goal is to encourage independent thinking, creative problem solving, and increased confidence in their own scientific abilities.

1. THE HEAT-LOSS TEST, p. 2

QUESTION: Which cups are best at keeping drinks hot?

WHAT STUDENTS WILL DO:

After covering test cups of hot water with foil and inserting thermometers, students will record how the water temperature changes over 1, 5, 10, 15, and 20 minutes, then graph the data.

MATERIALS FOR EACH GROUP:

4 coded test cups, 4 thermometers, aluminum foil, sharp pencil, measuring cup, timer, 4 rubber bands, 750 mL hot water (60 to 65°C), different-colored pencils.

Note: Heat water before class and put it into a large thermos to keep it hot and to make it easier for small groups to use.

OBJECTIVES:

To observe, measure, and understand heat transfer and heat loss; to develop temperature measurement and graphing skills.

CONCEPTS:

Heat transfer: Heat tends to move from hotter to cooler substances to reach thermal equilibrium.

Heat capacity: The quantity of heat transfer needed to increase or decrease the temperature of 1g of a substance 1°C.

DISCUSS:

1. What variable does covering the cups control? (*Losing heat via radiation.*) What other variables should be controlled?

2. Do you think you should pre-heat the cups for this test? (*Discuss responses to the first balloon.*)

DO YOU THINK YOU SHOULD HEAT THE TEST CUPS BEFORE DOING THIS TEST? WHY OR WHY NOT?

WRITE YOUR IDEAS HERE. *Pre-heating would bring all cups to the same starting temperature, so cups' (especially the ceramic cup's) heat capacity won't make a difference. Not pre-heating simulates the way cups are usually used. Either answer is defensible.*

3. What could have kept the ceramic cup from losing so much heat at the start? (*Pre-heating it. Discuss heat capacity.*)

4. Analyze the Heat-Loss Graph: Did water lose heat at the same rate across time, or did heat-loss rates change? Why? (*Heat loss slows down since heat transfer is proportional to the difference in temperature between the cups' contents and the surroundings.*)

5. Which do you think is more important, heat-loss rates over the first 10 minutes or the last 10 minutes? (*Discuss responses to the second balloon.*)

WHICH DO YOU THINK IS MORE IMPORTANT — HEAT-LOSS RATE OVER THE <u>FIRST</u> 10 MINUTES OR THE <u>LAST</u> 10 MINUTES? WHY?
As the cups' water cools, heat-loss rates slow down, so you're likely to see bigger differences at first. From the user's viewpoint, debate how quickly people drink hot liquids – and how long the cup should insulate.

ACTIVITIES:

- **Compute rates.** Using heat-loss data, students' can compute rates of temperature decrease (°C/minute) for each cup during the first and last time intervals of the test.

- **Estimate temperatures in cups between readings.** Use graphs to estimate minute-by-minute temperatures of the cups.

- **Test another variable** — the heat of the ceramic cup when hot water is poured in. Preheat the ceramic cup by filling it with hot water just before the test. Then pour that water out, add the hot test water, and see how the preheated cup's heat loss compares with its original heat loss.

- **Spreadsheet exercise.** If your class is working with computers, input data from this test and compute overall rate of temperature drop, minute-by-minute heat loss, and ratios of early rates to later rates.

2. COOL-TOUCH TEST, p. 4

QUESTION: Which cup stays cooler to the touch when filled with hot liquid?

WHAT STUDENTS WILL DO:
Students will use data on how hot the cups felt in Test 1 to give them Cool-Touch scores.

MATERIALS FOR EACH GROUP:
Data from Test 1.

OBJECTIVE:
To discover the relationship between insulating properties/heat conduction and how hot something feels.

CONCEPTS:

Conduction: Objects that feel hotter are conducting heat more rapidly from warmer substances to cooler ones.

Insulation: Materials that are less efficient at heat transfer, thereby keeping warm substances from losing heat and cooling off, are good insulators. Materials that trap air tend to be good insulators.

DISCUSS:

1. Is there a connection between a cup's heat loss and how hot it feels? Compare Test 2's scores with Test 1's. Are scores similar? What does that mean? (*Cups that feel the hottest are losing heat the fastest—the heat you feel is heat escaping. Cups that feel coolest are the best insulators.*)

2. Think about ceramic cup design. Why do you suppose most are made with handles?

3. THE HEAT-GAIN TEST, p. 4

QUESTION: Which cup is best at keeping drinks cold?

WHAT STUDENTS WILL DO:
Students will repeat the Test 1 procedure, recording how cool ice water in the test cups stays over 1, 5, 10, 15, and 20 minutes, then graphing their data.

MATERIALS FOR EACH GROUP:
4 coded test cups, covers and rubber bands from Test 1, 4 thermometers, 750 mL ice water (0 to 5°C), timer, measuring cup, different-colored pencils.

OBJECTIVES:
To reinforce concepts of heat transfer, conduction, and insulation; to develop skill at drawing and interpreting graphs; to infer relationships between results of two tests.

CONCEPTS:

Heat transfer, conduction: When liquids and cups are colder than the surrounding air, heat moves from the air to the cup and then to the liquid, warming them up. Your fingers may feel cold when holding some cups because heat is being conducted from your fingers to the cooler cup.

Insulation: Materials that resist heat transfer will prevent the warmer air from warming up the cooler liquid. (That's why insulation can keep homes warmer in winter and cooler in summer.)

DISCUSS:

1. Why did all cups have to start with the same water temperature? What other variables did we control? Are there any variables that we should have controlled but didn't?

2. Which cups did you think would do best in this test, cups that did best or worst in

the Heat-Loss Test? Did results of this test support your hypothesis? (*Discuss responses to the balloon and compare graphs and scores for Tests 1 and 3.*)

WHICH CUPS DID THE BEST IN THIS TEST—THE WINNERS OR LOSERS OF THE HEAT-LOSS TEST? WHY?
Cups that are good insulators should do well in both tests. A material that slows down heat transfer will work whether heat is entering or escaping.

3. What is the purpose of graphing the test results? Did graphs make it easier or harder to determine scores for Tests 1 and 3? Did graphs make it easier or harder to compare Tests 1 and 3? Why?

ACTIVITIES:

- **Have small groups compare their test results.** See how similar or varied their data are. Compare their Heat-Gain scores and graphs. Which is more consistent from group to group, the graphs or the scores? Why? (Which involves more interpretation of data? Does interpreting data add another variable?) If the groups' data differ, what are some possible reasons for the differences (variation)?

- **Control a different variable.** Repeat the test with 2 or 3 cups of the same type but different sizes. Discuss the effect of the surface area-to-volume ratio on heat loss.

- **Put data on a spreadsheet.** If the class is working with computers, enter data and compute rates of temperature rise. Compare with temperature-drop rates from Test 1.

TESTS STUDENTS WILL DESIGN THEMSELVES

Testing procedures are not provided for the following three tests. Each small group must devise its own plan and procedures. The goal is to encourage hands-on, common sense creativity and problem-solving by students. *There's no one "right" way to do these tests.* Encourage students to devise charts for recording data and to attach all data sheets to their Databooks.

WHAT DO YOU THINK MAKES A CUP EASY TO TIP OVER? HARD TO TIP OVER? WRITE YOUR HYPOTHESES HERE. *A small base, thin cylinder, light weight, and conical shape with large rim may make a cup tippy.*

4. THE TIP-OVER TEST, p. 6

QUESTION: Which cup is hardest to tip over?

POSSIBLE PROCEDURE:

Students may gradually tip the cups and use a protractor to measure the angles the cups will stay at before tipping over. (The cups may be empty or filled with sand or water.)

OBJECTIVES:

To encourage creative problem-solving; to understand design-weight interrelationships; to develop skill at ratios and measuring geometric shapes; to develop skills in designing controlled tests.

VARIABLES TO CONTROL:

Amount of weight (water or sand) added to cups; how evenly tipping force is exerted; whether cups are on a flat surface.

DISCUSS:

1. Have several groups describe how they tested for tippiness. Were test procedures similar? Were test results similar (did the groups find the same cups to be tippy and not tippy)? If yes, what does that mean? (*That their data are probably reliable.*) If not, what does that mean? Should tests be redesigned and repeated?

2. What makes a cup tippy — what was your hypothesis? Did your tests prove or disprove your hypotheses? (*Discuss responses to the balloon.*)

3. If the test cups are different heights and if you filled them before tipping them, what should you control—the height of the water (or sand) or the total amount of water (or sand)? Debate! (*The higher the water, the higher the center of gravity, which could make a cup less stable. But the more water, the greater the weight, which could make the cup more stable.*)

ACTIVITY:

Compute ratios of cup height to the diameter of its base; of the area of the base to the area of the rim; of height to volume, etc. Is there a relationship between these ratios and the cups' tippiness?

5. COMFORT TEST, p. 7

QUESTION: Which cup is more comfortable to use?

POSSIBLE PROCEDURE:

Using as many "testers" as possible, students will gather comfort-preference data on the cups. Testers will either score cups on a comfort scale, or (better) do paired comparisons: Choose the more comfortable of two cups, then repeat until all possible pairings have been judged.

OBJECTIVES:

To understand differences between collecting objective and subjective data; to become aware that more data lead to more reliable conclusions (especially with subjective data, which are less reliable and prone to error); to build skill at designing controlled tests.

VARIABLES TO CONTROL:

The number of testers; how clearly defined the comfort criteria are; the sequence in which cups are judged; whether cups are clean (or bent, dented, etc.); which pairs are compared, etc.

DISCUSS:

How many people did you have do this test? Why? Who were they? What groups did they represent (e.g., kid? adult?)? Do you think your results can predict how most other people would rate the cups' comfort? Why or why not? (*Discuss responses to the balloon.*)

WHEN TESTING SOMETHING LIKE COMFORT, IS IT BETTER TO GATHER <u>SEVERAL</u> PEOPLE'S JUDGMENTS OR TO MAKE ALL JUDGMENTS BY YOURSELF? WHY? *Consumer Reports would gather lots of people's judgments because people differ. The more people who do the test, the more likely it is that test results will predict others' opinions of the cups.*

6. TRASH TEST, p. 7

QUESTION: Which cup will take up the least space in a landfill?

POSSIBLE PROCEDURES:

After crushing disposable cups in a uniform manner, students could judge volume with a ruler or measuring cup; or they could measure volume more accurately by seeing how much water each crushed cup displaces. Test plans should also take into account the waste-difference between disposable and reusable cups over time.

OBJECTIVES:

To consider the environmental impact of consumer choices; to develop estimation and test-design skills; to discover ways of measuring volume of irregular solids.

CONCEPTS:

Solid waste disposal: Landfills are fast filling up because they tend to retard rather than promote degradation. In order to degrade, special conditions (light, moisture, biological agents, etc.) must be met. Most landfills don't meet these conditions: They pre-mix and cover all types of refuse. So the volume of trash is a primary concern.

DISCUSS:

1. How did you test? How big a difference in "crushed volume" did you find among the disposable cups? Why is volume of a disposable cup an important environmental consideration?

2. What are some other environmental issues to consider when selecting a disposable cup? (*Explore energy resource depletion and pollution in making the cups and transporting them to stores; water and energy needed to wash reusable cups.*)

3. Does a claim to be "degradable" or "recyclable" make one cup more earth-friendly than another? (*Explore what is needed for degradable cups to degrade and for recyclable cups to be recycled [a local recycling program for that material].*)

4. Should Trash Test scores and other environmental data be used to determine an overall rating of cups? Or should environmental issues be dealt with separately? Why?

ACTIVITIES:

- **Research and discuss the life-cycle of cups:** what they're made from, how they're made, the energy and pollution costs, and what's involved in "maintaining" them. Why have disposable cups become so popular?

- **Evaluate fast-food chains' drink cups:** What types of cups do chains use, why, and what are the alternatives?

- **Design the "perfect" drink cup for home use and for cafeteria use:** What will it be made of? How big will it be? What shape will it be? Will it be disposable or not?

INTERPRET YOUR TEST DATA, p. 8

Students have gathered data from all six tests. Now they have to figure out what it all means! Data alone can't say which cup is best. Like all facts, data have to be thought about, evaluated, and interpreted in a useful and meaningful way. If misinterpreted, data can mislead consumers rather than guide them.

WHAT STUDENTS WILL DO:

First, students will rank tests in order of importance, compile scores for the three most important tests (a method of "weighting"), rank cups from best to worst, and compute cost per cup, using label information. Next, they'll form conclusions and express "what it all means" in simple written sentences.

OBJECTIVES:

To understand the concept of weighting and rank-ordering; to evaluate other factors, like price and environmental impact.

MATERIALS FOR EACH GROUP:

Wrappers/packages from the cups with brand name and price information.

CONCEPT:

Weighted scores: Some tests measure more important qualities than other tests do. How cups score in important tests should count for more (have a greater impact on the cup's overall score). One simple way to "weight" scores is not to count in scores of less-important tests when compiling overall scores.

DISCUSS:

1. What are the three most important things a cup should do (from your page 8 rank order)? Why?

2. What are the pros and cons of just counting the three most important tests' scores? Average all six test scores and compare with the "weighted" scores. Does that change the cups' rank-order? If yes, which ranking seems most meaningful? Why?

3. Have students share their four conclusions. If they were the editorial staff of *Consumer Reports*, what would their article on disposable cups say? Why?

EXTRA ACTIVITY: PUT TOGETHER THE CLASS'S TEST DATA

CONCEPTS:

Sampling: The samples selected for testing can affect results.

Variation: Data can vary as a result of quality differences within a brand, making it advisable to repeat tests on multiple samples.

Measurement error: Measurements recorded during testing are subject to variation due either to measurement inaccuracy or differences in test conditions (e.g., if one group is working near a drafty window). An accurate measurement is closely repeatable from one test run to another.

ACTIVITY:

Make an enlarged copy of the chart on page 8 of this guide. Have all groups write their raw scores in the appropriate boxes. (Each box will have as many numbers as there are groups.) Average scores, then decide on Importance Factors for each test and determine weighted scores.

DISCUSS:

1. Did everyone who tested come up with the same raw scores for the test cups? Why not? Is it possible every cup A wasn't exactly the same? Can performance vary within a brand? Is it possible measurement errors were made? (*Explore rounding, different interpretations of scoring by testers.*)

2. How can we determine which measurements are most reliable (most likely to happen again if the test were repeated)? What if we performed each test several times instead of once? What if we based the cups' ratings on the whole class's raw scores combined, instead of just one group's?

3. Examine the class's raw data (on the chart). Which cup (if any) has very little variation in its scores? Which cup's performance could you predict with more confidence? (*The one with the least variation in scores.*) What might be some causes of the variation?

SEND YOUR RATINGS OF DISPOSABLE CUPS TO *CONSUMER REPORTS*

The class should fill in this chart and answer all questions about the cups. Attach a written summary of the class's conclusions. Then mail to the address below.

WHICH DISPOSABLE CUP IS BEST?

"RAW" SCORES

Write the class's combined scores for each test in the boxes below.
Are these ❏ mean scores or ❏ median scores? (Check *one*.)

TEST	A	B	C	D
1. Heat-Loss				
2. Cool-Touch				
3. Heat-Gain				
4. Tip-Over				
5. Comfort				
6. Trash				
TOTALS				

(Raw-Score Totals)

"WEIGHTED" SCORES

1. Assign Importance Factors to the tests. (3=*most* important, 1=*least* important)
2. Multiply the class's combined raw scores by the Importance Factors.

IMPORTANCE FACTOR:	A	B	C	D
1.				
2.				
3.				
4.				
5.				
6.				
TOTALS				

(Weighted-Score Totals)

(1) **Code**   **Brand**   **Type**

A _____ _____

B _____ _____

C _____ _____

D _____ _____

(2) How many small groups tested the cups? _____

(3) Date _____

(4) Person to contact (name and address):

_____

_____

_____

_____

(5) **Mail To:**

Consumer Reports
Education Division
101 Truman Avenue
Yonkers, New York 10703-1057

Testing Food Wraps helps students discover the science and technology governing the effectiveness of food wraps: How well food wraps keep air out of food **(oxygen permeability)**; how well wraps hold in moisture **(water vapor permeability)**; and which wraps are strongest **(tensile strength)**. It also builds scientific inquiry and testing skills by challenging students to make observations, control variables, hypothesize, and design testing procedures. Tests are open-ended: *There is no one answer, no desired conclusion.*

Collecting, analyzing, and interpreting the data also involve a variety of mathematics skills and concepts: weight calculations, addition and subtraction, averaging, graphing, and rates.

Tests are designed for groups of four. Students work together to conduct and plan tests, analyze data, solve problems, interpret results, and develop a scientific rating of the test wraps. Open-ended questions are asked throughout (and may be assigned as homework). The chart below links the tests students will perform with the science skills and concepts those activities help teach.

CURRICULUM SKILLS AND CONCEPTS

Test and Student Databook Page	Highlighted Skills	Science Concepts
Getting Started p. 1	Controlling Variables	Principles of Testing
The Air-Out Test p. 2	Controlling Variables, Using a Control	Oxygen Permeability, Molecular Action
Moisture-In Test p.4	Forming Hypotheses, Weighing, Graphing	Evaporation, Molds
The Tight-Seal Test p. 6	Designing a Test, Forming Hypotheses	Electrostatic Attraction
The Strength Test p. 7	Designing a Test, Controlling Variables	Tensile Strength, Paired Comparisons
Polarizing Experiments (Extra Test)	Observation, Inferring, Critical Thinking	Plastics, Polymers, Polarization, Light
Interpret Your Test Data p. 8	Mathematics, Ranking	Data Analysis, Weighted Scores, Sampling, Variation

MATERIALS NEEDED for each small group:

❏ **Test samples:**
3 different types of plastic wrap: polyethylene (*Handi-wrap* or *Glad Wrap*), polyvinyl chloride (*Reynolds Plastic Wrap* or *Borden Sealwrap*), and polyvinylidene chloride (*Saran Wrap*). 1 roll/package of each should suffice for 10 small groups.

❏ **For pre-planned tests:**
Covered plastic container, apple, knife, 3 small glasses, 3 rubber bands, 4 slices fresh white bread, balance.

CLASS-TIME REQUIREMENTS:

❏ To prepare for testing: 1/2 class period
❏ To conduct Tests 1 and 2: 2 class periods, spread out over one week
❏ To conduct Tests 3 and 4: 1 or 2 class periods
❏ For data analysis and interpretation: 1/2 class period

GETTING STARTED

1. Code test samples.

Leave test wraps in their packages (so they can be neatly rolled out and torn), but use adhesive to tape over brand names. Then code each wrap A, B, and C. Have a ruler and black marker pen by each package so students can measure the pieces they cut and write codes on them.

2. Distribute Student Databooks, one to each student group.

DISCUSS:

1. Discuss responses to the balloon on page 1. If you used different-sized pieces of wrap, would the tests be fair? *(The Databook has all pieces cut to 30-cm lengths.)*

> IF YOU USED DIFFERENT-SIZED PIECES OF EACH WRAP, WOULD THE TESTS BE FAIR? WRITE YOUR HYPOTHESIS HERE. *The size of each piece of food wrap is a variable to be controlled. A bigger piece could wrap tighter; a smaller piece would wrap looser. Test results would be due to these circumstances more than the wraps themselves.*

2. One thing that will vary in these tests is the food wraps: They are all different. But other things (like the temperature and humidity where wrapped foods are stored) shouldn't vary. Why not? *(If that happened, test results wouldn't necessarily be due to the wraps. It's best to test for one variable at a time. To do this, all test samples should be exposed to exactly the same conditions and procedures.)*

3. The goal of testing is to come up with reliable results — results that would probably be gotten again if the tests were repeated. How does controlling variables help you do that? What else should you pay attention to? *(Explore collecting data carefully and keeping good records, checking data, repeating tests.)*

TESTS ALREADY DESIGNED FOR STUDENTS

The first two tests describe the testing procedures students should follow. They involve observation and weighing activities over one week.

Allow student groups to work independently and solve problems among themselves. Wait until they've completed their testing before discussing or reviewing the tests. The goal is to encourage independent thinking, creative problem-solving, and increased confidence in their scientific abilities.

1. THE AIR-OUT TEST, p. 2

QUESTION: Which wrap keeps air out the best?

WHAT STUDENTS WILL DO:

Students will place 3 apple slices in glasses and cover each with a test wrap, then wrap 3 other slices directly in the test wraps. Two slices will be controls and left unwrapped. Students will judge how the wrapped slices compare with the unwrapped controls over the next two days.

MATERIALS FOR EACH GROUP:

3 coded wraps, covered plastic container, apple, knife, 3 glasses, 3 rubber bands.

OBJECTIVES:

To gain skill at making sequential observations; to understand oxygen permeability and the purpose of an experimental control.

CONCEPTS:

Oxidation: When certain foods are exposed to air, oxygen reacts with them, causing discoloration.

Oxygen permeability: Materials that allow oxygen to pass through are oxygen permeable. The extent to which a food wrap allows air to pass through it is a measure of its oxygen permeability.

Effects of temperature on molecules: Molecules of a gas (air, oxygen) gain energy and speed up when heated, but slow down when cooled. When moving slowly, fewer molecules collide with and permeate the wraps.

Control: How a sample would fare without any treatment (wrapping) helps to assess how much of a difference the test treatments (wraps) make in the first place. Controls provide an objective reference for making scoring judgments.

DISCUSS:

1. Discuss responses to the balloon. How did you control those variables? Were there any other variables that should have been controlled?

HOW LONG THE APPLE SLICES SIT BEFORE THEY'RE PUT INTO THE GLASSES IS A <u>VARIABLE</u>. SO IS HOW TIGHTLY YOU SECURE THE WRAPS TO THE GLASS. HOW WILL YOU CONTROL THESE VARIABLES? *Control the variables by putting all the slices into their glasses at the same time; cover them immediately; use rubber bands that are the same size; wrap them around each glass the same number of times.*

PLASTIC WRAP

2. What do you think would have happened if the test-wrapped apples were refrigerated? Would lowering the temperature affect the passage of air through the wraps? Why? (*Repeat the Air-Out Test but refrigerate the samples. Are the data different? Why?*)

3. Why were the unwrapped slices included in this test? Did they make it easier to assign Air-Out scores to the wraps? (*Explore the purpose of an experimental control.*)

4. Discuss responses to the second balloon. How do you think the plastic container would compare with the wraps? (*In their tests, Consumer Reports scientists found that plastic covered containers kept moisture in and air out better than plastic wraps.*)

2. MOISTURE-IN TEST, p. 4

QUESTION: Which wrap holds moisture in best?

WHAT STUDENTS WILL DO:
After wrapping bread with the test wraps, students will weigh the wrapped slices (and the control) right away and again after 1 day, 3 days, and 1 week. They'll subtract to find weight loss, graph their data, and interpret results.

MATERIALS FOR EACH GROUP:
3 coded wraps, 4 slices fresh white bread, balance (0.1g), different-colored pencils.

OBJECTIVES:
To discover how the movement of water vapor molecules through food wrap can cause food to dry out; to reinforce the skills of weighing and graphing.

CONCEPTS:

Evaporation: Water molecules near the surface of a moist solid (e.g., a bread slice) tend to vaporize into the drier air and escape. A barrier (like food wrap) can trap the moist air, which will slow down this process and keep moisture in the food.

Molds: A warm, moist culture fosters the growth of mold spores. If a wrap is excellent at keeping moisture in (and air out), mold may form on the bread after a week. The worse a wrap is at keeping moisture in, the slower molds will grow.

DISCUSS:

1. Discuss the first balloon. Why did the bread lose weight? Which lost more weight, the wrapped or unwrapped bread? Why does a food wrap cut down the weight loss? (*Explore evaporation and vapor permeability.*)

WHY DO BREAD SLICES LOSE WEIGHT? WHY DO SOME SLICES LOSE MORE WEIGHT THAN OTHERS? *Slices lose weight because water is evaporating from them and escaping through the wrap. The slices that lose the most weight will be the ones in the most water-permeable wraps.*

2. Discuss responses to the second balloon on page 5. When did the bread slices lose weight the *fastest*—at the beginning of the week or the end of the week? Why?

> THE GRAPH SHOWS HOW RATES OF WEIGHT-LOSS COMPARE. WHAT DOES THE STEEPEST GRAPH LINE MEAN? *The fastest weight loss.*

> DID EACH WRAP'S WEIGHT LOSS RATE SLOW DOWN OR SPEED UP? *Rates will slow down because after a while the bread has less moisture to lose.*

3. Open your week-old wrapped bread. Is mold growing on any slices? Is there more mold on some slices than on others? Is there a relationship between how much moisture the wrap kept in and how much mold is growing? Why? *(Explore molds.)*

4. What variables could have affected the results of this test? *(The number of thicknesses of wrap; how tightly the wrap was sealed; whether all bread was from the same loaf; whether one slice was an end piece; where the wrapped slices were placed [they'll lose moisture faster in a warm, dry place]; how accurately they were weighed, etc.)* Were these variables controlled? How?

5. Compare air permeability and water permeability of the test wraps (Tests 1 and 2). Did test wraps that allowed air in also allow moisture out? Are some wraps permeable to one and not the other?

ACTIVITY:

Test a different variable: temperature. Use just one plastic wrap to wrap several slices, then put them in places that have a different temperature and humidity (refrigerator, by a radiator or heater, in an incubator, under a hot light, etc.). Weigh over one week and compare data: Which conditions increase the rate of moisture loss? Which impede it? Why? *(Explore the effect of temperature on the activity of water vapor molecules and the effect of moisture/humidity on evaporation.)*

TESTS STUDENTS WILL DESIGN THEMSELVES

Testing procedures are not provided for the following two tests. Each small group must devise its own plan and procedures. The goal is to encourage hands-on, common sense creativity and problem-solving by students. There's no one "right" way to do these tests.

3. THE TIGHT-SEAL TEST, p. 6

QUESTION: How well does each wrap hold a seal?

OBJECTIVES:
To discover how to plan a fair test and collect reliable data; to think about the molecular make-up of food-wrap materials; to reinforce the importance of controlling variables.

POSSIBLE PROCEDURES:
Students may try to duplicate cling-demonstrations in TV ads. Or they may test for keeping gooey sauce in (wrap and store oil-soaked bread slices, seal-side facing down, weighing periodically to see how much weight/oil they lost). Or they could wrap salt or sand, place in a bag, and then shake to see which wrap loses the most; etc.

> DO YOU THINK "CLING" IS A GOOD TEST OF A WRAP'S SEAL? CAN A WRAP HAVE TOO MUCH CLING? WRITE YOUR HYPOTHESIS HERE. *Since all wraps are plastic, they can cling (be inherently adhesive, at least to themselves). Strong cling can indicate a good seal, but too much cling can make a wrap hard to use.*

CONCEPT:

Electrostatic attraction: Plastic wrap can cling to itself and to other containers (glass, plastic) because of electrostatic attraction between the polymer molecules in the plastic and other materials. If the attraction has electric properties (acts "magnetic"), wetting the wraps with oil or detergent solutions may neutralize those forces, as may a metal container.

DISCUSS:

1. What did you test for? What procedure did you follow? Why? What measurements did you make? What would you do differently next time?

2. What variables did you control? How did you control them? Are there other variables that you didn't control?

3. Did you find a difference in "cling" among the test wraps? *(Food wrap is composed of long polymer molecules, which are attracted to molecules in itself and other materials, leading to "cling." Differences in the polymers and additives will produce differences in cling.)*

4. THE STRENGTH TEST, p. 7

QUESTION: Which wraps are strongest?

OBJECTIVES:

To develop inquiry and testing skills by designing product tests; to explore paired comparison testing methods; to understand the concept of tensile strength; to reinforce the importance of controlling variables.

POSSIBLE PROCEDURES:

Utilizing the paired-comparison method, students could spring-clip together pairs of wraps, pull them in opposite directions to see which tears first, and keep eliminating the weaker wrap until the strongest wrap is identified. (Wraps should be pulled in both directions, horizontally and vertically, since they may be weaker in one direction.) Since wraps that stretch the most will tend to take the most force without tearing, students may pull on strips of the wraps and measure how far they stretch before tearing.

CONCEPTS:

Tensile strength is the ability to withstand pulling and stretching without tearing. It's affected by the direction in which the long polymer molecules run (the wrap will stretch more in that direction) and by plasticisers (chemicals that impart flexibility).

Paired-comparison testing: Pairing off test samples, choosing the better of each pair, comparing winners, and so forth until all but the best have been eliminated is a reliable way of evaluating products. It eliminates many hard-to-control variables. It's like the process of elimination.

DISCUSSION:

1. How did you test the wraps for strength? Did you find any relationship between how well a wrap stretched and how strong it was?

2. Discuss responses to the balloon.

COULD YOU MEASURE STRENGTH BY COMPARING PAIRS OF WRAPS AND ELIMINATING THE WEAKER ONE? *Comparing pairs — the process of elimination — is the easier way to test because fewer variables (like amount of force exerted and for how long) have to be measured. With special equipment, testing and measuring the wraps separately could give more accurate data.*

EXTRA TEST: POLARIZING EXPERIMENTS

QUESTION: Which plastic wraps change structure most when stretched? How does this explain the wrap's elasticity?

WHAT WILL HAPPEN:

When viewed between sheets of polarizing material, plastic film (wrap) appears to change color as it is stretched. This visually demonstrates that polymer molecules can be rearranged under the stress of stretching. Polarization will be most obvious along the areas of greatest stress.

MATERIALS:

Enough plastic polarizing sheets (available from *Edmund Scientific*, Barrington, NJ 08007) to provide each group with two 4-cm-by-4-cm pieces, a light source (classroom window), tape.

PROCEDURE:

1. Tape one polarizing sheet to the window. While looking at it, rotate the other polarizing sheet between it and your eye and observe how light transmission is reduced in certain positions. *(A polarizer transmits light waves vibrating in one direction and blocks the rest. Light can pass through two polarizers if they are lined up the same way, but it will be blocked if they're not lined up.)*

2. Rotate the polarizing sheet in your hand to the dark (non-aligned) position. Have someone hold a piece of plastic polyethylene wrap between the two polarizing sheets and rotate it slowly. It's molecular structure will make the effect more dramatic. What do you observe?

3. Stretch the plastic wrap while holding it at different angles between the polarizing sheets. What do you observe? *(The wrap may look different if you stretch it lengthwise and widthwise. A flexible plastic, it's composed of long polymer molecules tangled together like a plate of spaghetti. When stretched, the molecules line up along the direction of stretching and polarized light is altered into a rainbow of colors.)*

DEALING WITH DATA

Students have gathered data and assigned raw scores for all food-wrap tests. Now they have to figure out what it all means!

Data alone can't say which food wrap is best. Like all facts, data have to be thought about, evaluated, and interpreted in a useful and meaningful way. If misinterpreted, data can mislead consumers instead of guiding them. There's no one right way to deal with data.

- While "dealing with data," students will be using basic mathematics skills as well as learning statistics in a hands-on way. They will also be saying "what it all means" — expressing in simple written sentences what their tests revealed about food wraps. Data are seen as a means to an end, rather than an end in themselves.

- The Databooks have students analyze and interpret the data their small group collected. Much can be learned by having small groups compare their results and combine their data to come up with class results (see the Extra Activity on the following page).

INTERPRET YOUR TEST DATA, p. 8

OBJECTIVES:

To understand that data can be combined in different ways; to develop skill at interpreting data, ranking, and expressing scientific findings in simple language.

WHAT STUDENTS WILL DO:

After deciding which tests are more important, students will assign them Importance Factors and multiply raw scores by those factors to determine weighted scores. Then they'll rank food wraps from best to worst in the ratings chart, compute cost of using, and give additional information.

CONCEPT:

Weighting: Some tests measure more important qualities than other tests. How a food wrap scores in important tests should count for more (have a greater impact on the wrap's overall score).

DISCUSS:

1. What are the most important things a food wrap should do? Which food-wrap tests did you give an Importance Factor of 3 (*most* important)? Why?

2. What are the pros and cons of weighting scores—of making important tests' scores count for more? Did weighting the scores change the wraps' ranking order? *(Have each group add unweighted scores and rank-order wraps, then compare that with their weighted-score rankings. Which is more meaningful? Why?)*

3. What are some "one-day" wrap jobs? What are some jobs that require the wrap to work several days? Is there a difference in which wrap is better for the "short" jobs and which is better for the "long" ones? *(Discuss the ratings students gave the wraps for one-day and several-day jobs in the ratings chart.)*

4. What about the covered plastic container—would it ever be preferable to a disposable food wrap? What are the environmental costs and benefits of a reusable rather than a disposable wrap?

5. What were your conclusions (question 6 on page 8)? Have small groups share their findings and advice.

EXTRA ACTIVITY: PUT TOGETHER THE CLASS'S TEST DATA

CONCEPTS:

Sampling: The samples selected for testing can affect results.

Variation: Data can vary as a result of differences within a brand, making it advisable to test several samples. Variation can also arise from uncontrolled variables or changes in testing conditions.

Measurement error: Measurements recorded during testing are subject to variation due either to measurement inaccuracy or differences in test conditions (e.g., if one group left its wrapped slices in a hotter area). A reliable measurement is closely repeatable from one test run to another.

ACTIVITY:

Make an enlarged copy of the chart on the following page. Have all groups write their raw scores in the appropriate boxes. (Each box will have as many numbers as there are groups.) Have the class calculate means or medians, assign Importance Factors to the tests, and determine weighted scores.

DISCUSS:

1. Did everyone who tested come up with the same raw scores for the test wraps? Why not? Is it possible every piece of wrap A wasn't exactly the same? Can performance vary within a brand? Is it possible measurement errors were made? *(Explore rounding, accuracy, different interpretations and scoring by testers.)*

2. How can we determine which measurements are most reliable (most likely to happen again if the tests were repeated)? What if we performed each test several times instead of once? What if we based the wraps' ratings on the whole class's raw scores combined, instead of just one group's?

3. Examine the class's raw data (on the chart). Which wrap (if any) has very little variation in its test scores? Which wrap's performance could you predict with more confidence? *(The one with the least variation in scores.)*

SEND YOUR RATINGS OF FOOD WRAPS TO *CONSUMER REPORTS*

The class should fill in this chart and answer all questions about the food wraps. Attach a written summary of the class's conclusions. Then mail to the address below.

WHICH FOOD WRAP IS BEST?

"RAW" SCORES

Write the class's combined scores for each test in the boxes below.
Are these ❑ mean scores or ❑ median scores? (Check *one*.)

TEST	A	B	C
1. Air-Out			
2. Moisture-In			
3. Tight-Seal			
4. Strength			
TOTALS			

(Raw-Score Totals)

"WEIGHTED" SCORES

1. Have the class vote to assign Importance Factors to the tests. (3=*most* important; 1= *least* important)
2. Multiply the class's combined raw scores by the Importance Factors.

IMPORTANCE FACTOR:	A	B	C
1.			
2.			
3.			
4.			
TOTALS			

(Weighted-Score Totals)

(1) **Code** **Brand**

A _____

B _____

C _____

(2) How many small groups tested the food wraps? _____

(3) Date _____

(4) Person to contact (name and address):

_____

_____

_____

_____

(5) **Mail To:**

Consumer Reports
Education Division
101 Truman Avenue
Yonkers, New York 10703-1057

PRENTICE HALL

PRODUCT TESTING ACTIVITIES by Consumer Reports

TESTING GLUES

Testing Glues helps students discover the science and technology governing the performance of glues: how well the glues bond wood **(adhesion, tension, force)**; how well glues stand up to environmental variables **(temperature effects, solubility)**; how fast glues dry **(evaporation, film formation)**; how well glues bond different materials **(adhesion, surface properties of solids)**; appearance of glued materials **(solubility)**. It also builds scientific inquiry and testing skills by challenging stu-dents to form hypotheses, control variables, analyze data, and design testing procedures themselves. *There is no one right answer, no desired conclusion.*

Tests are designed for groups of four. Students work together planning tests, analyzing data, solving problems, and developing a scientific rating of the glues. The chart below links the tests students will perform with the science skills and concepts those testing activities help teach.

CURRICULUM SKILLS AND CONCEPTS

Test and Student Databook Page	Highlighted Skills	Science Concepts
Getting Started p. 1	Controlling Variables, Blind Testing	Principles of Testing
Prepare Test Samples, p. 2	Reading Directions, Measuring	Evaporation
The Strength Test p. 3	Measuring, Controlling Variables	Adhesion, Tension
The Torture Test p. 4	Comparing, Forming Hypotheses	Solvents, Temperature
The Drying-Speed Test, p. 5	Controlling Variables	Evaporation, Porosity
Stick-To-Stuff Test p. 6	Designing a Test	Adhesion, Properties of Solids
The Appearance Test p. 7	Controlling Variables, Designing a Test	Solvents
Interpret Your Test Data, p. 8	Analyzing Data, Forming Conclusions	Weighted Scores, Variation

CLASS-TIME REQUIREMENTS:

❑ To prepare test samples: 1 class period
❑ To conduct Tests 1 through 3: 3 class periods
❑ To conduct Tests 4 and 5: 2 class periods (or home assignments)
❑ For data analysis and interpretation: 1 class period

MATERIALS NEEDED for each small group:

❑ **Test samples:** 4 different glues (white glue, household cement, rubber cement, and mucilage, white paste, or glue stick). Don't include epoxy or instant glues. Household cement isn't water-soluble, so have a solvent like acetone (nail polish remover) available. Keep contain-ers closed to prevent drying.

❑ **For pre-planned tests:** 48 15-cm-by-2-cm wood strips (tongue depres-sors, available at phar-macies), 24 2-inch spring clips, ruler, pen or pencil, heavy twine, bathroom scale, tape, sink, water, aluminum foil, marker, timer, 4 wood sticks, 12 cotton swabs.

GETTING STARTED

1. Code test samples.

Although students must read each glue's label (for application directions), they should identify the glues by code letter rather than brand name. Blind testing is standard scientific procedure for keeping tester bias from skewing test results.

Code test samples in advance (or have a student who won't be testing the glues code test samples). Cover all brand-name identification on glue containers with a marker or tape, being sure not to cover label directions. Code the glues A, B, C, and D.

2. Distribute Student Databooks, one to each student group.

DISCUSS:

1. What is the point of testing glues? What can you learn? How can you use test results?

2. One thing that will vary in these tests is the glues. But other things (like drying place and time) shouldn't vary. Why not? (*Results wouldn't necessarily be due to the glues. It's best to test for one variable at a time. To do this, all test samples should be exposed to exactly the same conditions and procedures.*)

3. What's more important for a tester to do: control variables by using the same amount of each glue or follow each glue's application directions? Discuss responses to the balloon on page 1.

HOW MUCH GLUE YOU USE AND HOW YOU APPLY IT ARE <u>VARIABLES</u>. BUT SOME GLUES' <u>DIRECTIONS</u> TELL YOU TO USE LESS OR TO APPLY IT IN A SPECIAL WAY. WHAT SHOULD A TESTER DO?
It depends on what you're testing for. If you want to know which glue is stronger drop for drop, control the amount used. If you want to know which will work best in real-life use, follow its directions.

PREPARE TEST SAMPLES, p. 2

WHAT STUDENTS WILL DO:

Students will record each glue's directions for use, then follow those directions to bond 6 pairs of sticks with each glue. They will mark each pair with the test glue's code, clamp them with spring clamps, and leave them in the same place overnight to dry.

OBJECTIVES:

To prepare glued samples for strength and torture tests; to reinforce the importance of reading directions and controlling variables.

MATERIALS FOR EACH GROUP:

Test glues, 48 15-cm-by-2-cm wood sticks (tongue depressors), 24 2-inch spring clips, ruler, pen or pencil, glues' directions.

DISCUSS:

1. Discuss the glues' directions. Which directions are similar? Which are different? Do you think it's a good idea to clamp all glued pairs together, even if the directions don't call for that? Why or why not? (*Clamping aids bonding by maintaining maximum contact between the glue and the glued surfaces. Clamping all wood strips gives all glues this benefit, thereby controlling a variable.*)

2. Discuss responses to the balloon.

EACH TEST GLUE CONTAINS A SOLVENT AND A SUBSTANCE THAT WILL STICK TO THINGS. WHEN THE GLUE IS EXPOSED TO AIR, ITS SOLVENT EVAPORATES, MAKING THE GLUE SET.

GEE, THEN I GUESS IT'S IMPORTANT TO PUT ALL GLUED WOOD IN THE <u>SAME PLACE</u> TO DRY. WHY?
Variations in temperature and humidity affect how fast the glues' solvents will evaporate (and therefore how fast they dry). Putting glued wood in the same place controls these variables.

TESTS ALREADY DESIGNED FOR STUDENTS

The first three tests describe the testing procedures students should follow. Allow student groups to work independently and solve problems among themselves. Wait until they've completed their testing before discussing or reviewing the tests. The goal is to encourage independent thinking, creative problem-solving, and increased confidence in their scientific abilities.

1. THE STRENGTH TEST, p. 3

QUESTION: Which glue forms the strongest bond with wood?

WHAT STUDENTS WILL DO:
Students will apply increasing tension to a glued joint by pulling it up with twine until it fails. One student will stand on the sticks; a second will stand on the scale and pull the twine; a third will read the scale to see how much weight is applied before the glued joint breaks.

MATERIALS FOR EACH GROUP:
Wood-strip pairs glued with A, B, C, and D (2 of each), heavy twine (4 meters), tape, bathroom scale.

OBJECTIVES:
To understand adhesion and ways of measuring force (tension); to reinforce the importance of controlling variables.

CONCEPTS:
Adhesion is a tendency of one substance to stick to another. Most synthetic glues consist of polymers — huge molecules (assembled from simpler molecules) that are strong and very attracted to other substances. The bonding of materials involves adhesion between the molecules in the glue and those on the surfaces of the materials to be bonded.

Tension is the stress exerted on materials by applying force, causing the materials (here the glue and wood) to stretch, elongate, bend, or break. (In this test, the tension force is measured in pounds, using a bathroom scale.)

DISCUSS:

1. What variables might affect the results of the tests? *(The size of the area glued; how close your feet are to the bond and how fast you pull on the twine; how uniformly the glue was applied; warping of the wood, etc.)*

2. How could you control these variables? *(Keep glued areas the same size; have your feet overlap strips the same distance; pull the twine slowly and evenly; examine wood strips for warping before testing.)*

3. Could the wood break before the bond fails? *(Yes, if the affinity of the glue for the wood is greater than the internal strength of the wood — or if there's a defect in the wood.)* How can you tell if a break in the wood is due to strong glue or weak wood? *(Repeat several times. If the wood keeps breaking, it's most likely that the glued joint is stronger than the wood.)* Discuss students' responses to the balloon.

WHAT DOES IT MEAN IF THE WOOD STRIP BREAKS BEFORE THE GLUED JOINT BREAKS? WHAT SCORE WOULD YOU RECORD FOR THAT GLUE? *If the wood breaks first it means the glue bond is stronger than the forces holding the wood together — or the wood strip had a defect. If you test again and the same thing happens, the glue deserves a score of 5.*

Puller → ← Holder

Recorder →

ACTIVITY:
Test for variation. Prepare another 6 sets of wood strips glued with the test glues. Then repeat the Strength Test multiple times and compare results. Discuss sources of variation *(variation in wood strips, variables like pulling strength and measurement error).*

2. THE TORTURE TEST, p. 4

QUESTION: Which glue holds up best under difficult conditions?

WHAT STUDENTS WILL DO:
Using the technique described in Test 1, students will measure the strength of the test glues' bonds after exposure to heat and water.
Note: Students have to leave glued strips on a radiator for five to seven days before doing this test.

MATERIALS FOR EACH GROUP:
Sticks glued with A, B, C, and D (4 of each), sink of water, twine, tape, bathroom scale.

OBJECTIVE:
To understand the effect of temperature on evaporation, drying, and adhesion.

CONCEPTS:
Heat and cold: Environmental conditions may dry out or in some way weaken a glue's adhesive grasp on materials.
Solvents: Some glue bonds that harden as their solvents evaporate can be weakened or broken if their solvents are reapplied. Some glues with water-based solvents may weaken in water.

DISCUSS:
1. Did heat affect how strong a glue's bond was? *(Compare results of the Strength Test and this test. Heat can weaken some glues.)* Why do you think heat affects some glues' bonds? *(Heat accelerates evaporation or degradation, which can dry out the glue.)*

2. What new variables had to be controlled in this test? *(Temperature, temperature variations, length of soaking, etc.)*

IF A GLUE DISSOLVES OR WEAKENS IN WATER, WHAT TYPE OF SOLVENT DO YOU THINK IT HAD? WRITE YOUR HYPOTHESIS HERE. *A glue that weakens in water probably has a water-based solvent. Test glues that didn't weaken in the water may not be water soluble — or they may just require a longer dunking!*

3. THE DRYING-SPEED TEST, p. 5

QUESTION: Which test glue dries the fastest?

WHAT STUDENTS WILL DO:
Students will apply equal amounts of the glues to equal areas of a non-absorbent material (aluminum foil) and touch them with cotton swabs every 30 seconds to determine how long they take to dry.

MATERIALS FOR EACH GROUP:
4 coded test glues, aluminum foil, ruler, marker pen that will write on aluminum foil, timer, 4 wood sticks to use as glue applicators, 12 cotton-swab sticks.

OBJECTIVES:
To understand evaporation and how it can be affected by environmental conditions; to reinforce the importance of controlling variables.

CONCEPTS:
Evaporation: Many commonly used glues form bonds via the evaporation of their solvent. Evaporation is affected by the surface area (how much glue is exposed to air) and the temperature and humidity of the air. Increasing the surface area without increasing the amount of glue and/or increasing the temperature will increase the rate of evaporation and thus decrease drying time. Increased humidity, on the other hand, decreases the rate of evaporation and increases drying time.
Porosity: The farther apart a material's fibers are, the more it will allow liquid molecules to enter and fill the spaces. With glues, that increases the surface area from which solvents can evaporate and speeds drying time. (Note that several glues' labels specify instructions for "porous" and "nonporous" materials.)

DISCUSS:
1. What variables could affect this test? *(Air temperature, humidity, porosity of the materials glues are put on, the thickness of the glue, how hard you press with the cotton swab, etc.)* Why? *(Explore the concept of evaporation.)*

2. How would you control these variables? *(Discuss responses to the balloon.)*

HOW THICK YOU SPREAD THE GLUE AND HOW HARD YOU PRESS ON THE COTTON SWAB ARE <u>VARIABLES</u>. HOW WILL YOU CONTROL THEM? *Thicker globs of glue will take longer to dry, so use the same amount of each glue and spread it over the same area. When pressed lightly the cotton swab may stop at the surface film and not detect wet glue underneath. So use the same firm pressure on all glues. (Perhaps have the same person check all four glues.)*

3. What variable is controlled by using aluminum foil rather than paper? *(Foil doesn't absorb glue; paper does. Aluminum foil is not porous while paper is. Soaking into the surface will speed drying because it increases the surface area from which a glue's solvent can evaporate.)*

4. How might drying time affect the best way to glue two surfaces together? *(With a slow-drying glue, clamps or clips have to hold the surfaces together as the glue dries. Instant glues, which don't set by evaporation but by other chemical activity, demand precise alignment because they set immediately.)*

ACTIVITY:

Test drying speed on other surfaces. Repeat the test using a variety of materials including paper, cardboard, cloth, plastic, metal, glass, and the like. Students should determine whether there is a correlation between porosity and drying time. *(Drying time will be faster on more porous surfaces.)* Repeat this activity on a single surface, but make surface area the variable: Spread the same amount of glue over different surface areas and compare drying times. *(Drying time will be faster on larger surface areas.)*

TESTS STUDENTS WILL DESIGN THEMSELVES

Testing procedures are not provided for the following two tests. Each small group must devise its own plan and procedures. The goal is to encourage hands-on, common sense creativity and problem-solving by students. There's no one "right way" to do these tests.

4. STICK-TO-STUFF TEST, p. 6

QUESTION: Which glue works on the most kinds of materials?

POSSIBLE PROCEDURES:
Students may choose to bond identical materials to each other (plastic to plastic, glass to glass, etc.) or bond different materials to each other (paper to plastic or metal to cotton fabric, etc.), then apply weights to one side of the bond and see how much the bond can support.

OBJECTIVES:
To reinforce the concept of adhesion and the importance of controlling variables; to learn how to design a controlled, scientific test.

CONCEPT:
Adhesion: Glues will adhere differently to different surfaces because of their molecular make-up. The more complex a glue's molecules are, the more different types of materials it will be attracted to.

DISCUSS:

1. What combination of materials do people commonly glue together? *(Leather, china, plastic, wood, metal, and cloth.)*

2. What properties of a glue make it work best with a particular material? *(A glue works best if its molecules have a strong attraction for the molecules on the surface of a material.)*

3. When doing these tests, what variables should be controlled? *(Amount of glue used, surface area of joint, thickness and evenness of glue, drying time, temperature, humidity.)*

4. Will glues bond the same, no matter what the materials are that you're trying to glue? Discuss responses to the balloon.

> WILL THE TEST GLUES WORK DIFFERENTLY ON PLASTIC, CHINA, CLOTH, PAPER, AND WOOD? WRITE YOUR HYPOTHESIS HERE. HOW CAN YOU TEST YOUR HYPOTHESIS?
> *A glue will work differently on different materials. Test this hypothesis by applying the same glue to different materials and determining the strength of each bond.*

5. THE APPEARANCE TEST, p. 7

QUESTION: Which glues leave the materials they're applied to looking best?

POSSIBLE PROCEDURES:
Students might use different glues to bond the same materials, then evaluate the materials' appearance after the glues have dried. Some glues may crinkle or discolor paper; some may dissolve paint or plastic.

OBJECTIVES:
To see how glues and their solvents affect materials they're applied to; to gain skill at designing controlled tests.

CONCEPT:
Solvents: Solvents in glues may also be solvents for the materials they're applied to. (Household cement will dissolve certain plastics; rubber cement can discolor photographs after a while).

DISCUSS:

1. What are some gluing problems? Discuss responses to the first balloon.

> WHAT PROBLEMS DO SOME MATERIALS HAVE WITH GLUES? HOW COULD YOU TEST TO SEE IF THE TEST GLUES HAVE THESE PROBLEMS?
> *Staining, puckering, bubbling, crinkling, discoloring, roughening, stickiness, unevenness, and the like. Test by applying glues and judging how the glued materials look.*

2. What do you think is responsible for these problems? *(Discuss responses to the second balloon.)*

> WHICH DO YOU THINK IS RESPONSIBLE FOR MOST GLUE PROBLEMS, THE ADHESIVE MATERIALS IN THE GLUE OR THE GLUE'S SOLVENT? WHY?
> *The adhesive or the solvent could be responsible for glue problems. For example, an adhesive may stain a material, while a solvent may expand and crinkle it.*

DEALING WITH DATA

Students have gathered data and assigned raw scores for all the glue tests. Now they have to figure out what it all means!

Data alone can't say which glue is best. Like all facts, data have to be thought about, evaluated, and interpreted in a useful and meaningful way. If misinterpreted, data can mislead consumers instead of guiding them. There's no one right way to deal with data.

- Page 8 (Interpret Your Test Data) has students "weight" scores to make important tests count for more, then rank glues from best to worst.

- While dealing with data, students will be using basic mathematics skills as well as learning simple statistics concepts in a hands-on way. They will also be saying "what it all means"—expressing in simple written sentences what their tests revealed about glues. Data are seen as a means to an end, rather than the end itself.

- The Databooks have students analyze and interpret the data their small group collected. Much can be learned by having small groups share results and combine data to come up with *class* results (see the Extra Activity on the following page).

INTERPRET YOUR TEST DATA, p. 8

WHAT STUDENTS WILL DO:

Students will assign Importance Factors to the tests; multiply the glues' scores by those factors to determine weighted scores; then rank the glues from best (highest weighted score) to worst and write out their conclusions and advice.

OBJECTIVES:

To understand the concept of weighted scores; to interpret data and form conclusions.

MATERIALS:

Brand names and prices of the glues.

CONCEPT:

Weighted scores: Some tests measure more important characteristics than other tests. How glues score in important tests should count for more (have a greater impact on the glues' overall rankings).

DISCUSS:

1. Why is it necessary to develop a weighting system? *(Certain factors are more important than others in determining the overall ranking of a glue. A weighting system takes such factors into account.)*

2. What "Importance Factors" did you give each test? Why? Which tests should count more? Why?

3. What other thing could you have tested and/or judged the glues for? *(Cost, packaging, ease of use, applications of glues, toxicity, ease of cleaning up spilled glue.)* Might those things have affected the glues' rankings?

4. How important is price compared to how well a glue works? When does price become an influencing factor? When should price be ignored? *(Price becomes an influencing factor when choosing among glues with similar performance ratings. If an inexpensive glue is inadequate for the intended use, price should be ignored.)*

EXTRA ACTIVITY: PUT TOGETHER THE CLASS'S TEST DATA

ACTIVITY:

Post an enlarged copy of the chart on the following page. Have all groups write their raw scores in the appropriate boxes. (Each box will have several scores.) Then average the scores, assign Importance Factors to the tests, and determine the class's weighted scores.

CONCEPTS:

Variation: Data can vary as a result of differences in test materials (e.g., wood strips). Repeating tests a number of times make results more reliable.

Measurement error: Measurements recorded during testing are subject to inaccuracies due to uncontrolled variables or the imprecision of measuring devices and procedures.

DISCUSS:

1. How did your group's ranking of glues compare with that of other groups? Did everyone who tested come up with the same raw scores for the glues? Did they have the same rank orders? If not, why not? Were some variables not controlled? Is it possible that measurement errors were made? *(Evaluate the chances for error in the measurements that were taken, the impact of using different weighting systems or testing methods, and how interpretations of scoring may have varied from tester to tester.)*

2. How can we determine which measurements are most reliable (most likely to happen again if the test were repeated)? What if we performed each test several times instead of once? What if we based glue ratings on the whole class's raw scores combined instead of just one group's?

3. Examine the class's raw data (on the chart). Which glue (if any) has very little variation in its data (the small groups' test scores are similar)? Which glue has wide variation in its scores? Which glue's performance could you predict with more confidence? *(The one with the least variation in scores.)*

The class should fill in this chart and answer all questions about the glues. Attach a written summary of the class's conclusions. Then mail to the address below.

WHICH GLUE IS BEST?

"RAW" SCORES

Write the class's combined scores for each test in the boxes below.
Are these ❑ mean scores or ❑ median scores? (Check *one*.)

TEST	A	B	C	D
1. Strength				
2. Heat				
3. Water				
4. Drying-Speed				
5. Stick-to-Stuff				
6. Appearance				
TOTALS				

(Raw-Score Totals)

"WEIGHTED" SCORES

1. Assign Importance Factors to the tests. (3=*most* important; 1=*least* important)

2. Multiply the class's combined raw scores by the Importance Factors.

IMPORTANCE FACTOR:	A	B	C	D
1.				
2.				
3.				
4.				
5.				
6.				
TOTALS				

(Weighted-Score Totals)

(1) **Code** **Brand** **Type**

A _____ _____
B _____ _____
C _____ _____
D _____ _____

(2) How many small groups tested the glues?_____

(3) Date_____

(4) Person to contact (name and address):

_____

_____

_____

_____

(5) **Mail To:**

**Consumer Reports
Education Division
101 Truman Avenue
Yonkers, New York 10703-1057**

PRENTICE HALL
PRODUCT TESTING ACTIVITIES by Consumer Reports

TESTING JEANS

Testing Jeans helps students discover the science and technology behind jeans' construction, style, and fashion: observing the fabric weave **(fabric structure and strength)**; testing shrinkage **(molecular structure of fibers, effects of heat)**; testing color-fastness **(oxidation, bleaching)**; judging zippers **(mechanical devices)**; evaluating construction qualities **(stress/force on seams, clothing construction)**; and seeing how well the fabric breathes **(absorption and evaporation)**. In addition, students will be making observations, forming hypotheses, and controlling variables.

Collecting and analyzing data also build counting and measuring skills.

Tests are designed for groups of four. Students work together to conduct and plan tests, analyze data, solve problems, and develop scientific ratings of jeans. A series of pre-tests on fabric swatches allows for destructive testing to explore denim fabrics. The tests on real jeans combine evaluations of fabric and clothing construction. The chart below links the tests students will perform with the science skills and concepts those testing activities help teach.

CURRICULUM SKILLS AND CONCEPTS

Test and Student Databook Page	Highlighted Skills	Science Concepts
Getting Started p. 1	Controlling Variables, Blind Testing	Principles of Testing
Strong or Wimpy Weave?, p. 2	Observing, Forming Hypotheses	Fabric Structure and Strength
Is Pre-shrunk Important? p. 3	Measuring, Controlling Variables, Designing a Test	Structure of Fibers, Heat
The Color Test p. 4	Observing, Inferring	Oxidation, Bleach
Zipper Test p. 5	Observing, Analyzing	Mechanical Devices, Clothing Construction
Seams-and-Pocket Test, p. 6	Observing, Analyzing, Calculating	Clothing Construction
Does-It-Breathe? Test, p. 7	Designing a Test, Controlling Variables	Absorption, Evaporation
Interpret Your Test Data, p. 8	Rank-ordering, Polling, Forming Conclusions	Representative Samples

MATERIALS NEEDED
for each small group:

❑ **Test samples:**
Fabrics for pre-tests: 30-cm-by-30-cm swatches of 100% cotton denim, cotton/polyester denim, cotton/spandex denim, and woven shirt material (or an old shirt), all blue. (Denims should be new and never washed for optimal results in the shrinkage pre-test.)
Jeans for tests: 4 pairs of jeans. (Ask students to bring in relatively new jeans.)

❑ **For pre-planned tests:**
Magnifying glass, bright light, needle, tweezers, scissors, laundry marker, ruler, heavy cardboard, bleach, large beaker, aluminum foil, rubber band, tape, safety goggles, protective clothing, water.

CLASS-TIME REQUIREMENTS:

❑ To conduct Pre-test 1: 1 class period
❑ To conduct Pre-tests 2 and 3: 2 class periods, 1 day apart
❑ To conduct Tests 1 through 3: 2 class periods
❑ For data analysis and interpretation: 1 class period

GETTING STARTED

1. Prepare test samples in advance.

Fabric swatches for pre-tests: Since the pre-tests' objective is to help students learn about denim fabrics, the swatches should be identified by name, not code. (The same swatches can be used for all three pre-tests.)

Jeans to be tested: Since students should do blind testing, all brand names should be hidden and the jeans coded A through D. A practical way to do this is to staple or stitch coded patches over brand names and logos. (Small groups could do this, then exchange coded jeans with another group.)

2. Distribute Student Databooks, one to each group.

DISCUSS:

1. What do you like about jeans? What do you dislike? Could product testing reveal whether jeans have the characteristics you like (or dislike)? How? *(Encourage students to brainstorm and keep notes. They may want to do the tests they think of later on.)*

2. Is "style" something you can test jeans for? *("Style" is more a reflection of the taste of the wearer than the quality of the jeans themselves. But you could poll to find which styles are popular and see how the test jeans compare.)* "Style" isn't one of the things you'll be testing for in this unit. Should it be? How would you test for it?

3. Might people think some brands of jeans are better than others? Might they think there's a link between brand name and quality or price and quality? Is it important that testers not know the brand names of the jeans they're testing? Why or why not? *(Discuss responses to the page 1 balloon.)*

> IF YOU THINK A CERTAIN BRAND OF JEANS IS BEST, MIGHT YOU EXPECT IT TO DO BEST (OR SECRETLY ROOT FOR IT TO WIN)? COULD THAT AFFECT THE WAY YOU JUDGE THE JEANS?
> *People sometimes use a brand they think is better to define "quality" in their minds—sometimes without knowing it! Testers may be extra critical while evaluating store brands, for example, or extra lenient when examining a popular brand.*

TESTS ALREADY DESIGNED FOR STUDENTS

The following pre-tests and tests describe the testing procedures students should follow. Allow student groups to work independently and solve problems among themselves. Wait until they've completed their testing before discussing or reviewing the tests. The goal is to encourage independent thinking, creative problem-solving, and increased confidence in their scientific abilities.

PRE-TEST 1 — STRONG OR WIMPY WEAVE?, p. 2

QUESTION: What makes denim strong?

WHAT STUDENTS WILL DO:

Students will examine four fabric swatches and the four coded test jeans to identify weave direction, thread colors, tightness of weave, and twill or plain weaves.

MATERIALS FOR EACH GROUP:

Swatches of blue 100% cotton, polyester blend, and stretch denims, swatch of plain woven shirt fabric, 4 coded jeans, bright light, magnifying glass, needle, tweezers.

OBJECTIVES:

To observe fabric structures and weaves; to infer a link between type of weave and fabric strength; to build skill at making observations and forming hypotheses.

CONCEPTS:

Structure of fabric: Fabric is produced when threads are woven together. "Warp" threads, the basic structure of the fabric, run lengthwise from the back of the loom to the front. "Filling" threads are the crosswise threads that pass over and under the warp threads.

Weaves: Plain weave, formed when filling fibers go over then under *single* warp fibers, looks like a checkerboard. Twill weave, formed when filling fibers interlace *more than one* warp fiber, has a compact diagonal appearance. (Both weaves are illustrated in the Student Databook.) True denim is a twill weave of white filling fibers and colored (usually blue) warp fibers.

DISCUSS:

1. What similarities did you find among the three denim fabrics? *(All three should have the diagonal-looking weave, lock threads in tightly, and not let you see through.)* What did you find with the test jeans? *(If they're all denim, they will be similar.)*

2. Were any denims noticeably heavier or lighter than the others? What do you think accounts for the difference in weight? *(The weight of the threads used to weave the denim. They may be heavy or light.)*

3. How does a twill weave lock in threads? *(Filling threads interlace more than one warp thread, making threads lie very tight and close together. If one comes loose, another will hold it.)*

4. When you can see through a fabric, what are you actually looking through? *(Tiny holes between threads where they're woven together. The more holes there are or the bigger the holes are, the easier it is to see through the fabric.)*

5. How would having fewer spaces between threads affect a fabric's strength? *(Discuss responses to the balloon.)*

DOES HAVING LESS SPACE BETWEEN THREADS MAKE A WEAVE WEAKER OR STRONGER? WRITE YOUR HYPOTHESIS HERE. *It would make the fabric stronger because threads would be packed so tightly that even if one broke, it couldn't unravel. It's like detangling string —the looser the knots, the more easily it's detangled.*

PRE-TEST 2   IS PRE-SHRUNK IMPORTANT?, p. 3

QUESTION: How much will denim shrink if it's not pre-shrunk?

WHAT STUDENTS WILL DO:

After tracing 20-cm-by-20-cm squares on the denim swatches, students will wash and dry the swatches (at home), measure to see if the squares shrank, and record lengthwise and widthwise shrinkage.

MATERIALS FOR EACH GROUP:

3 denim swatches from Pre-Test 1, laundry marker, ruler, heavy cardboard, scissors. **(Note: For optimal results, the fabrics should be new and never washed.)**

OBJECTIVES:

To reinforce understanding of fabric structure; to develop skill at measuring and designing a test.

CONCEPT:

Structure of fibers: When treated with hot water, molecules in cotton fibers change shape, thereby shortening the threads. In the process of weaving, threads are stretched, but return to their natural shorter length when washed. Depending on the weave, threads are stretched more in one direction than the other, so lengthwise and widthwise shrinkage will differ.

DISCUSS:

1. Why were *new* samples of denim used in this pre-test? *(Fabric will shrink the most the first time it's washed. After that, shrinkage will be much less.)* What causes shrinking? Why does new fabric shrink more than fabric that's already been washed? *(Discuss the structure of fibers concept.)* How can you tell if jeans are pre-shrunk before you buy them? *(Appearance can tell: Acid-washed, bleached, or other treatments mean they've been pre-shrunk. Also, labels may say pre-shrunk. Most jeans sold today are pre-shrunk.)*

2. What variables were controlled in this test? *(Size of the squares, washing and drying temperature and time, etc.)* What are some possible sources of measurement error? *(Accuracy and precision of measurements both before and after washing.)*

3. In your testing, which fabric shrank the most? *(Shrinkage for 100% cotton denims may be as much as 10%, less than 1% for cotton spandex, and virtually nothing for polyester blends.)* Did the fabrics shrink more lengthwise or widthwise? Why do you think that happened? *(Discuss the first balloon.)*

IN THE WEAVING PROCESS, LENGTHWISE THREADS ARE STRETCHED TIGHTER THAN THREADS THAT RUN WIDTHWISE. WHICH THREADS ARE LIKELY TO SHRINK MORE? WRITE YOUR HYPOTHESIS HERE.
The threads that are stretched more during weaving will shrink more, since washing lets them return to their natural length. Since the warp (lengthwise) threads were stretched more, they will shrink more.

DO PRE-SHRUNK JEANS SHRINK, TOO? DESCRIBE HOW YOU COULD TEST YOUR OWN JEANS FOR SHRINKAGE THE NEXT TIME YOU WASH THEM.
Instead of marking a 20-cm square with laundry marker, use chalk and sew over it with thread. Then wash, dry, and measure again as in Pre-Test 2.

4. You probably don't want to mark up your good jeans with a laundry marker, so how could you test your jeans to see if they still shrink? *(Discuss responses to the second balloon.)*

ACTIVITY:

Compute percent of shrinkage. How much will jeans made of the test fabrics shrink? More than the total amount of shrinkage measured on a 20-cm-by-20-cm square! Convert length and width shrinkage data to *percents*. *(Have students divide cm shrunk by the original 20 cm. Multiply the answer by 100.)* Multiply the length of the jeans by the lengthwise shrinkage percent and the width by the widthwise percent.

PRE-TEST 3 — THE COLOR TEST, p. 4

QUESTION: Which fabrics are dyed with indigo and likely to bleach and fade?

WHAT STUDENTS WILL DO:

Students will cut strips of the denim swatches, dip one end in the bleach solution, tape the other end to the top of the beaker, and let them soak overnight. The next day, students will compare the bleached and non-bleached fabrics and judge the color change. *(Easy bleaching indicates use of a natural [indigo] dye; resistance to bleaching indicates a synthetic dye.)* Students will read jeans' care labels to identify fabrics, note how swatches of similar fabrics bleached, and infer how the test jeans would bleach.

CAUTION: Make sure students wear safety goggles and protective clothing when doing this test.

MATERIALS FOR EACH GROUP:

3 denim swatches, 4 coded test jeans, 0.5% solution of chlorine bleach, large beaker, aluminum foil and rubber band (to cover beaker), scissors, tape, safety goggles, protective clothing, water.

Note: Mix the bleach solution beforehand. Add 20 mL of 5% chlorine bleach (Clorox®) to 180 mL water.

OBJECTIVES:

To observe oxidation and how bleaches work; to gain skill at making visual observations and comparisons.

CONCEPT:

Oxidation and bleaching: Bleaching is an oxidation/reduction reaction. Most liquid household bleaches contain sodium hypochlorite as their active ingredient. Upon dilution with water and heat it breaks down into chlorine, which reacts with the dye and oxidizes it, changing the color.

DISCUSS:

1. How does bleaching remove color (or stains) from fabrics? *(Explore the oxidation and bleaching concept.)* What variables were controlled in this test? *(Strength of bleach solution, soaking time, temperature of solution.)*

2. Which fabric bleached the most? the least? What could you infer about the type of dye those fabrics used? *(100% cotton will bleach the most because it uses natural indigo dyes. Over time, light — especially sunlight — can also bleach indigo. The polyester blend is likely to bleach the least because it uses synthetic dyes.)*

3. Which type of fabric is made from natural fiber? *(100% cotton.)* Which fabric do you think uses natural (indigo) dyes? *(100% cotton. Discuss responses in Box 3 in the Databook.)* Which fabric contains synthetic fibers and dyes? *(Polyester blend and spandex cotton.)* Which fabric do you think is most likely to fade over time? *(100% cotton.)*

1. ZIPPER TEST, p. 5

QUESTION: Which jeans have the best zipper?

WHAT STUDENTS WILL DO:
Students will switch from testing fabric swatches to testing jeans. They will evaluate the test jeans' zippers for how well they're sewn in and mechanical performance, give jeans scores for each, then find average scores.

MATERIALS FOR EACH GROUP:
4 coded test jeans.

OBJECTIVES:
To introduce clothing construction principles; to explore the mechanics of a zipper; to gain skill at making observations and evaluations.

CONCEPTS:
Zipper mechanics: A zipper is a slide fastener. When you pull it up, two small wedges exert enough force to make its metal teeth lock together. When you pull a zipper down, a third wedge forces the teeth apart. How well the teeth and wedges are made and positioned will affect how well the zipper operates.

Clothing construction: The number of stitches, zipper placement, and the strength of sewing thread indicates how well a garment is made.

DISCUSS:
1. How does a zipper work? *(Explore the zipper mechanics concept.)* What differences did you find among the test jeans' zippers? Which do you think is the bigger concern, how well the zipper works or how well it's sewn in? Why?

2. What variables were controlled in this test? *(Discuss responses to the balloon.)*

HOW HARD YOU PULL ON THE ZIPPER IS A <u>VARIABLE</u>. WHAT OTHER VARIABLES HAVE TO BE CONTROLLED IN THIS "ZIP-IT" TEST? *Variables include how taut the jeans are held, how fast you zip, how hard you pull the edges apart, how you determine scores.*

3. What variables weren't controlled? *(The possibility that zipper problems were caused by rough use, since the jeans aren't brand new; the possibility that other samples of the same jeans brand and model could vary in zipper quality or construction.)* Could these variables be controlled? How? *(Yes, by testing new jeans and by testing several samples of each brand-model.)*

ACTIVITY:
Analyze zippers. Bring in broken zippers and old clothes with zippers that can be "stress tested." First analyze the broken zippers: What went wrong? How can other zippers be tested for these defects? Form hypotheses: Is there a link between the size of a zipper's teeth and how strong it is? Is there a link between what the teeth are made of (metal or plastic) and the zipper's strength? Then use the zippers on the old clothes to test these hypotheses. *(Try zipping over increasingly larger objects to exert increasing stress on zippers. Have the zipped-up fabric support increasing amounts of weight over time to judge strength.)*

2. SEAMS-AND-POCKET TEST, p. 6

QUESTION: How well-made are the jeans?

WHAT STUDENTS WILL DO:
Students will examine each pair of jeans, looking for the 10 construction features described in the Databook. Jeans will get a check for each feature they have. Jeans with the most checks will get the highest scores.

MATERIALS FOR EACH GROUP:
4 coded test jeans.

OBJECTIVES:
To understand basics of clothing construction; to make visual observations and judgments.

CONCEPT:

Clothing construction: Certain construction features make clothes stronger and better able to resist ripping at the seams. They include double-stitched seams, straight untwisted seams, no broken threads, and rivets or bartacks in places where stress is likely to be greatest.

DISCUSS:

1. Which construction details did *all* the test jeans have? Which details did only one or two have? What problems could those jeans have later on?

2. Judging from your data, is there a big or small difference in how well made jeans are? Explore whether price differences among jeans appear to be related to the quality of the jeans' construction. *(Price differences are more likely to be due to other things like special pre-treatments and marketing costs.)*

ACTIVITY:
Conduct a "Jeans Day" test. Judge construction details of a much larger sampling of jeans by inviting the class (or the school) to bring in jeans from home and putting all the jeans to the Zipper and the Seams-and-Pocket tests. Sort jeans by brand name and tally scores for similar brands: Are different samples of the same brand consistent (all well made or all poorly made)?

A TEST STUDENTS WILL DESIGN THEMSELVES

Testing procedures are not provided for the following test. Each small group must devise its own plan and procedure. The goal is to encourage hands-on, common sense creativity and problem-solving by students. There's no one "right" way to do this test.

3. DOES-IT-BREATHE? TEST, p. 7

QUESTION: Which jeans let air and moisture pass through best?

POSSIBLE PROCEDURE:
Students could tightly cover glasses of weighed and measured water with the jeans fabric, then measure loss of water by evaporation a day or two later.

OBJECTIVES:
To understand how to design a test; to reinforce the importance of controlling variables.

DISCUSS:

1. Which fabric would let water escape best, one that absorbed water fast or slow? *(Discuss responses to the balloon.)*

DO YOU THINK THERE IS ANY LINK BETWEEN HOW FAST A FABRIC LETS WATER VAPOR ESCAPE AND HOW FAST IT DRIES? WRITE YOUR HYPOTHESIS HERE. *Since cotton is more absorbent than the other fibers, it will absorb more water. As a result it may dry more slowly.*

2. Describe your testing procedure. What was your hypothesis? What measurements did you take? What variables did you control? How did you decide scores?

DEALING WITH DATA

Students have gathered data and assigned raw scores for all the jeans tests. Now they have to figure out what it all means!

Data alone can't say which pair of jeans is best. Like all facts, data have to be thought about, evaluated, and interpreted in a useful and meaningful way. If misinterpreted, data can mislead consumers instead of guiding them. There's no one right way to deal with data.

INTERPRET YOUR TEST DATA, p. 8

WHAT STUDENTS WILL DO:

Each student will poll 15 people, asking them to rank-order jeans features. Students will then determine which jeans performed best in the features that are most important, according to the poll.

OBJECTIVES:

To understand the concepts of surveying, representative samples, and weighted scores; to interpret data and form conclusions.

MATERIALS:

Jeans' brand names and prices when new.

DISCUSS:

1. Have the small groups compare results of their polls: Are their average rankings of the 10 jeans features similar or different? If different, why? *(Did they survey the same types of people? Were the people representative samples? What groups did they represent? Did the small groups interpret results differently?)*

2. Which type of fabric do people prefer, based on their responses to your poll? *(Link how people felt about shrink-resistance, fade-ability, and color to the fabrics most likely to deliver those qualities, based on Pre-Tests 1 through 3.)*

3. Other important features of jeans are their style and fit — features that weren't tested for. Should they have been tested for? If so, how? If not, why not? *(Dicuss responses to question 5 on page 8 of the Databook. Is style a matter of preference that doesn't affect the quality of jeans? Why or why not?)*

EXTRA ACTIVITY: PUT TOGETHER THE CLASS'S TEST DATA

Rather than combining scores for jeans A through D (which aren't the same brand for all groups), have students combine scores on the basis of the jeans' *price ranges*. Each group should rank its jeans from most expensive to least expensive. Then tabulate the class's scores on that basis.

ACTIVITY:

Post an enlarged copy of the chart on the following page. Have all groups write their raw scores for the test jeans *based on the jeans' relative cost (from most to least expensive)*. Each box will have several scores. Then determine how important each test is and assign Importance Factors (3 = *most* important; 2 = important; 1 = *least* important). Multiply test scores by Importance Factors and add to find weighted scores of costly, moderately-priced, and inexpensive jeans.

DISCUSS:

1. Could we compare small groups' ratings of expensive and inexpensive jeans? What might it tell us? *(Whether there's any link between the price and quality of the jeans tested.)*

2. Do you think your small group's ratings of the brands you tested can predict how good those brands are? *(Explore variation: Another sample of each brand might be better or worse than the one you tested. You'd need to do these tests on several samples of each brand-model to be able to predict quality with confidence.)*

3. Is there a relationship between the jeans' prices and how well they performed in these tests? (Are the most expensive jeans always the highest scoring jeans?) Were any inexpensive jeans as good as costly ones? What do you think the extra cost of high-priced jeans pays for? *(Explore everything from style to marketing and advertising costs.)*

SEND YOUR RATINGS OF JEANS TO *CONSUMER REPORTS*

The class should fill in this chart and answer all questions about the jeans. Attach a written summary of the class's conclusions. Then mail to the address below.

WHICH JEANS ARE BEST?

"RAW" SCORES

Write the class's combined scores for each test in the boxes below.
Are these ❑ mean scores or ❑ median scores? (Check *one*.)

TEST	Most Costly Jeans	Second Most Costly	Third Most Costly	Least Costly Jeans
1. Zipper				
2. Seams/ Pocket				
3. Does-It-Breathe?				
TOTALS				

(Raw-Score Totals)

"WEIGHTED" SCORES

1. Assign Importance Factors to the tests. (3=*most* important; 1=*least* important)
2. Multiply the class's combined raw scores by the Importance Factors.

IMPORTANCE FACTOR:	Most Costly Jeans	Second Most Costly	Third Most Costly	Least Costly Jeans
1.				
2.				
3.				
TOTALS				

(Weighted-Score Totals)

(1) Please list the brand names and prices of the jeans in each price category. (Each small group should write its most costly brand, second-most costly brand, etc.)

MOST COSTLY JEANS & PRICES:

_____

_____

SECOND MOST COSTLY JEANS & PRICES:

_____

_____

THIRD MOST COSTLY JEANS & PRICES:

_____

_____

LEAST COSTLY JEANS & PRICES:

_____

_____

(2) Person to contact (name and address):

_____

_____

_____

(3) **Mail To:**

**Consumer Reports
Education Division
101 Truman Avenue
Yonkers, New York 10703-1057**

TESTING LIP BALMS

PRODUCT TESTING ACTIVITIES by Consumer Reports

PRENTICE HALL

Testing Lip Balms brings together topics in biology, chemistry, and physics: the lips **(anatomy and physiology of skin)**; the drying of lips **(evaporation and physical properties of substances)**; components of lip balms **(chemical and physical properties of waxes and oils)**; staying-power of lip balms **(water solubility, interaction of skin and waxes)**; moisture barriers **(impermeable substances)**; durability of lip balms **(effects of temperature on substances and mixtures)**. In the process of performing the various tests, students will learn how to apply the scientific method to solve problems. They will develop and test hypotheses, identify and control variables, collect and interpret data, and draw meaningful conclusions.

Tests are designed for groups of four. Students work together to conduct tests, analyze data, solve problems, and develop a scientific rating of lip balms. The chart below links tests students will perform with the science skills and concepts those testing activities help teach.

CURRICULUM SKILLS AND CONCEPTS

Test and Student Databook Page	Highlighted Skills	Science Concepts
Getting Started p. 1	Controlling Variables, Blind Testing	Principles of Testing
The Lip Test p. 2	Experimenting, Controlling Variables	Skin Structure, Nerve Density
The Evaporation Test, p. 3	Forming Hypotheses, Calculating, Controlling Variables	Evaporation Rates, Properties of Oil
The Waxy-Oily Test, p. 4	Tactile Judgments, Controlling Variables	Esters, Reference Standards
Stay-On Test p. 5	Controlling Variables, Observation	Insolubility, Water Repellency
Moisture-Barrier Test, p. 6	Controlling Variables, Visual Judgments	Impermeable Substances, Experimental Controls
All-Temperatures Test p. 7	Designing a Test, Forming Hypotheses	Effect of Temperature on Solids
Interpret Your Test Data, p. 8	Analyzing Data, Forming Conclusions	Weighted Scores

CLASS-TIME REQUIREMENTS:

- ❏ For Pre-Tests 1 and 2: 1 class period, split over 2 days
- ❏ For Tests 1 and 2: 1 class period
- ❏ For Test 3: 1 class period, split over 2 days
- ❏ For Test 4: 1 class period
- ❏ For data analysis and interpretation: 1 class period

MATERIALS NEEDED
for each small group:

- ❏ **Test samples:** 4 different lip balms (preferably 2 sticks and 2 tubes)

- ❏ **For pre-planned tests:** 3 pencils, blindfold, white tissue paper (gift wrap), magnifying glass, mirror, 3 same-sized beakers, ruler, marker (for glass), water, stirrer, medicine dropper, balance, vegetable oil, fan, candle wax or crayon, washable-ink marker, paper towels, large pot and water, tissues, liquid soap, petroleum jelly, cup, scissors, food coloring, tape, pen, cardboard, small beaker.

GETTING STARTED

1. Code test samples.

Students should conduct blind tests of the four lip balms — they shouldn't know brand names until the testing is completed. Black out or tape over all brand names on each lip balm, then code the lip balms A through D. Keep a record of brand names and prices (for step 5 of Data interpretation, page 8 of the Student databook).

2. Distribute Student Databooks, one to each group.

DISCUSS:

1. What are the purposes of lip balm? What symptoms would indicate that you might need a lip balm?

2. How do lip balms differ from other substances you put on your skin? How are they similar?

3. Why did we code the test samples? *(So that testers won't be biased by what they think about a brand.)* What things other than brand name could give away the identity of the lip balms? *(Color, aroma, the shape or size of the container, etc.).* How might you keep these clues from giving away a lip balm's brand name (and influencing your judgments)? *(Blindfold yourself and have a partner apply the lip balms on you.)*

4. If testers were to apply the lip balms to their lips, why couldn't they share test samples? *(That would be unsanitary and spread germs.)* How could you test the lip balms without applying them to your lips? *(Apply them to your wrist-forearm, as the following tests instruct. Discuss responses to the page 1 balloon.)*

LIP BALMS CAN'T BE SHARED BY TESTERS BECAUSE THAT WOULD SPREAD GERMS. SHOULD EACH TESTER GET HIS OR HER OWN SAMPLES TO TEST? SHOULD ONLY ONE PERSON TEST? OR SHOULD THE TESTS BE DONE ON NON-LIP SURFACES? WHY? *Giving each tester samples for the test could be expensive and having one person test would not give sufficient data, thus testing on a wrist-forearm might be the best solution.*

TESTS ALREADY DESIGNED FOR STUDENTS

Testing procedures are described for the following tests. Allow student groups to work independently and solve problems among themselves. Wait until they have completed their testing before discussing or reviewing the tests. The goal is to encourage independent thinking, creative problem solving, and increased confidence in their scientific abilities.

PRE-TEST 1 — THE LIP TEST, p. 2

QUESTION: How are lips different from other parts of the skin?

WHAT STUDENTS WILL DO:

Students will compare the lips with other parts of the skin for dryness or oiliness, the presence of pores and hairs, and sensitivity.

MATERIALS FOR EACH GROUP:

3 pencils, blindfold, white tissue paper (gift wrap), magnifying glass, mirror.

OBJECTIVES:

To become aware of some properties of lips; to understand that nerve density varies in different body surfaces; to gain skill at making observations.

CONCEPTS:

The anatomy and physiology of skin vary depending on where the skin is. Skin is a protective organ, with greater protections (hair, sebaceous glands) on parts most exposed to the elements. Skin is also a sensory organ, possessing nerve cells that are sensitive to stimuli such as heat, cold, pain, and pressure. Furthermore, since the lips have special sensory tasks from eating to speaking to kissing, they have a greater supply of nerve cells than skin surfaces. The outline of the lips is the junction between skin and the mucous membrane that lines the mouth. The part of the lips that lip balms are applied to isn't technically skin and doesn't have the natural protections (hair and sebaceous glands) that skin has.

DISCUSS:

1. What are some basic functions of skin, the body's largest organ? *(Protective, sensory.)* How are the lips similar? How are they different? *(Discuss responses to the first balloon.)*

> WHAT SPECIAL JOBS DO LIPS HAVE? LIST EVERYTHING YOU CAN THINK OF.
> *Sensing the heat of foods, speaking, eating and drinking, whistling, kissing, smiling, frowning, or making other expressions.*

2. Which was oilier, lips or skin? *(Skin.)* Which was dryer? *(Lips.)* Which had no hair follicles? *(Lips.)* What skin characteristics do lips *not* have? *(They don't sweat, secrete oil, grow hair. Discuss responses to the second balloon.)*

> ARE LIPS MORE LIKE THE SKIN ON YOUR FACE OR THE LINING INSIDE YOUR MOUTH? WRITE YOUR OBSERVATIONS HERE.
> *Lips share more characteristics of the inner mouth because they are extensions of the mucous membrane that lines the mouth.*

3. Which surface seems to have nerve cells closer together? Explain your answer. *(The lips, because they could sense the number of pencil points whereas the skin on the arm couldn't.)*

PRE-TEST 2 — THE EVAPO-RATION TEST, p. 3

QUESTIONS: Does air moving over lips dry them out? Can an oily coating reduce moisture loss?

WHAT STUDENTS WILL DO:

Students will discover that water protected by a layer of oil will not evaporate as fast as water alone, then relate that finding to lips. They will prepare and weigh three beakers of water (two covered by oil), set a fan on two of them overnight, then weigh each beaker and see which lost the most water.

MATERIALS FOR EACH GROUP:

3 beakers (all the same size), ruler, marker that will write on glass, water, medicine dropper, balance, stirrer, vegetable oil, fan.

OBJECTIVES:

To understand evaporation and how oil acts as a vapor barrier; to practice forming hypotheses and controlling variables.

CONCEPTS:

Evaporation rate of a substance depends on the physical properties of the substance, temperature, humidity, surface area, and whether the surface of the substance is exposed to moving air. Because of its physical properties, oil tends to evaporate much slower than water.

Properties of oil: Oil is not soluble in water and is less dense than water, so it will float on water and form a vapor barrier, reducing the water's evaporation rate.

DISCUSS:

1. What variables did you control? How? *(Discuss responses to the first balloon.)*

> THE TEMPERATURE AND HUMIDITY WHERE THE BEAKERS ARE LEFT OVERNIGHT ARE <u>VARIABLES.</u> SO IS THE POSSIBILITY OF SPILLING WATER. HOW WILL YOU CONTROL THOSE VARIABLES?
> *Put the beakers in the same room and as close together as possible so temperature and humidity won't vary. Handle beakers carefully and put them in a place where they won't be disturbed.*

2. Which beaker did you think would lose the most weight? Why? What was your hypothesis? *(Discuss responses to the second balloon.)*

THE "OIL" BEAKER IS LIKE NORMAL SKIN. "WIND AND NO OIL" IS LIKE THE LIPS. "WIND AND OIL" IS LIKE LIPS WITH LIP BALM ON. WHICH DO YOU THINK WILL LOSE THE MOST MOISTURE OVERNIGHT? WHY? WRITE YOUR HYPOTHESIS HERE.

"Wind and no oil" (like lips). The beaker containing water alone will lose the most moisture because a large surface of water is exposed to lots of air (due to "wind"). A layer of oil reduces the water's exposure to air — and oil evaporates much slower than water.

3. Which beaker actually lost the most weight? *(The one representing the unprotected lips.)* Did that prove or disprove your hypothesis?

4. Based on your results, what would you infer about the composition of lip balms? *(One component is an oily substance — white petrolatum.)*

1. THE WAXY-OILY TEST, p. 4

QUESTIONS: Which lip balms are dry and waxy? Which are wet and oily?

WHAT STUDENTS WILL DO:

Students will apply candle wax and vegetable oil (reference standards), then a lip balm, compare the lip balm to the standards, determine where the lip balm falls on a waxy-oily scale, then repeat this sequence to test the other lip balms. *Tests will be done on forearms, not lips. Students should go on to Test 2 before washing the lip balms off.*

MATERIALS FOR EACH GROUP:

4 coded lip balms, candle wax or crayon, vegetable oil, washable-ink marker, paper towels.

OBJECTIVES:

To understand standards of reference; to make sensory observations.

CONCEPTS:

Esters: Waxes and vegetable oils belong to the same chemical family, esters. In general, at room temperature most oils are liquids, while waxes are solids that do not feel oily. Both, however, are insoluble in water. And both can be used as vapor barriers on the skin.

Standards of reference: Descriptive words like waxy and oily need to be given a measurable meaning so testers' judgments (and the data collected) will be comparable. Standards use specific references (like vegetable oil) to define what these words mean.

DISCUSS:

1. How big a difference in lip-balm texture did you find? *(In general, lip balms in a tube will be oilier than stick-type lip balms.)*

2. Did most students agree on the lip balms' waxy-oily description? Why or why not? *(If not, were some variables not controlled? Were the reference standards clear? Did the order in which the lip balms were tested affect results? Should different groups have tested the lip balms in different sequences?)*

3. What variables should have been controlled? Were they? If so, how? *(Discuss responses to the balloon.)*

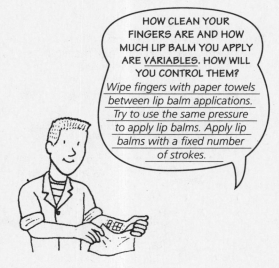

HOW CLEAN YOUR FINGERS ARE AND HOW MUCH LIP BALM YOU APPLY ARE UNDERLINED VARIABLES. HOW WILL YOU CONTROL THEM?

Wipe fingers with paper towels between lip balm applications. Try to use the same pressure to apply lip balms. Apply lip balms with a fixed number of strokes.

4. What properties do you think waxes and oils share? *(They are insoluble in water and can coat and protect the skin.)*

5. What properties are unique to waxes? *(Waxes are solids that do not have an oily feel.)* to oils? *(Most oils, especially vegetable oils, are liquids.)*

2. STAY-ON TEST, p. 5

QUESTION: Which lip balm stays on best?

WHAT STUDENTS WILL DO:
Immediately after Test 1 (with the lip balms still on), students will apply a reference standard (petroleum jelly) and then subject the lip balms to "wear" by dunking their arms into soapy water. Then they'll pour plain water over their arms to see how well the lip balms repel water compared to the standard. (Repelling water is an indication that the lip balms are still on.)

MATERIALS FOR EACH GROUP:
4 coded lip balms already applied on students' arms, tissues, large pot or sink, water, liquid soap, petroleum jelly, cup.

OBJECTIVE:
To understand the relationship between water repellency and insolubility.

CONCEPTS:
Insolubility means being incapable of dissolving in a liquid. With lip balms, the oil or petrolatum is incapable of being dissolved in water.

Water repellency: the capacity of being resistant but not impervious to water.

DISCUSS:

1. What variables had to be controlled in this test? *(Discuss responses to the balloon.)*

HOW HARD YOU BLOT YOUR FOREARM IN STEP 1 IS A VARIABLE. WHAT OTHER VARIABLES SHOULD BE CONTROLLED IN THIS TEST? *How hard and long you agitate your arm under water, how much lip balm you'd applied in Test 1, how long the lip balms have been on your arm, how precisely you compared them with the petroleum jelly, etc.*

2. What do you think makes lip balm wear off? *(Breathing, eating, drinking, talking, laughing, licking lips, wiping mouth, etc.)* Which did this test simulate?

3. MOISTURE-BARRIER TEST, p. 6

QUESTION: Which lip balm forms the best moisture barrier?

WHAT STUDENTS WILL DO:
Students will apply the lip balms and petroleum jelly to tissue paper and place a drop of colored water on each and on an untreated control. The next day, students will see how much water (color) each section let pass through. (A good moisture barrier would block out all color.)

MATERIALS FOR EACH GROUP:
4 coded lip balms, petroleum jelly, white tissue paper, scissors, food coloring, tape, medicine dropper, paper towels, pen, cardboard, small beaker, water.

OBJECTIVES:
To understand the concept of vapor barriers and the purpose of an experimental control; to reinforce the importance of controlling variables.

CONCEPTS:
Experimental controls provide an objective reference for scoring. They also show how something would fare without any treatment with the test samples.

Impermeable substances are substances that will not allow liquids to pass through.

DISCUSS:

1. Did all groups get the same results? If not, why not? How did they control variables? *(Discuss responses to the balloon.)*

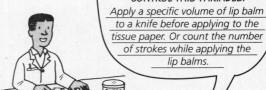

HOW MUCH LIP BALM YOU APPLY IS A VARIABLE. BUT THAT'S HARD TO MEASURE SINCE EACH LIP BALM HAS A DIFFERENT APPLICATOR. HOW COULD YOU CONTROL THIS VARIABLE? *Apply a specific volume of lip balm to a knife before applying to the tissue paper. Or count the number of strokes while applying the lip balms.*

2. What ingredient of lip balm might be blocking moisture? *(Petrolatum.)* Why can this ingredient block the loss of moisture from lips? *(It's impermeable.)*

3. What did the blank, untreated section represent? *(The experimental control.)*

A TEST STUDENTS WILL DESIGN THEMSELVES

Testing procedures are not provided for the next test. Each small group must devise its own procedures, identify the materials needed, and decide which variables to test and which to control. The goal is to encourage independent thinking, appreciation and use of scientific techniques, and the drawing of valid conclusions.

4. ALL-TEMPERATURES TEST, p. 7

QUESTION: Which lip balms can survive hot and cold temperatures?

POSSIBLE PROCEDURE:
Students could judge how easy the lip balms are to apply to their forearms at room temperature, then compare how easy they are to apply after leaving them refrigerated and after leaving them in a warm place.

OBJECTIVES:
To reinforce testing skills by designing a test; to understand relationships between heating and melting and between cooling and hardening; to reinforce the importance of controlling variables.

CONCEPT:
Temperature changes and effects on solids: Increasing the temperature increases molecular activity in solids, making them start to liquefy (melt). Decreasing the temperature slows molecular activity and makes viscous solids (like wax and oil) become harder (more solid). Lip balms may be formulated to minimize the effects of temperature change by raising the melting point and lowering the hardening point.

DISCUSS:
1. Did some lip balms withstand temperature extremes better than others? Do lip balms that are solids and lip balms in tubes react differently?

2. What was your hypothesis on the way heat and cold would affect lip balms? *(Discuss responses to the balloon.)*

HOW MIGHT <u>HEAT</u> AND <u>COLD</u> AFFECT THE CONSISTENCY OF LIP BALMS? WRITE YOUR HYPOTHESIS HERE. *Heat may soften the consistency of lip balms; cold may harden their consistency.*

3. In general, how does warming a wax or oil affect its physical properties? *(Warming increases molecular activity, thereby making waxes soft and oils more fluid.)*

4. In general, how do cold temperatures affect waxes and oils? *(Cold reduces molecular activity, making oils start to solidify.)*

ACTIVITY:
How different oils react to temperature change. Do all oils respond in the same way to different temperatures? Students should obtain small samples of margarine and various vegetable oils such as olive oil, corn oil, soybean oil, and safflower oil. These should be exposed to various temperature conditions and the effects compared. Students should be asked to develop hypotheses to account for their observations. (For one thing, the oils are made of different substances, each of which has different physical properties.)

DEALING WITH DATA

Students have gathered data and assigned raw scores for all tests. Now they have to figure out what it all means!

Data alone can't say which lip balm is best. Like all facts, data have to be thought about, evaluated, and interpreted in a useful and meaningful way. If misinterpreted, data can mislead consumers instead of guiding them. There's no one right way to deal with data.

INTERPRET YOUR TEST DATA, p. 8

WHAT STUDENTS WILL DO:
Students will assign Importance Factors to the three lip-balm tests, then multiply each test's scores by these factors to calculate weighted scores, which will determine the lip balms' ranking order. Data obtained from the waxy-oily test will be included separately in the ratings chart. Data from the pre-tests will be used in the students' written conclusions.

OBJECTIVES:
To understand the concept of "weighting" scores so important qualities count for more; to build skill at interpreting data and forming conclusions.

CONCEPT:
Weighted scores: Some tests measure characteristics that are more important than others. How lip balms scored in the important tests should have a greater impact on the lip balms' overall ranking.

DISCUSS:
1. Were there any factors that you felt should have been tested but were not? If so, what were they? (*Aroma, appearance, applicator design, etc.*)

2. What are the most important qualities for a lip balm to have? Why? Which tests did you think were most important? Why?

3. What are the pros and cons of weighting scores? Did weighting the scores change the lip balms' ranking order? (*Have each group interpret its data without weighting scores and compare with the weighted scores. Which is more meaningful? Why?*)

EXTRA ACTIVITY: PUT TOGETHER THE CLASS'S TEST DATA

CONCEPTS:
Variation: Data can differ as a result of uncontrolled variables and of using people as measuring instruments.

Measurement error: Measurements taken during testing are not 100 percent precise. A reliable measurement is closely repeatable from one test run to another.

ACTIVITY:
Make an enlarged copy of the chart on the following page. Have all groups write their raw scores in the appropriate boxes. (Each box will have as many numbers as there are groups.) Then have the class assign Importance Factors to the tests, determine weighted scores, and decide the overall class ranking of the lip balms.

DISCUSS:
1. Did everyone who tested the lip balms come up with the same raw scores? Why or why not? Is it possible variables were controlled differently (or not controlled at all)? What are other possible sources of variation?

2. How can we determine which measurements are most reliable (most likely to happen again if the tests were repeated)? What if we performed each test several times instead of just once? What if we based the lip balms' ratings on the class's combined scores instead of on just one group's scores?

3. Examine the class's raw scores (on the chart). Which lip balm (if any) has very little variation in its individual test scores? Which lip balm's performance could you predict with more confidence? (*The one with the least variation in scores.*)

4. What's the best way to tally the groups' raw scores — figure out means, medians, or modes? (*Try all three. Do scores differ? Do rankings differ? Which scoring method is more appropriate?*)

SEND YOUR RATINGS OF LIP BALMS TO *CONSUMER REPORTS*

The class should fill in this chart and answer all questions about the lip balms. Attach a written summary of the class's conclusions. Then mail to the address below.

WHICH LIP BALMS ARE BEST?

"RAW" SCORES

Write the class's combined scores for each test in the boxes below.
Are these ❑ mean scores or ❑ median scores? (Check *one*.)

TEST	A	B	C	D
1. Stay-On				
2. Moisture-Barrier				
3. All-Temps.				
TOTALS				

(Raw-Score Totals)

"WEIGHTED" SCORES

1. Assign Importance Factors to the tests. (3-*most* important; 1-*least* important)

2. Multiply the class's combined raw scores by the Importance Factors.

IMPORTANCE FACTOR:	A	B	C	D
1.				
2.				
3.				
TOTALS				

(Weighted-Score Totals)

(1) **Code** **Brand** **Waxy or oily?**

A _____ _____

B _____ _____

C _____ _____

D _____ _____

(2) How many small groups tested the lip balms? _____

(3) Date _____

(4) Person to contact (name and address):

_____

_____

_____

_____

(5) **Mail To:**

Consumer Reports
Education Division
101 Truman Avenue
Yonkers, New York 10703-1057

PRENTICE HALL
PRODUCT TESTING ACTIVITIES by Consumer Reports

TESTING NAIL ENAMEL

None of the tests in this unit require students to put on nail enamel. *All* students can participate. If they prefer, students may substitute other types of enamels (such as model paints or home enamels) for nail enamels and test them, following the procedures in this unit.

Testing Nail Enamel helps students discover the science and technology governing the performance of enamels. Students will discover which enamels go on smoothest (**viscosity and evaporation**); which have the best hiding power (**opacity and pigments**); and which chip more easily than others (**surface adhesion**). It also builds scientific inquiry and testing skills by challenging students to form hypotheses, control variables, and design testing procedures themselves. *There is no one right answer, no desired conclusion.*

Tests are designed for groups of four. Students work together planning tests, analyzing data, and developing a scientific rating of the enamels. The chart below links the tests students will perform with the science skills and concepts those testing activities help teach.

CURRICULUM SKILLS AND CONCEPTS

Test and Student Databook Page	Highlighted Skills	Science Concepts
Getting Started, p. 1	Controlling Variables, Blind Testing	Principles of Testing
The Put-On Test p. 2	Controlling Variables, Number Lines	Viscosity, Solvents, Evaporation
Glossy-Finish Test p. 3	Observation, Paired-Comparison Testing	Glossiness, Pigments
Hardness Test p. 4	Controlling Variables, Observation	Film Hardness (Polymers)
Cover-Up Test p. 5	Controlling Variables, Observation	Opacity
The Chip-and-Peel Test, p. 6	Designing a Test, Controlling Variables	Adhesion
Appearance Test p. 7	Designing a Test, Observation	Nature of Paints
Interpret Your Test Data, p. 8	Analyzing Data, Forming Conclusions	Weighted Scores

MATERIALS NEEDED for each small group:

❑ **Test samples:** 4 different nail enamels (or 4 enamel paints), all the same color (red, preferably) and ranging in price from inexpensive to expensive.

❑ **For pre-planned tests:** 1 large plastic soda bottle with label cleaned off, heavy scissors, marker pen, ruler, bright light, pencils, emery board or fine sandpaper, pencil sharpener, magnifying glass, clear nail polish, aluminum foil.

CLASS-TIME REQUIREMENTS:

❑ To prepare for testing: 1 class period
❑ To conduct Tests 1 through 4: 2 or 3 class periods
❑ To conduct Tests 5 and 6: 2 class periods
❑ For data analysis and interpretation: 1 class period

GETTING STARTED

1. Code test samples.

Students should do "blind tests" of the nail enamels — they should not know the brand names or prices of the test samples.

Code test samples in advance (or have a student who won't be testing the enamels code test samples for the small groups). Cover all brand-name identification on nail enamel bottles. Code them A, B, C, and D. Keep a record of the codes and their brand names and prices, but keep this secret until testing is completed.

2. Distribute Student Databooks, one to each student group.

DISCUSS:

1. One thing that will vary in these tests is the enamels. But other things (like amount used and drying time) shouldn't vary. Why not? *(Results wouldn't necessarily be due to the nail enamel. It's best to test for one variable at a time. To do this, all test samples should be exposed to exactly the same conditions and procedures.)*

2. Discuss responses to the balloon. Can price or ads make certain brands seem to be superior? (Which do people often think is better—an inexpensive product or an expensive one? Why? How do ads make cosmetic products like nail enamel appealing?)

KNOWING A NAIL ENAMEL IS EXPENSIVE OR SEEING ITS ADS COULD MAKE YOU <u>THINK</u> IT'S THE BEST. COULD THAT AFFECT HOW YOU JUDGE THE NAIL ENAMELS? EXPLAIN.
Feeling a certain product is superior can affect judgments about it, especially subjective judgments (when making visual assessments rather than taking measurements). That could bias test results in favor of that product.

3. Why is each test nail enamel assigned a code letter? *(Discuss how blind testing helps reduce bias in scientific experiments. Does bottle shape give away brand names? Could that be controlled?)*

TESTS ALREADY DESIGNED FOR STUDENTS

The first four tests describe the testing procedures students should follow. Allow student groups to work independently and solve problems among themselves. Wait until they've completed their testing before discussing or viewing the tests. The goal is to encourage independent thinking, creative problem-solving, and increased confidence in their scientific abilities.

1. THE PUT-ON TEST, p. 2

QUESTION: Which nail enamel goes on best?

WHAT STUDENTS WILL DO:

Students will apply the test enamels to squares drawn on a clean strip cut from a plastic bottle and rate how they go on.

MATERIALS PER GROUP:

Coded enamels, large plastic bottle with label cleaned off, heavy scissors, marker pen, ruler. **Note: It may be a good idea to cut the 12-cm-by-4-cm strip from the plastic soda bottle in advance.**

OBJECTIVES:

To understand solvents and evaporation; to reinforce controlling variables.

CONCEPTS:

Solvents: Nail enamel consists of **lacquers** (synthetic organic coatings made up of polymers that dry hard and clear) and **pigments** (color particles) dissolved in **solvents,** which keep the enamel liquid. When exposed to air, the solvent evaporates and the polymers and color pigments harden onto the nail. (Nail polish remover is a solvent that redissolves the enamel.)

Evaporation is a phase change from liquid to gas, occurring when a liquid comes into contact with drier air. Enamels harden by evaporation of their solvents. If evaporation happens too fast, the enamel may be bumpy; too slow, it may take long to dry.

Viscosity: The smoothness of application depends in part on **viscosity,** the resistance of a liquid to flow. Thicker enamels have a higher viscosity and go on less easily than thinner ones, but are also less runny.

DISCUSS:

1. What variables had to be controlled in this test? *(Ventilation, temperature, thickness of application, etc.)* Discuss responses to the balloon. Why is the amount of time the bottle stays open a variable? *(Because the solvent in nail enamel is very volatile — it evaporates quickly. Point out that the paint-like smell from an open bottle is the solvent evaporating. Leaving a bottle open can thicken — dry out — the polish.)*

> HOW LONG THE NAIL ENAMEL BOTTLE STAYS OPEN AND HOW MANY STROKES YOU USE ARE TWO <u>VARIABLES</u>. HOW WILL YOU CONTOL THEM?
> *Close each bottle right after using it; time how long bottle A is open, then keep the others open that amount of time; count how many strokes you use to fill square A, then repeat for the other enamels.*

2. How does an enamel's *viscosity (resistance to flow)* affect how thickly and smoothly it goes on? *(If an enamel is too viscous/thick, it will go on lumpy; if it's too thin, it'll go on thin and runny.)* Which test enamel had the best viscosity?

2. GLOSSY-FINISH TEST, p. 3

QUESTION: Which enamel dries to the glossiest finish?

WHAT STUDENTS WILL DO:
Students will place the enameled squares from Test 1 under a bright light and judge which reflects a pencil point most clearly.

MATERIALS PER GROUP:
Enameled squares from Test 1, bright light, 2 sharpened pencils.

OBJECTIVES:
To understand glossiness; to build skill at making sensory observations and judgments; to practice using the paired-comparison method of testing.

CONCEPTS:
Glossiness is the ability of a surface to reflect an image. The glossier the surface, the clearer it will bounce back light waves and the sharper the reflected image will be.

Lacquer and color pigments: The lacquer in nail enamel dries hard and clear and is very glossy, but color pigments can interfere with the lacquer's glossiness. Since nail enamels' lacquers and pigments vary, so will their glossiness.

DISCUSS:

1. What variables had to be controlled so you could make fair comparisons? *(The type, intensity, and placement of the light source; angle at which you look at the reflection; where on the test square you place the pencil.)*

2. Is it easier to compare two enamels with each other or to judge them all at once? Which do you think gives more reliable data? *(Paired comparison testing lets you compare without having to define standards of glossiness and without having to utilize more complex scoring scales. By comparing every possible pairing of test samples, you can arrive at a valid ranking of test samples.)*

3. Discuss responses to the balloon. Did you find a difference in the way the test squares felt? How did the square you ranked as most glossy feel compared to the square you ranked as least glossy?

> NOW CLOSE YOUR EYES AND <u>FEEL</u> THE TEST SQUARES. DOES THE GLOSSIER ENAMEL FEEL DIFFERENT? HOW? WHY?
> *Glossier enamels will have more "drag"—they will seem stickier to the touch. Glossier enamels are smoother—and that means more skin will be in contact with the enamel. The greater the surface contact between finger and enamel, the more the finger will seem to "stick."*

3. HARDNESS TEST, p. 4

QUESTION: Which nail enamel is the hardest when dry?

WHAT STUDENTS WILL DO:
Using the enameled squares from Test 1, students will try to etch initials into each enamel with a pencil, then judge which enamel dried to the hardest finish.

MATERIALS PER GROUP:
Enameled squares from Test 1, emery board or fine sandpaper, pencil sharpener, pencil, magnifying glass.

OBJECTIVES:
To reinforce paired-comparison testing methods; to introduce polymers; to reinforce controlling variables.

CONCEPT:
Polymers are long molecules made by joining many smaller molecules. Because of the length and shape of their molecules, polymers form plastic-like materials (including hard lacquer films of nail enamels) that are strong yet pliable.

DISCUSS:
1. Discuss responses to the balloon.

> WHAT <u>VARIABLES</u> COULD AFFECT HOW MUCH AN ENAMEL'S SURFACE IS SCRATCHED?
> *Variables include how sharp the pencil was; how hard its point was; how hard you pressed; and the angle of the pencil to the enamel.*

2. How did the results of this hardness test compare with the results of the glossiness test? Do you think these qualities are related? *(Both glossiness and hardness are due to the lacquer [the hard, clear polymer coating] used in the nail enamel. Make a graph of the enamels' hardness and glossiness scores to help investigate how the two may relate.)*

4. COVER-UP TEST, p. 5

QUESTION: Which nail enamel has the most "hiding power"?

WHAT STUDENTS WILL DO:
After applying a clear base coat (to prevent seepage), students will paint over four gray to black bars with the enamels and see if any bars are visible through the enamels.

MATERIALS:
4 coded enamels, clear nail polish (base coat), aluminum foil.

OBJECTIVES:
To evaluate the opacity, or hiding power, of each nail enamel; to control variables.

CONCEPT:
Opacity is the ability to block out light rays. Enamels with less pigment will have less hiding power. So will enamels with coarsely ground pigments. (Pigments are insoluble — they are ground up to mix with the dissolved polymer. How finely they're ground affects how well they remain dispersed in the enamel.)

DISCUSS:
1. Discuss responses to the balloon. *(With nail enamels, applicators are part of the "product." You have two variables: the nail enamel and the applicator.)*

> HOW MANY BRUSH STROKES YOU USE AND HOW THICKLY YOU APPLY THE BASE COAT AND ENAMELS ARE <u>VARIABLES</u>. HOW WILL YOU CONTROL THEM?
> *These variables can be controlled by using the same number of dips into each enamel, applying just one coat, and not "painting over" your first tries (or painting over all first tries the same number of times).*

Foil

2. Is there a relationship between hiding-power and glossiness (Test 2)? Graph glossiness and cover-up scores and compare. *(More opaque products contain more pigment and may have less gloss.)*

TESTS STUDENTS WILL DESIGN THEMSELVES

Testing procedures are not provided for the following two tests. Each small group must devise its own plan and procedures. The goal is to encourage hands-on, common-sense creativity and problem-solving by students. There's no one "right way" to do these tests.

5. THE CHIP-AND-PEEL TEST, p. 6

QUESTION: Which nail enamel resists chipping and peeling the best?

POSSIBLE PROCEDURES:
Students could perform a variety of "torture tests" on the enameled squares after devising some way to count or measure the amount of force, degree of flexion, etc.

OBJECTIVES:
To understand how to design a controlled test; to observe properties of lacquers (polymers).

CONCEPTS:
Adhesion is the molecular attraction exerted between the surfaces of different substances in contact with each other (e.g., enamel and fingernail).

Plastics are polymers. They can be brittle or flexible materials: Some shatter when bent, while others bend easily. Some are insoluble, while others (like nail enamels) dissolve easily and dry to a hard film when the solvent evaporates.

DISCUSS:

1. What was your testing plan? Did you test on a plastic bottle or real nails? Why? What data did you collect? How did you use your data to arrive at scores?

2. What variables did you control? Were any variables not controlled? *(Variables could have included how the plastic-bottle squares were flexed, how and with what force scratches and blows were applied to test squares, etc.)*

3. Discuss responses to the balloon. What are the pros and cons of doing chip-and-peel tests on real nails? *(Pros: It's a real-use test. Cons: It would require weeks, and involve controlling numerous variables.)*

> WHAT TORTURE TESTS COULD YOU DO ON PLASTIC-BOTTLE NAILS THAT YOU COULDN'T DO ON REAL NAILS? *Almost any torture test (scraping, hanging, smashing) could not be done on real nails.*

6. APPEARANCE TEST, p. 7

QUESTION: Which is the best-looking nail enamel?

POSSIBLE PROCEDURES:
Students could designate one person to be a "model" and apply the test enamels for the rest of the group to judge. Or they could use the enamels on bumpy surfaces (like an orange) to judge ridge-filling ability. Or they could apply enamels to fake fingernails and judge overall appearance.

OBJECTIVES:
To design a controlled test; to reinforce the importance of controlling variables.

DISCUSS:

1. Did you have trouble deciding which characteristics make a good-looking nail enamel? What might have helped? *(Surveying nail-enamel users.)* What characteristics did you look for in your tests? Why?

Speech bubble:
SHOULD APPEARANCE TESTS BE DONE ON REAL NAILS OR ON A VARIETY OF "FAKE" SURFACES (OR BOTH)? *Either way is valid. Doing both would let you double-check your results.*

2. How did you test? What data did you collect? Discuss responses to the balloon. What surfaces did you use for the appearance test? What were the reasons for your decision?

3. Could knowing a nail enamel's brand name or price affect your judgment of its appearance? Could ads influence you? Could the appearance of a nail enamel's bottle or applicator give away its brand? Could that variable be controlled? If so, how? *(Perhaps have a third party apply the enamels so testers can judge without seeing the bottles.)*

EXTRA TEST: AGING TEST
(Approximate time: 2 weeks)

As nail enamels age (and are opened and closed), they are prone to thickening, drying out, and discoloration. Exposure to heat and cold can also affect them.

QUESTION: Do nail enamels in the bottle deteriorate with age?

MATERIALS:
4 test nail enamels, same materials as for Tests 1 through 6.

PROCEDURE:

1. Open the bottles for 20 minutes every day to simulate use. (This is an "accelerated" test. Nail enamels aren't used that often.)

2. After 2 weeks, repeat tests 1 through 5 to evaluate viscosity, smoothness, chip resistance, hiding power, and shine.

3. Compare 2-week scores with the scores obtained when the enamels were new.

4. Base enamels' "aging" score on how close they stayed to their original quality.

DEALING WITH DATA

Students have gathered data and assigned raw scores for all the nail enamel tests. Now they have to figure out what it all means!

Data alone can't say which nail enamel is best. Like all facts, data have to be thought about, evaluated, and interpreted in a useful and meaningful way. There's no one right way to deal with data.

- Page 8 (Interpret Your Test Data) has students "weight" scores to make important tests count for more, then rank nail enamels from best to worst.

- While dealing with data, students will perform calculations and learn simple statistics concepts in a hands-on way. They will also express in writing what their tests revealed about nail enamels.

- Much can be learned by having small groups compare results and combine data to come up with *class* results (see the following page).

INTERPRET YOUR TEST DATA, p. 8

WHAT STUDENTS WILL DO:
Students will assign Importance Factors to the tests; multiply the enamels' scores by those factors to determine weighted scores; rank the enamels from best (highest weighted score) to worst; and write out their conclusions and advice.

OBJECTIVES:
To understand the concept of weighted scores; to interpret data and form conclusions.

MATERIALS:
Brand names and prices to decode test enamels.

DISCUSS:
1. What Importance Factors did you give each test? Why? Should tests for the more important things count more? Why or why not?

2. Is there a relationship between a nail enamel's price and its quality? Do any of the qualities you tested for seem related to price?

EXTRA ACTIVITY: PUT TOGETHER THE CLASS'S DATA

CONCEPTS:
- **Variation:** Data can vary as a result of quality differences within a brand, making results more reliable if tests are repeated a number of times.

- **Measurement error:** Measurements recorded during testing are subject to inaccuracies due to uncontrolled variables or the imprecision of measurements.

ACTIVITY:
Post an enlarged copy of the chart on the following page. Have all groups write their raw scores in the appropriate boxes. (Each box will have several scores.) Then average the scores, assign Importance Factors to the tests, and determine the class's weighted scores.

DISCUSS:
1. Did everyone who tested come up with the same raw scores for the nail enamels? Did they have the same rank orders? If not, why not? Is it possible every nail enamel A wasn't exactly the same? Can performance vary within a brand? Is it possible that measurement errors were made? *(Explore different methods of testing and different interpretations of scoring by testers.)*

2. How can we determine which measurements are most reliable (most likely to happen again if the test were repeated)? What if we performed each test several times instead of once? What if we based nail enamel ratings on the whole class's raw scores combined, instead of just one group's?

3. Examine the class's raw data (on the chart). Which nail enamel (if any) has very little variation in its data (the small groups' test scores are similar)? Which enamel has wide variation in its scores? Which nail enamel's performance could you predict with more confidence? *(The one with the least variation in scores.)* What might be some causes of variation? *(Explore subjective vs. objective data.)*

4. What's the better way to tally the small groups' scores — calculate means or medians? *(Have some students do it one way and others the other way. Are scores different? Which is more appropriate?)*

SEND YOUR RATINGS OF NAIL ENAMELS TO *CONSUMER REPORTS*

The class should fill in this chart and answer all questions about the nail enamels. Attach a written summary of the class's conclusions. Then mail to the address below.

WHICH NAIL ENAMEL IS BEST?

"RAW" SCORES

Write the class's combined scores for each test in the boxes below.
Are these ❑ mean scores or ❑ median scores? (Check *one*.)

TEST	A	B	C	D
1. Put-On				
2. Glossy-Finish				
3. Hard-ness				
4. Cover-Up				
5. Chip/Peel				
6. Appear-ance				
TOTALS				

(Raw-Score Totals)

"WEIGHTED" SCORES

1. Assign Importance Factors to the tests. (3=*most* important; 1=*least* important)
2. Multiply the class's combined raw scores by the Importance Factors.

IMPORTANCE FACTOR:	A	B	C	D
1.				
2.				
3.				
4.				
5.				
6.				
TOTALS				

(Weighted-Score Totals)

(1) **Code**   **Brand**
A _____
B _____
C _____
D _____

(2) How many small groups tested the nail enamels?_____

(3) Date_____

(4) Person to contact (name and address):

_____

_____

_____

_____

(5) **Mail To:**

Consumer Reports
Education Division
101 Truman Avenue
Yonkers, New York 10703-1057

PRENTICE HALL

PRODUCT TESTING ACTIVITIES by Consumer Reports

TESTING ORANGE JUICE

Testing Orange Juice helps students discover the science and technology involved in evaluating orange juice: finding taste preferences **(sampling and paired comparisons)**; identifying ideal orange juice **(standards of reference, the sense of taste)**; measuring juices' vitamin C content **(chemical reactions, titration)**; and how juices' packaging affects the environment **(degradability, volume)**. Collecting, analyzing, and interpreting the data also involve counting and measuring, ratios, number lines, graphing, and basic statistics (variation, sampling, measurement error).

Tests encourage cooperative learning. They are designed for groups of four. Students work together to conduct and plan tests, analyze data, solve problems, and develop a scientific rating of orange juice. The chart below links the tests students will perform with the science skills and concepts those testing activities help teach.

CURRICULUM SKILLS AND CONCEPTS

Test and Student Databook Page	Highlighted Skills	Science Concepts
Getting Started p. 1	Controlling Variables, Blind Testing	Principles of Testing
The Real-Thing Test p. 2	Sensory Observation, Measuring, Averaging	Sensory System, Standards of Reference
The I-Like-It Test p. 4	Controlling Variables, Ratios, Number Lines	Paired-Comparison Testing
Vitamin C Survival Test, p. 5	Measuring, Recording Data, Titrating	Chemical Reactions, Titration, Vitamins
The Pulp Test p. 6	Designing a Test, Controlling Variables	Fruits
The Packaging Test p. 7	Designing a Test, Research Skills	Degradability, Packaging
Interpret Your Test Data, p. 8	Ranking, Making and Interpreting Graphs	Weighted Scores, Variation

CLASS-TIME REQUIREMENTS:

❑ To prepare for testing: 1 class period.
❑ To conduct Test 1: 1 class period
❑ To conduct Test 2: 1 class period.
❑ To conduct Test 3: 1 class period.
❑ To conduct Tests 4 and 5: 1 or 2 class periods (or assign as homework).
❑ For data analysis and interpretation: 1 class period

MATERIALS NEEDED for each small group:

❑ **Test samples:**
3 orange juices. Try to mix type and prices: frozen concentrate, bottled, and cartoned; costly and inexpensive. (Frozen concentrates should be prepared the day before and all 3 test samples should be refrigerated in identical non-metallic covered containers.)

❑ **For pre-planned tests:**
Commercially prepared fresh-squeezed orange juice, paper cups, orange rind, lemon juice, sugar, water, ruler, marker pen, paper, small beaker, small graduated cylinder, stirrer, cornstarch, iodine solution (2% tincture of iodine antiseptic), medicine dropper.

GETTING STARTED

1. Prepare test samples in advance.

Orange juices should be stored in covered containers coded A to C for students to pour from. (Frozen juice should be reconstituted and refrigerated to the same temperature as the other samples.) Preparations should be done by someone who will not be doing these tests. Save the containers and labels for data-interpretation activities.

CAUTION: Before testing, ask if any students have an allergy to citrus fruits or are on a restricted-sugar diet (perhaps for diabetes). If so, they shouldn't do any of the tasting in this test. They can, however, help prepare and blind-code the juices as well as participate in the non-tasting tests.

2. Distribute Student Databooks, one to each group.

DISCUSS:

1. One thing that will vary in these tests is the orange juice. But other things (like how they're stored and their temperature when tasted) shouldn't vary. Why not? *(Differences could be due to the uncontrolled variables. Discuss responses to the page 1 balloon.)*

TEMPERATURE AFFECTS HOW ORANGE JUICE TASTES. HOW COULD YOU CONTROL THIS VARIABLE? *After preparing and coding, chill to the same temperature.*

2. The goal of testing is to come up with *reliable* results (results that would probably be gotten again if the tests were repeated) and *valid* results (results that reflect actual differences among the products). How does controlling variables help you do that? What else should you pay attention to? *(Collect data carefully and keep good records, check data.)*

TESTS ALREADY DESIGNED FOR STUDENTS

The first three tests describe the testing procedures students should follow. Allow student groups to work independently and solve problems among themselves. Wait until they've completed their testing before discussing or reviewing the tests. The goal is to encourage independent thinking, creative problem-solving, and increased confidence in their scientific abilities.

1. THE REAL-THING TEST, p. 2

QUESTION: Which juice tastes most like fresh-squeezed orange juice?

WHAT STUDENTS WILL DO:

Students will taste sugary and plain water to identify sweet and not sweet, then taste the juices and mark where they fall between those extremes. They'll follow a similar process to measure sourness and orange flavor. Then they'll measure how far from fresh-squeezed each juice is on the scales and use that to determine scores.

MATERIALS FOR EACH GROUP:

For each tester: coded test juices and fresh-squeezed*, orange-rind slice, 1 tsp lemon juice, 1 tbsp sugar, water, 7 small paper cups per tester, ruler, marker pen. **Prepare the sugar water and lemon water in advance (1 tbsp sugar in 125 mL water and 1 tsp lemon juice in 125 mL water).**

* *Note: Commercially prepared orange juices are often a blend of varieties of oranges. If you squeeze just one type of orange, it may not represent overall "orange" taste.*

OBJECTIVES:

To use standards of reference; to become aware of different types of orange juice tastes and how the tongue works; to develop sensory-observation skills.

CONCEPTS:

Standards of reference: A standard describes words like sweet, sour, and flavor relative to a specific reference that can be defined, so testers' judgments (and the data collected) will be comparable.

Tastes and the tongue: There are four basic tastes (sweet, sour, salty, and bitter). Taste buds that detect these tastes are in certain locations on the tongue: sweet at the tip; bitter at the back; salty and sour on the sides.

Sense of taste: The mouth and nose are a sensory system that can be trained to discriminate tastes, flavors, and intensity. Like vision and touch, the sense of taste can become a scientist's tool.

DISCUSS:

1. Why did you taste sugar water and define "sweet" rather than just taste for sweetness in general? What variables does this control? (*Explore how a standard of reference controls each taster's definition of "sweet."*)

2. Discuss responses to the balloon. Which is the better way to test for taste qualities: to gulp the sample fast or sip it slowly? Why?

WHAT IS THE BEST WAY TO JUDGE A JUICE— GULP IT OR SIP IT SLOWLY? WHY? WRITE YOUR HYPOTHESIS HERE. *Sipping slowly and letting juice linger in the mouth give the taste buds time to "observe" individual qualities.*

3. Why were the test juices' scores based on how close they came to fresh-squeezed? Can a juice be too sweet or too sour, or have too much flavor? (*More sweetness or sourness than fresh-squeezed is a taste defect.*)

4. Do you think sweetness, sourness, and orange flavor are equally important in determining how good a juice tastes? Or is one of those characteristics more important than the others? Which one? Why? (*See weighting activity.*)

5. How accurate do you think taste observations can be? What can you do to make them more accurate? (*Explore things like sipping slowly, focusing on taste, maybe closing eyes.*)

ACTIVITIES:

- **Weight the test data** and compute weighted scores for the juices. Which taste characteristic is more important? How much more important is it? (Two times? Three times?) Decide, then use that number to multiply the test juices' distance from OJ for that characteristic. Compute the weighted *Total distance from OJ* and use the number line to find weighted scores. Does "weighting" make the results more meaningful? Why or why not?

- **Do pH tests on the juices.** See if the sourest-tasting juice is the most acidic (and see how the test juices compare with the pH of fresh-squeezed).

2. THE I-LIKE-IT TEST, p. 4

QUESTION: Which juice's flavor is preferred by more people?

WHAT STUDENTS WILL DO:
Students will taste pairs of test juices and choose the preferred one until all possible combinations of juices have been compared. The juice selected the most times wins.

MATERIALS FOR EACH GROUP:
1/4 cup coded test juices and 4 paper cups per tester, water, paper.

OBJECTIVES:
To understand the concept of paired-comparison testing; to develop skill with ratios and number lines; to reinforce the importance of controlling variables.

CONCEPT:
Paired-comparison testing: The process of comparing all different combinations of test samples and choosing the preferred one makes it easier to control variables. This method is particularly useful in sensory testing where standards of reference (for scoring flavor, texture, etc.) may be particularly difficult to define.

1. Which do you think is a more scientific way to test for taste preferences: paired comparisons (as you did here) or tasting all three together and choosing the one you like best? Why?

2. Discuss responses to the balloon. (*Explore how preference testing differs from testing for sensory characteristics.*)

> IS IT POSSIBLE FOR A JUICE THAT WAS <u>NOT</u> CLOSEST TO FRESH-SQUEEZED IN TEST 1 TO <u>WIN</u> THIS TEST? WHY OR WHY NOT?
> *Yes. Preference testing is different from testing sensory characteristics. People could prefer a sweeter, more flavorful taste than that of fresh-squeezed.*

3. How could these variables have affected the results of this test:
- The temperature of the juices.
- Being compared to a strong-flavored juice.
- Being tasted first.
- Being tasted last.
- Ad claims for one of the brands.

Which of these variables were *not* controlled in this test? (*Being tested first and last.*) Which were controlled? How were they controlled?

ACTIVITY:

Ratios: Express test data as ratios of wins to times tested. Explore how the "margin of error" gets smaller as the number of times tested gets larger. (Or use the analogy of an exam: If an exam has 100 questions and you get one wrong, that's one point; if the exam has two questions and you get one wrong, that's 50 points.)

3. VITAMIN C SURVIVAL TEST, p. 5

QUESTION: Do some orange juices have more vitamin C than others?

WHAT STUDENTS WILL DO:

Students will do a titration using iodine and cornstarch to measure each juice's vitamin-C content. (Iodine reacts with cornstarch and changes color, but only after it has reacted with all the vitamin C that's present. Students will count the number of drops of iodine an orange juice-cornstarch solution takes before changing color. The more it takes, the more vitamin C the juice has.)

MATERIALS FOR EACH GROUP:

3 coded test juices (10 mL of each), small glass or beaker, stirrer, cornstarch, small graduated cylinder, 2% tincture of iodine solution, medicine dropper.

OBJECTIVES:

To introduce the molecular nature of chemical reactions; to become familiar with the concept of titration and practice doing it; to reinforce the importance of accurately measuring and recording data and controlling variables.

CONCEPTS:

Molecules and chemical reactions. Molecules react more rapidly with some substances than with others. When those substances are used up, less-favored reactions may take place. Iodine is more reactive with vitamin C than with cornstarch, so it reacts to decompose all the vitamin C. Only then will iodine start reacting with the cornstarch.

Titration is a method of measuring how much of a substance (vitamin C) is present in a solution by gradually adding a reactant (iodine) and seeing how much is needed to "use up" that substance. When the reactant begins to react with a secondary substance — an "indicator" (cornstarch) — it forms a compound that changes the solution's color, signaling the end point of the titration.

Vitamins as a group are essential to health. Vitamin C is found in high concentrations in citrus fruits.

DISCUSS:

1. Exposure to air and heat can kill off vitamin C. How could orange juice have lost vitamin C between the tree and your glass? (*Juices are exposed to air and heat during processing.*)

2. What was happening in the orange juice-cornstarch solution when you added iodine but the color stayed orange? (*Iodine was reacting with vitamin C.*) What was happening when you added iodine and the color changed? (*Iodine was reacting with cornstarch.*) Which do you think iodine is more strongly reactive with: vitamin C or cornstarch? Why? (*Vitamin C, because it reacts with that first.*)

3. How did this experiment show the amount of vitamin C in the juices? (*The juice changed color after the vitamin C was used up. The more iodine that took, the more vitamin C was present.*) Discuss responses to the balloon.

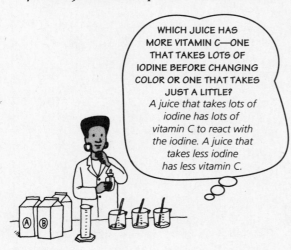

WHICH JUICE HAS MORE VITAMIN C—ONE THAT TAKES LOTS OF IODINE BEFORE CHANGING COLOR OR ONE THAT TAKES JUST A LITTLE?
A juice that takes lots of iodine has lots of vitamin C to react with the iodine. A juice that takes less iodine has less vitamin C.

4. What variables were very important to control in this experiment? (*Counting the exact number of iodine drops, stirring before judging color, using the same amount of each test juice.*) What variable did you not have to control? Why? (*The amount of cornstarch because you just had to note when the iodine started to react with it.*)

5. Have small groups compare data. Did every group get the same number of drops? If not, what could be some reasons? (*Were variables controlled? Were data accurate? Did groups have the same definition of "color change"?*) Did the groups' rankings of the juices vary? (*If rankings were the same, the groups might have controlled variables differently but consistently.*)

TESTS STUDENTS WILL DESIGN THEMSELVES

Testing procedures are not provided for the following two tests. Each small group must devise its own plan and procedures. The goal is to encourage hands-on, common sense creativity and problem-solving by students. There's no one "right" way to do these tests.

4. THE PULP TEST, p. 6

QUESTION: Do some juices have more pulp than others?

POSSIBLE PROCEDURE:

Students could copy Test 1: Make a Pulp Scale and mark where fresh-squeezed OJ falls, then test the other juices to see how close they come to fresh. They could do this using either sensory tests (taste) or measurement tests (pour a measured amount of each juice through cheesecloth and count or weigh the pulp left behind).

OBJECTIVES:

To understand how to design a controlled test; to reinforce the importance of defining standards of reference when testing.

CONCEPT:
Nature of fruits: Citrus fruits contain tiny juice sacs.

DISCUSS:

1. Discuss responses to the first balloon.

YOU COULD DO SENSORY (TASTE) OR PHYSICAL (MEASURING) TESTS TO JUDGE PULP. WHICH WOULD GIVE BETTER DATA? WRITE YOUR OPINION HERE.
Sensory testing (e.g., paired comparisons) can help identify which juice's pulpiness people prefer. Physical tests can measure how much pulp juice has.

2. What variables did you control? How did you control them? *(The volume of juice measured, the method of catching the pulp, counting method, etc.)*

3. Discuss responses to the second balloon. How did you determine how much pulp was the right amount?

IS <u>MORE</u> PULP ALWAYS BETTER? CAN A JUICE BE <u>TOO</u> PULPY? HOW COULD YOU DETERMINE HOW MUCH PULP IS JUST RIGHT? WRITE YOUR HYPOTHESIS HERE.
Preferences will vary. Could compare with real juice, do taste-preferences tests, etc.

5. THE PACKAGING TEST, p. 7

QUESTION: Which juice package adds the least to landfill waste problems?

POSSIBLE PROCEDURES:

Students might crush and measure the crush-volume of each container, then relate to number-of-servings per container. (For example, is the ratio of servings per cubic centimeter of waste greater for bottled juices than for frozen concentrates?)

Students might also research the materials juice containers are made of and analyze the energy and resources consumed to make them. Students may also research whether the community has programs to recycle those materials.

OBJECTIVES:

To develop skill at analyzing a problem and creating ways to test; to develop awareness of environmental consequences of packaging; to develop research skills.

CONCEPT:

Degradability: Most of the nation's solid waste goes to landfills, which are fast filling up. Landfills often retard rather than promote degradability. In order to degrade, special conditions (light, moisture, biological agents, etc.) must be met. Most landfills don't have conditions that support degradability: They pre-mix and cover all types of refuse, making everything degrade slowly. So the characteristic that most affects landfill problems is the volume of trash dumped there; degradability is important only if that particular material is composted or treated specially.

DISCUSS:

1. Discuss responses to the first balloon. How did you test? Why?

WHICH IS MORE IMPORTANT TO TEST FOR: WHETHER THE JUICE CONTAINER IS DEGRADABLE OR THE LANDFILL SPACE THAT CONTAINER TAKES UP? WRITE YOUR IDEAS HERE.
If you have a local program that degrades the type of material a juice container is made of, then a container's degradability is important. Otherwise, the volume the juice container takes up will be more important.

2. How do the test juices' containers compare? Is any type of container significantly more earth-friendly than another? How do all manufactured containers compare with "nature's container" (orange peels)?

3. Discuss responses to the second balloon. When doesn't it make a difference whether a juice's packaging is recyclable (or degradable)?

EVEN IF A CONTAINER IS RECYCLABLE, IT DOESN'T MAKE A DIFFERENCE UNLESS YOU RECYCLE IT. WHAT DOES YOUR COMMUNITY RECYCLE? (THIS MAY TAKE SOME RESEARCH!) WRITE YOUR FINDINGS HERE.
Check with Sanitation Department, town hall, or local environmental groups.

INTERPRET YOUR TEST DATA, p. 8

Students have gathered data and assigned raw scores for all five orange juice tests. Now they have to figure out what it all means!

Data alone can't say which juice is best. Like all facts, data have to be analyzed, evaluated, and interpreted in a meaningful way. If not interpreted, all the testing was a waste of time. If misinterpreted, data can mislead consumers instead of guiding them.

WHAT STUDENTS WILL DO:

Students will decide which tests are more important, assign Importance Factors to the tests, then multiply juices' scores by those factors to arrive at weighted scores. They will also rank the juices in order of performance, fill in brand names, compute price per serving, and use symbols to give additional information.

OBJECTIVES:

To understand the concept of weighting; to gain practice in making and interpreting charts.

CONCEPT:

Weighting: Some tests measure more important characteristics than other tests. How juices score in important tests should count for more (have a greater impact on the juices' overall rankings).

DISCUSS:

1. What are the most important things an orange juice should do? Which tests did you think were most important? Why?

2. Did one juice do best in all the important tests or were different juices best at different things? How would you decide which juice to buy?

3. What are the pros and cons of weighting scores? Did weighting the scores change the juices' rank order? *(Have each group interpret its data without weighting scores. Which ranking is more meaningful? Why?)*

EXTRA ACTIVITY: PUT TOGETHER THE CLASS'S TEST DATA

CONCEPTS:

Variation: Data can vary as a result of uncontrolled variables; of changes in testing conditions (like where the juices were tested); and of using people as measuring instruments (for taste).

Measurement error: Measurements taken during testing are subject to variation due to measurement inaccuracy (like how carefully distances on scales were measured) or to different testing conditions (like defining titration end-points). A reliable measurement is closely repeatable from one test run to another.

ACTIVITY:

Make an enlarged copy of the chart on the following page. Have all groups write their raw scores in the appropriate boxes. (Each box will have as many numbers as there are groups.) Then have the class average the scores assign Importance Factors to the tests, and determine weighted scores.

DISCUSS:

1. Did everyone who tested come up with the same raw scores for the test juices? Why not? Is it possible measurement errors were made? Were some variables *not* controlled?

2. How can we determine which measurements are most reliable (most likely to happen again if the tests were repeated)? What if we performed each test several times instead of once? What if we based the juices' ratings on the class's raw scores combined, instead of on just one group's scores?

3. Examine the class's raw data (on the chart). Which juice (if any) has very little variation in its individual test scores? Which juice's performance could you predict with more confidence? *(The one with the least variation in scores.)*

4. What's the best way to tally the groups' raw scores — figure out means, medians, or modes? *(Try all three. Do scores differ? Which is more appropriate?)*

SEND YOUR RATINGS OF ORANGE JUICES TO *CONSUMER REPORTS*

The class should fill in this chart and answer all questions about the orange juices. Attach a written summary of the class's conclusions. Then mail to the address below.

WHICH ORANGE JUICE IS BEST?

"RAW" SCORES

Write the class's combined scores for each test in the boxes below.
Are these ❏ mean scores or ❏ median scores? (Check *one*.)

TEST	A	B	C
1. Real-Thing			
2. I-Like-It			
3. Vitamin C			
4. Pulp			
5. Packaging			
TOTALS			

(Raw-Score Totals)

"WEIGHTED" SCORES

1. Assign Importance Factors to the tests. (3 = *most* important, 1 = *least* important)
2. Multiply the class's combined raw scores by the Importance Factors.

IMPORTANCE FACTOR:	A	B	C
1.			
2.			
3.			
4.			
5.			
TOTALS			

(Weighted-Score Totals)

(1) **Code** **Brand** **Type**

A _____ _____

B _____ _____

C _____ _____

(2) How many small groups tested the orange juices?_____

(3) Date _____

(4) Person to contact (name and address):

_____

_____

_____

_____

(5) **Mail To:**

Consumer Reports
Education Division
101 Truman Avenue
Yonkers, New York 10703-1057

PRENTICE HALL

PRODUCT TESTING ACTIVITIES by Consumer Reports

TESTING PAPER TOWELS

Testing Paper Towels helps students discover which towels perform certain tasks best and the science behind their performance. Students will discover why water climbs up paper towels **(capillary action)**; why some paper towels absorb more water than others **(porosity, fiber structure of paper)**; why some paper towels are stronger than others **(paper structure)**; and why some paper towels leave lint behind **(fiber length)**. They will also judge

a reusable alternative to paper towels (a sponge) and explore the environmental impact of disposable products.

Tests are designed for groups of four. Students will work together to conduct and plan tests, collect and analyze data, solve problems, and develop a scientific rating of the test towels. The chart below links the tests students will perform with the science skills and concepts those testing activities help teach.

CURRICULUM SKILLS AND CONCEPTS

Test and Student Databook Page	Highlighted Skills	Science Concepts
Getting Started p. 1	Controlling Variables, Blind Testing	Principles of Testing
Quick-Climb Test p. 2	Observation, Time Calculations	Capillary Action, Evaporation
Big-Spill Test p. 3	Controlling Variables, Measuring Liquids	Porosity
Dry-Strength Test p. 4	Testing Paired Comparisions	Nature of Paper, Variation
Wet-Strength Test p. 5	Designing a Test	Nature of Paper
Rough-Scrub Test p. 6	Controlling Variables	Abrasion
Shedding Test p. 6	Designing a Test, Observation	Linting, Paper Fibers
Analyze Your Test Data p. 7	Mathematics Skills, Graphing	Weighted Scores
Interpret Your Test Data p. 8	Critical Thinking, Forming Conclusions	Variation, Mean and Median

MATERIALS NEEDED
for each small group:

❑ **Test samples:** 3 brands of paper towels (1 roll of each should suffice for 10 small groups). Try to include 1- and 2-ply samples. 1 sample should be an inexpensive store brand.

❑ **For pre-planned tests:** Ball-point pen, beaker, tape, water, scissors, long pencil, ruler, timer, books for stacking, measuring cup, sponge, spring clip.

CLASS-TIME REQUIREMENTS:

❑ To prepare for testing: 1 class period
❑ To conduct Tests 1 to 6: 3 class periods
❑ For data analysis and interpretation: 1 or 2 class periods

GETTING STARTED

1. Distribute Student Databooks, one to each student group.

DISCUSS:

1. What could we learn from testing paper towels? (Could our towel choices save us money? affect the environment?)

2. What paper-towel commercials have you seen? What do they claim? What do they demonstrate? Do you think other paper towels might also be able to make those claims or perform those demonstrations? What non-disposable products might do the job just as well?

2. Code test samples.

Students should do "blind tests" of the towels — they should not know the brand name of the towels they test. They should identify the test samples by code letter rather than brand name.

Prepare test samples in advance: Remove packaging and all brand-name identification from towels. Code the test towels A, B, and C. (Write codes on the end of the rolls.) Write codes on packages, too, and keep them hidden until all testing is completed.

> COULD ADVERTISING CLAIMS AFFECT THE WAY YOU JUDGE PAPER TOWELS? HOW COULD YOU CONTROL THIS VARIABLE?
> *Ad claims can create an image of superiority, which could subtly influence judgments (even if we don't "believe" the claims).*

1. Discuss responses to the page 1 balloon. Explore biases: Which do people often think is better: store or national brands? advertised or no-name brands? How might these biases form?

2. Why is each test paper towel assigned a code letter? (*Discuss how coding test samples helps to eliminate bias from scientific experiments.*)

TESTS ALREADY DESIGNED FOR STUDENTS

The first three tests describe the testing procedures students should follow. Allow student groups to work independently and solve problems among themselves. Wait until they've completed their testing before discussing or reviewing the tests. The goal is to encourage independent thinking, creative problem-solving, and increased confidence in their scientific abilities.

1. QUICK-CLIMB TEST, p. 2

QUESTION: Which towel soaks up water the fastest?

WHAT STUDENTS WILL DO:
After cutting and measuring a strip of each towel, students will put its bottom edge in water and time how long it takes the water to climb 10 cm.

MATERIALS FOR EACH GROUP:
3 coded test towels (1 sheet of each), ballpoint pen, beaker, water, scissors, tape, long pencil, ruler, timer, books for stacking.

OBJECTIVES:
To compare rates of absorption; to discover how capillary action works; to understand evaporation; to reinforce the importance of controlling variables.

CONCEPTS:

Capillary action: When students place paper towel strips into a beaker of water, the water will climb the strip via **capillary action.** Water molecules "adhere" (stick) to the paper fibers and keep moving up to drier (and higher) fibers.

Evaporation: The water molecules also keep moving from the paper into the drier air by **evaporation.** By checking the 30-second marks on each paper-towel strip, students can see that the water's climbing rate slows down as it moves up the strip due to evaporation. It stops moving up the strip when capillary action is supplying water *up* at the same rate the water in the strip is evaporating *out.*

HMMM...THIS TOWEL FEELS SOFT AND THICK. THIS ONE FEELS HARD AND THIN. WHICH ONE WILL WATER CLIMB UP FASTER?

WRITE YOUR HYPOTHESIS HERE. *Soft and thick towels have more fibers and more space between fibers. That gives water more room to move and more surface area to stick to. So water should climb them faster.*

DISCUSS:

1. Discuss the balloon. What was your hypothesis? Did your tests prove or disprove that hypothesis? What do your test results suggest about the nature of paper? of liquids? How did the water climb up the paper? *(Explore capillary action and evaporation.)*

2. Which type of paper towel scored better: thick or thin? 1-ply or 2-ply? Why? *(In general, the towels with more "puff" are likely to perform better.)*

ACTIVITY:

Calculate capillary action rates (how fast the water climbed). During the test, students marked the water level on their towel strips every 30 seconds. Have students use those data to graph height vs. time and compare rates at the beginning and near the end of the water's climb. Did the rate at which the water was climbing slow down? Why? *(The surface that the water was evaporating from increased as the water climbed. As that surface area grew, more water evaporated. So the rate of climb slowed down.)*

2. BIG-SPILL TEST, p. 3

QUESTION: Which paper towel absorbs the most water?

WHAT STUDENTS WILL DO:

Students will pour 250 mL of water into a cup, soak 2 sheets of each towel in the water and measure the amount of water left, then subtract to determine how much water the towels absorbed.

MATERIALS FOR EACH GROUP:

3 coded test towels (2 sheets of each), measuring cup, water, timer, sponge (optional).

OBJECTIVES:

To make judgments based on careful measurement; to introduce the concept of porosity; to compare paper towels with a reusable alternative.

CONCEPT:

Porosity: Paper towels absorb liquids because their fibers are far enough apart to let liquid molecules fill in the spaces. Some towels have bigger spaces between fibers—they are more porous.

WHAT CONDITIONS HAVE TO BE THE SAME FOR ALL PAPER TOWELS IN THIS TEST?

WRITE THE VARIABLES TO CONTROL HERE. *Amount of water in the glass, how long they drip, water lost by splashing, being eye-level when measuring water, etc.*

DISCUSS:

1. Discuss responses to the first balloon: What variables did you identify? How could you control them? How would not controlling them have affected the test?

2. Did different small groups get the same data? If not, why did data differ? *(Explore the possibility of measuring error: How precisely can you measure with a measuring cup? How could you get more precise data?)*

3. Suggest that students repeat this test three times and average their data. Or combine groups' data. Are results different? How consistent were the results? Which would you trust more: a single test's results or the average of several tests? (*The average of several tests is more reliable.*)

4. Discuss the second balloon. What was your hypothesis? Did your test data support this hypothesis? How important is it to limit usage of disposable products? Should the sponge become part of this test project? (If so, how can it be built in?)

HOW WOULD A SPONGE COMPARE? WRITE YOUR HYPOTHESIS HERE. THEN TEST TO SEE IF YOU'RE RIGHT. *The sponge will probably soak up more water than the towels. (Debate what size sponge to test.) A kitchen-use size sponge would be most realistic.*

5. Discuss scores. (*In general, towels with more "puff" are likely to be more porous and to absorb more.*) Examine winning and losing paper towels with a magnifying glass. Which ones have bigger fibers? Which have fibers that are farther apart? Which are more porous?

ACTIVITY:

Develop a weight-test for absorption. Design a test based on the weight of water absorbed. Compare with the volume test: Are rankings the same? Which test do you think is better? Why?

3. DRY-STRENGTH TEST, p. 4

QUESTION: Which paper towel is strongest when dry?

WHAT STUDENTS WILL DO:

First students will see if each towel is stronger lengthwise or widthwise; then they'll see which of the three towels is the strongest. To do so, they'll spring-clip two towel strips together and pull in opposite directions and see which tears first.

MATERIALS FOR EACH GROUP:

3 coded test towels (2 sheets of each), scissors, spring clip, tape, pencil, ruler.

OBJECTIVES:

To understand testing via paired comparisons; to understand variation and reasons for repeating tests; to see how the orientation of a paper's fibers affects its strength.

DISCUSS:

1. Did you find a difference in strength between lengthwise and widthwise strips? What makes paper stronger in one direction? (*Long fibers running in that direction and overlapping. The perpendicular direction is weaker because there's less overlap between fibers.*)

2. When you repeated the widthwise vs. lengthwise test, did the same strip always break? If not, what might be some reasons? (*Might the paper have been nicked and weakened? Were both papers tugged exactly the same?*) Did repeating these tests make your data more reliable? Why or why not?

3. Discuss scores: Towels with longer fibers are likely to be stronger. But is strongest always best? How much strength do you need for normal use? When *don't* you need strength? When *do* you need it?

ACTIVITY:

Double-check for strength. Repeat Step 7 of the Strength Test, but compare the losing (weaker) strips instead of the winning ones. Is the strongest towel also the least weak? (*A towel could be very strong in one direction but very weak in the other. When testing for strength, it's a good idea to dou-*

TESTS STUDENTS WILL DESIGN THEMSELVES

Testing procedures are not provided for the following three tests. Each small group must devise its own plan and procedures. The goal is to encourage hands-on, common sense creativity and problem solving by students. There's no one "right way" to do these tests.

4. WET-STRENGTH TEST, p. 5

QUESTION: Which paper towel is strongest when wet?

POSSIBLE PROCEDURES:
The procedure could be similar to the Dry-Strength test. Or it could entail supporting a cup and saucer on a wet towel and measuring how much water the cup holds before the towel tears. (*Do this with unbreakable materials over a full sink.*)

OBJECTIVES:
To understand what's involved in designing a test; to control variables; to apply knowledge of the nature of paper.

VARIABLES TO CONTROL:
How much water is applied to "wet" the towel; where and how the water is applied to the towel; whether the towel is held along its long fibers or across them; the force applied to the towel, etc.

WOULD <u>WETTING</u> A PAPER TOWEL MAKE IT STRONGER OR WEAKER? WRITE YOUR HYPOTHESIS HERE. *Wetting paper loosens its weave. When its fibers are loose, they don't hold together as well. So the paper is weakened by wetting it.*

DISCUSS:
1. Discuss the balloon. What was your hypothesis? Did your data prove or disprove it?

2. What was your testing plan? What variables did you control? What did your test reveal? What could you have done differently to make your test more informative?

3. Compare your results in this test with the results of the Dry-Strength test. Is there a relationship? If a towel is stronger than the others when dry, will it be stronger than the others when wet? (*Discuss responses to the Data Analysis question.*)

ACTIVITY:
Can you rig the coffee-cup-on-a-towel test to make one towel seem stronger? You've seen the commercials. Now try it in class, but use this trick: Hold the towel you want to seem strong so its fibers run between your hands. Hold the other towels the other way. Does that make a difference? (*Do this over a sinkful of water to catch any spills and to cushion the cup's fall if the towel tears.*)

5. ROUGH SCRUB TEST, p. 6

QUESTION: Which towel tears the least when scrubbing rough surfaces?

POSSIBLE PROCEDURE:
Wet each towel with a set amount of water, rub it on a rough surface (brick), count the number of "rubs" before it shreds.

OBJECTIVE:
To apply an understanding of controlling variables and the structure of paper in designing a scientific test.

VARIABLES TO CONTROL:
Type of surface; force of scrubbing; amount of water used to wet the paper towel; length of each scrub; how the towel is folded; judgment of when "shredding" has occurred, etc.

DISCUSS:
1. What test procedure did you follow? What variables did you control? What measurements did you make? How scientific were these measurements?

2. Did you have trouble judging the point at which a towel was "shredding"? Were you able to quantify this (measure it exactly)? Explain.

3. Are there any variables you could have controlled more effectively?

6. SHEDDING TEST, p. 6

QUESTION: Which towel is least "linty"?

POSSIBLE PROCEDURES:
Use each towel to clean a window or dark fabric, then examine the object with a magnifying glass and count the amount of lint left behind. Or use a towel, then let it dry and shake it over black paper. Count the fibers it leaves.

OBJECTIVE:
To determine the causes of linting; to demonstrate an understanding of variables and test design.

VARIABLES TO CONTROL:
How clean the window is; force of strokes; number of strokes; amount and kind of cleaner used; wetness of towel.

DISCUSS:

1. What test procedure did you follow? What variables did you control? Were you able to measure data objectively?

2. Where do you think lint comes from? Think of the structure of paper: Do you think it's from long or short fibers? Which are likely to be looser? to fall out more easily? *(High quality papers contain longer short fibers, so they're less likely to shed lint. The best quality papers are made with cotton rag. Less expensive papers, like paper towels, are usually made from wood pulp, which gives shorter fibers.)*

DEALING WITH DATA

Students have gathered data and assigned raw scores for all six paper towel tests. Now they have to figure out what it all means.

Data alone can't say which paper towel is best. Like all facts, data have to be thought about, evaluated, and interpreted in a useful and meaningful way. If misinterpreted, data can mislead consumers instead of guiding them. There's no one right way to deal with data.

- Page 7 (Analyze Your Test Data) has students put their data together in two different ways: simply adding up raw scores and weighting them to make important tests count for more. Which is better? Students will have to make that decision on page 8 (Interpret Your Test Data).

- While dealing with data, students will be using basic mathematics skills as well as learning statistics concepts in a hands-on way. They will also be saying "what it all means"— expressing in simple written sentences what their tests revealed about paper towels. Data are seen as a means to an end, rather than an end in themselves.

- The Databooks have students analyze and interpret the data their small group collected. Much can be learned by having small groups compare their results and combine their data to come up with *class* results.

ANALYZE YOUR TEST DATA, p. 7

WHAT STUDENTS WILL DO:
Students will first add up each paper towel's raw scores and draw a bar graph of the results in the Databook. Then students will assign Importance Factors to each test, multiply raw scores by the tests' Importance Factors, and draw a bar graph of the results.

OBJECTIVE:
To see that data can be combined in different ways.

WHICH PAPER TOWEL DO YOU THINK IS THE BEST? WHY? *Discuss reasons why students chose the towel they did. (This is just a way of checking data analysis for sense.)* DO YOUR TEST DATA SUPPORT YOUR HYPOTHESIS? LET'S SEE!

DISCUSS:

1. What "Importance Factors" did you give to each test? Why? Should tests for more important things count more in the scoring?

2. Did your weighted scores change the ranking of the paper towels? Are weighted scores more or less meaningful than raw scores? Why?

INTERPRET YOUR TEST DATA, p. 8

OBJECTIVES:

To consider the importance of price and environmental impact and to determine which paper towel is the "winner."

MATERIALS FOR EACH GROUP:

Original packaging from paper towels (so students can identify brand name, price, and number of towels per roll).

DISCUSS:

1. What are the pros and cons of each scoring method? Which did you use? Why? *(Remember, there's no one answer — it's the thinking process that counts.)*

2. Which test towel is least expensive? Should price be factored into the overall ranking of paper towels or should it be dealt with separately? Why?

3. Should people consider the environmental impact of using disposable towels? Why or why not? Did you test a sponge? How did it compare with the paper towels? Would it ever be preferable to paper towels?

EXTRA ACTIVITY: PUT TOGETHER THE CLASS'S TEST DATA

CONCEPTS:
- **Variation:** Data can vary as a result of quality differences within a brand, making results more reliable if tests are repeated a number of times.
- **Measurement error:** Measurements recorded during testing may not be 100 percent precise due to uncontrolled variables or the imprecision of measurements.

ACTIVITY:

Post an enlarged copy of the chart on the next page of this guide. Have all groups write their *raw* scores in the appropriate boxes. (Each box will have several scores.) Then average scores, assign Importance Factors to the tests, and determine the class's weighted scores.

DISCUSS:

1. Did everyone who tested come up with the same raw scores for the paper towels? Why not? Is it possible every towel A wasn't exactly the same? Can performance vary within a brand? *(Yes. That's why it's best to test several samples of each brand.)*

2. How can we determine which measurements are most reliable (most likely to happen again if the tests were repeated)? What if we performed each test several times instead of once? What if we based paper-towel ratings on the whole class's data, instead of just one group's?

3. Examine the class's raw data on the chart. Which towel, if any, has very little variation in its data (the small groups' test scores are similar)? Which towel has wide variation in its scores? Which towel's performance could you predict with more confidence? *(The one with the least variation in scores.)*

4. What's the better way to tally the small groups' raw scores — figure out means or medians? *(Have some students do it one way and others the other way. Compare: Are scores different? Which is more appropriate?)*

SEND YOUR RATINGS OF PAPER TOWELS TO *CONSUMER REPORTS*

The class should fill in this chart and answer all questions about the paper towels. Attach a written summary of the class's conclusions. Then mail to the address below.

WHICH PAPER TOWEL IS BEST?

"RAW" SCORES

Write the class's combined scores for each test in the boxes below.
Are these ❑ mean scores or ❑ median scores? (Check *one*.)

TEST	A	B	C
1. Quick-Climb			
2. Big-Spill			
3. Dry-Strength			
4. Wet-Strength			
5. Rough-Scrub			
6. Shed-ding			
TOTALS			

(Raw-Score Totals)

"WEIGHTED" SCORES

1. Assign Importance Factors to the tests. (3=*most* important; 1=*least* imortant)

2. Multiply the class's combined raw scores by the Importance Factors.

IMPORTANCE FACTOR:	A	B	C
1.			
2.			
3.			
4.			
5.			
6.			
TOTALS			

(Weighted-Score Totals)

(1) **Code   Brand   Type**
(1- or 2-ply?)

A _____ _____

B _____ _____

C _____ _____

(2) How many small groups tested the paper towels? _____

(3) Date _____

(4) Person to contact (name and address):

_____

_____

_____

(5) **Mail To:**

Consumer Reports
Education Division
101 Truman Avenue
Yonkers, New York 10703-1057

Testing Popcorn helps students discover the science and technology governing the performance of popcorn: why popcorn pops **(heat and phase change of water)**; why some popcorns pop better than others **(variation, predicting, ratios)**; whether some brands pop bigger than others **(volume of an irregular solid, density)**; whether some brands are more healthful than others **(fat, caloric content)**; and how serving sizes and weights compare **(ratios)**.

Students will also learn how to design scientific tests, control variables, and record and analyze data. They will discover that there's no "right" answer, no one way to test.

Tests are designed for groups of four. Students work together to conduct and plan tests, analyze data, solve problems, and develop a scientific rating of popcorn. The chart below links tests students will perform with the science skills and concepts those testing activities will help teach.

CURRICULUM SKILLS AND CONCEPTS

Tests and Student Databook Page	Highlighted Skills	Science Concepts
Getting Started p. 1	Controlling Variables, Blind Testing	Principles of Testing
The Popping Process p. 2	Observation, Weighing	Phase Changes
The Pop/Flop Test p. 3	Counting, Graphing, Controlling Variables	Variation, Predicting
The Big-Pop Test p. 4	Weighing and Measuring, Controlling Variables	Volume of Solid, Density
The Yum/Yuck Test p. 5	Designing a Test	Sensory Testing
Health Test p. 6	Critical Thinking, Measuring	Nutrition, Calories
Analyze Your Test Data, p. 7	Analyzing Data, Graphing	Weighted Scores
Interpret Your Test Data, p. 8	Critical Thinking	Statistics

CLASS-TIME REQUIREMENTS:

❏ To prepare and do Pre-test: 1 class period
❏ For Tests 1 and 2: 1 or 2 class periods
❏ For Tests 3 and 4: 1 class period
❏ For data interpretation and discussion: 1 class period

MATERIALS NEEDED
for each small group:

❏ **Test samples:** 3 different brands of unpopped popcorn without oil/fat. (Bags of microwave popcorn contain globs of fat, so they would not be comparable.) Include one less-expensive store brand. One 16-ounce jar of each brand should suffice for 10 small groups.

Keep unpopped kernels in covered plastic containers. (Kernels shouldn't be exposed to air for extended periods.)

❏ **For pre-planned tests:** Nonstick 2-liter pot and stove or hot plate for popping, aluminum foil, cheesecloth, string, balance, popper, timer, 3 2-liter bowls, glass, measuring cup, rubber bands.

GETTING STARTED

1. Distribute Student Databooks, one to each student group.

DISCUSS:

1. What do you like and dislike about popcorn? What can we learn by testing different brands of popcorn?

> HAVING A FAVORITE BRAND CAN AFFECT THE WAY YOU JUDGE THE TEST POPCORNS.

> **HOW COULD YOU CONTROL THIS VARIABLE?** *Find some way to keep testers from knowing the popcorns' brand names until after the testing is done. One way is to identify test samples by codes instead of brand names.*

2. Discuss responses to the balloon. Scientific experiments usually test for one variable at a time — the other variables have to be "controlled" (made the same for all popcorns tested). What is the variable we're testing? (*The three popcorns.*) What variables must we control? (*Popping method, tester bias, added ingredients, measurement methods, etc.*)

2. Code test samples. p. 1

Students should do "blind tests" of the popcorns: They should not know the brand names of the popcorns they're testing. They should identify the test samples by code letter rather than brand name.

Prepare test samples in advance: Transfer popcorn kernels to covered plastic containers coded A, B, and C. Write codes on popcorn labels, too, and keep hidden until all testing is completed.

PRE-TEST — THE POPPING PROCESS, p. 2

QUESTION: What puts the pop in popcorn?

WHAT STUDENTS WILL DO:

Students will weigh unpopped kernels (of just *one* popcorn), pop them without oil, observe steam escaping, then weigh the popped puffs and observe that weight was lost.

MATERIALS:

Unpopped popcorn (1 brand only), non-stick pot (2 liters), stove or hot plate, aluminum foil, cheesecloth, string, balance.

OBJECTIVES:

To understand the concept of phase change of water to steam; to develop problem-solving and measuring skills.

CONCEPT:

Phase change: Water in the starchy interior of the kernel turns into superheated steam, swelling the starch grains and building enough pressure to burst the hard outer shell.

DISCUSS:

1. What did you observe coming through the cheesecloth? What was your hypothesis? Discuss responses to the balloon. (*If the steam is hard to see, hold a piece of aluminum foil over the popper to make steam condense.*)

> WHAT DO YOU SEE COMING THROUGH THE CHEESECLOTH? WHERE IS IT COMING FROM?

> WRITE YOUR OBSERVATIONS AND HYPOTHESIS HERE. *Steam is coming through the cheesecloth. The water in the unpopped kernels turns to steam when heated. The steam forces the kernels to pop, then escapes.*

2. Did the popcorn's weight change? What caused that to happen? (*Loss of moisture.*)

ACTIVITY:

What prevents a kernel from popping? Form hypotheses, then test them. (*Soak kernels overnight; puncture their shells with a pin.*)

TESTS ALREADY DESIGNED FOR STUDENTS

The first two tests describe the testing procedures students should follow. Allow student groups to work independently and solve problems among themselves. Wait until they've completed their testing before discussing or reviewing the tests. The goal is to encourage independent thinking, creative problem solving, and increased confidence in their scientific abilities.

1. THE POP/FLOP TEST, p. 3

QUESTION: Which popcorn has the fewest flops?

WHAT STUDENTS WILL DO:
For each test popcorn, students will count 100 kernels, pop them, count the unpopped kernels, draw a bar graph of the results, then interpret that graph to score the popcorns.

MATERIALS:
3 test popcorns (50 mL each), popper (non-oil), 3 2-liter bowls labled A, B, and C.

OBJECTIVES:
To understand the concept of variation and how to factor it into scientific tests; to appreciate the importance of controlling variables; to reinforce graphing skills; to calculate ratios.

CONCEPTS:
Variation: Every kernel of a brand isn't identical: Some kernels may have less moisture or have punctured shells and not pop, while others may be fine. Two handfuls of the same brand may not have the same pop/flop distribution.

Predicting: Observing how a product performs under test conditions enables scientists to predict how it may perform in the future. The more observations a prediction is based on, the more accurate it's likely to be.

DISCUSS:

1. What variables did you control? *(Discuss the balloon.)*

THE AMOUNT OF OIL (IF YOU USE ANY) AND THE TEMPERATURE OF THE POPPER WILL AFFECT HOW MANY KERNELS POP.

HOW WILL YOU CONTROL THESE VARIABLES? *Measure and use the exact same amount and type of oil with each popcorn; wipe the pan clean between poppings; use the same temperature setting when popping.*

2. Why might some kernels pop and others not pop? *(Too much or no moisture, punctured shells, and stale kernels could prevent popping.)*

3. If you had counted out half as many kernels (50 instead of 100), do you think your Pop/Flop *ratio* would be the same? What if you counted out twice as many (200)? If you got different ratios, which would be more accurate? *(The one with more kernels, because it's more representative. Combine small groups' data to illustrate the concept.)*

4. How could you predict the Pop/Flop ratio of a popcorn? *(Pop some and determine the ratio.)* How could you make your prediction more accurate? *(Pop several samples.)*

ACTIVITIES:

• **Predictions.** Have students pop the same popcorn several times and compare to see how consistent its pop-to-flop ratio is. Then predict its probable pop-to-flop ratio and test to confirm that prediction.

• **Percents.** Since students started with 100 kernels, the number of unpopped kernels is also the "flops percent" (flops per 100). Express pops and flops as percents.

2. THE BIG-POP TEST, p. 4

QUESTION: Which popcorn pops biggest?

WHAT STUDENTS WILL DO:

After weighing a glass and finding its volume, students will fill it with popped popcorn, then weigh the popcorn and measure its volume by seeing how much water it displaces.

MATERIALS:

3 bowls of popped popcorn from Test 1, glass, measuring cup, cheesecloth, rubber band, balance.

OBJECTIVES:

To gain experience measuring the volume of an irregular solid; to reinforce the concepts of variation and controlling variables; to build counting and measuring skills; to understand density.

CONCEPTS:

Volume of an irregular solid can be calculated by measuring how much of a fluid-like substance (water, sand) it displaces.

Density is a measure of how light or heavy a substance is in relation to its volume. Water is a standard for density measurements, with a density of 1.0 (it weighs one gram per cubic centimeter). Substances (like popcorn) whose density is less than 1.0 float on water. Substances whose density is greater than 1.0 sink.

DISCUSS:

1. Is measuring the volume of a popcorn puff different from measuring the volume of a perfect cube or ball? Is it harder to measure an irregular shape?

2. Is the procedure you followed a good way to measure the volume (size) of a piece of popcorn? (*The water had filled the glass completely, so the volume of water displaced reflects the volume of the popcorn.*)

3. Why wouldn't the method work if the cheesecloth cover were loose and some popcorn floated above the rim? (*See density discussion above.*)

HOW QUICKLY YOU POUR THE WATER IN STEP 5 IS AN IMPORTANT VARIABLE.

WHY? HOW WILL YOU CONTROL IT? *If poured very slowly, water will soak into the popcorn. You have to measure before this happens. Control this by timing how fast you pour and doing the same for all popcorns.*

4. Why wouldn't it work if you poured water very slowly? (*Discuss responses to the balloon.*)

5. How did you determine what each popcorn's score should be: by size of puffs or by weight? Which is more important, size, weight, or how the two are related? (*Introduce density — weight per unit of volume.*)

ACTIVITIES:

• **Compute density of popcorn by the glassful.** Divide each popcorn's weight by its volume (data are in Box 3 of the Databook). Should popcorn have low or high density? Why? Would density be a good measure of Big-Pop scores?

• **Compare density and volume of popped popcorn and unpopped kernels.** Use the data in Box 3 of the Databook. Count out the same number of *unpopped* kernels, weigh them, measure volume, and compute density. Then compare density of popped and unpopped popcorns.

A TEST STUDENTS WILL DESIGN THEMSELVES

Testing procedures are not provided for the Yum/Yuck Test. Each small group must devise its own procedures, and identify the materials needed and the variables to be controlled. The goal is to encourage hands-on, common-sense creativity and problem solving.

3. THE YUM/YUCK TEST, p. 5

QUESTION: Which popcorn is the tastiest?

POSSIBLE PROCEDURES:
Students could test for preference (which popcorn is liked by the most people) or sensory qualities (how popcorns measure up to taste and texture criteria).

OBJECTIVES:
To design a test and identify and control variables; to understand roles of taste and texture in sensory evaluations.

DISCUSS:

1. What should a popcorn taste-test look for? How did you measure taste preferences? Discuss responses to the balloon.

> WHAT MAKES POPCORN YUMMY? WHAT MAKES IT YUCKY? DESCRIBE WHAT A POPCORN TASTE-TEST SHOULD LOOK FOR.
> *Popcorn flavor, absence of off-tastes (burned, rancid, cardboard flavor), light crispy texture, absence of sharp hulls, etc.*

2. Did you test popcorn with or without butter and salt? Why?

3. What variables did you control? (*Popping method? Added flavorings? Time elapsed between popping and tasting? How the popped popcorn was stored? Tester bias?*)

4. HEALTH TEST, p. 6

QUESTION: Are some popcorns better for you than others?

WHAT STUDENTS WILL DO:
Using a chart in the Databook, students will compare plain, buttered, caramel, and cheese popcorns, then compute the extra weight and calories the flavorings add.

MATERIALS:
(Optional) Bags of buttered, caramel-coated, and cheese-flavored popcorn.

OBJECTIVES:
To compare the calorie content of popcorns with different flavorings; to understand nutrition concepts; to develop critical thinking and measuring skills.

> WOW! A CUPFUL OF CHEESE POPCORN IN THIS CHART WEIGHS A LOT MORE THAN PLAIN. WHAT COULD ACCOUNT FOR ALL THAT EXTRA WEIGHT?
> *The cheese that's added adds weight. The weight is the total weight of the added cheese and the popcorn,*

ACTIVITIES:

- **What's a serving?** Have students pile popcorn into a bowl until they have what they consider to be one serving. Measure it. Compute the weight, calories, and fat for that many cups of plain, oil-cooked, caramel, and cheese-flavored popcorns using the Databook chart.

- **Weigh for yourself.** If students have the optional bags of popcorn, weigh a cupful of each. Why does the same volume of different popcorns weigh different amounts? (*The flavorings add weight.*)

- **Analyze microwave popcorn in bags.** Open the bags (unpopped), separate the kernels from the globs of fat, and weigh each. What is the weight of the fat? Take the bottom of the bag apart. How is it different from plain bags? (*Microwave bags contain a plate called a susceptor, which heats up first and then pops the kernels.*)

EXTRA TEST: POPPING METHOD

Popping method might affect a popcorn's pop-to-flop ratio and texture and perhaps its density as well. At *Consumer Reports*, popcorn tests are repeated on different types of poppers (hot air, microwave, etc.), and popcorns sometimes score differently. In this case, the popping method becomes the variable tested for.

QUESTION: Would the test popcorns get different scores in a different kind of popper?

MATERIALS:
3 test popcorns, different type of popper than used before, materials for Pop/Flop Test (p 3).

PROCEDURE:

1. Repeat the Pop/Flop Test on page 3 of the Student Databook, using a different popper.

2. Repeat the Yum/Yuck Test (as students designed it) on page 5.

3. Compare the test popcorns' scores on both types of poppers. Are scores the same or different?

DISCUSS:

1. Might some popcorns work well in some poppers but not others? Why?

2. What if you use a popper that requires oil? Could oil affect popping conditions? taste? (*Reinforce the importance of controlling variables.*)

WHICH POPCORN DO YOU THINK IS BEST? WHY? *Ask students to give reasons for their hypotheses.*

LET'S SEE IF THE DATA YOU COLLECTED SUPPORT YOUR HYPOTHESIS!

DEALING WITH DATA

Students have gathered data and assigned raw scores for all four popcorn tests. Now they have to figure out what it all means.

Data alone can't say which popcorn is best. Like all facts, data have to be thought about, evaluated, and interpreted in a useful and meaningful way. If misinterpreted, data can mislead consumers instead of guiding them. There's no one right way to deal with data.

- Page 7 (Analyze Your Test Data) has students put their data together in two ways — by adding up raw scores and by weighting them to make important tests count for more.

- Page 8 has students rank popcorns from best to worst and express their conclusions in simple written sentences.

- Much can be learned by having small groups combine data to come up with class results (see the following page).

ANALYZE YOUR TEST DATA, p. 7

WHAT STUDENTS WILL DO:
After adding up each popcorn's raw scores, students will draw bar graphs of the results, then assign each test an Importance Factor, multiply to weight scores, and compare weighted scores to raw scores.

OBJECTIVE:
To see that data can be summarized in different ways.

DISCUSS:

1. What Importance Factors did you give each test? Why? Should tests for the more important things count more?

2. Did your Weighted Scores change the ranking of the popcorns? Are these scores more or less meaningful than the raw scores?

3. Which popcorn did you think was best? Was that popcorn ranked number one in your raw scores? in your weighted scores? If not, what do you think happened? (*This is just a way of double-checking results. If results seem wrong, check data again.*)

INTERPRET YOUR TEST DATA, p. 8

OBJECTIVES:

To determine which popcorn is the "winner."

DISCUSS:

1. What scoring method did you think was more meaningful? Why? *(Discuss reasons students gave in their Databooks.)*

2. Do you think the popcorn that won your test will always be the best choice for everyone? Why or why not?

3. Do you think the popcorn that won your test will pop best in every type of popper? *(When Consumer Reports tests popcorn, it pops the test-sample brands in different types of poppers. In the past, it has found that the type of popper does make a difference in how a popcorn performs.)*

4. Discuss the groups' conclusions (how they answered the questions on page 8):

- Which popcorn should the class choose if it's trying to raise money? *(How important are taste, puffiness, and price?)*

- Which is the best kind of popcorn if you're trying to lose weight? *(Review the calories added by oil, cheese, and caramel from page 6 of the Databook. Plain popcorn is best.)*

- Which popcorn would you want to be able to buy in the cafeteria? *(How important would taste, puffiness, and cost be?)*

- Which popcorn would you recommend to friends? Why?

5. Popcorn can be an inexpensive and pretty healthful snack. How do you think it compares to potato chips and cheese-puff snacks? *(Suggest that students read labels and compare. Base comparisons on the volume of one serving, not the weight.)*

EXTRA ACTIVITY: PUT TOGETHER THE CLASS'S TEST DATA

CONCEPTS:

- **Sampling:** The samples selected for testing can affect results.

- **Variation:** Data can vary as a result of quality differences within a brand, making it advisable to repeat tests a number of times.

- **Multiple testing:** Conclusions derived from more data are more reliable.

ACTIVITY:

Make a large copy of the chart on page 8 of this guide. Have all groups write their raw scores in the appropriate boxes. (Each box will have several scores.) Then assign Importance Factors to each test and determine weighted scores.

DISCUSS:

1. Did everyone who tested come up with the same raw scores for the popcorns? Why or why not? *(Is it possible every popcorn kernel wasn't exactly the same? Might testers have interpreted test findings differently?)*

2. How can we determine which test results are most reliable (most likely to happen again if the test were repeated)? What if we performed each test several times instead of once? What if we based popcorn ratings on the whole class's scores?

3. Examine the class's raw data (on the chart). Which popcorn (if any) has very little variation in its data (the small groups' test scores are similar)? Which popcorn has wide variation in its scores? Which popcorn's performance could you predict with more confidence? *(The one with the least variation.)*

SEND YOUR RATINGS OF POPCORN TO *CONSUMER REPORTS*

The class should fill in this chart and answer all questions about the popcorns. Attach a written summary of the class's conclusions. Then mail to the address below.

WHICH POPCORN IS BEST?

"RAW" SCORES

Write the class's combined scores for each test in the boxes below.
Are these ❑ mean scores or ❑ median scores? (Check *one*.)

TEST	A	B	C
1. Pop/Flop			
2. Big-Pop			
3. Yum/Yuck			
4. Health			
TOTALS			

"WEIGHTED" SCORES

1. Assign Importance Factors to the tests. (3=*most* important; 1=*least* important)

2. Multiply the class's combined raw scores by the Importance Factors.

IMPORTANCE FACTOR:	A	B	C
1.			
2.			
3.			
4.			
TOTALS			

(1) **Code**   **Brand**

   A   _____

   B   _____

   C   _____

(2) Popping method? _____

(3) How many small groups tested the popcorns?_____

(4) Date_____

(5) Person to contact (name and address):

_____

_____

_____

_____

(6) **Mail To:**

Consumer Reports
Education Division
101 Truman Avenue
Yonkers, New York 10703-1057

Testing Shampoos integrates basic chemical and physical science concepts with personal hygiene: how soaps and detergents behave in hard water **(solubility, mineral composition of water)**; what affects ease of combing **(friction, lubrication)**; whether special formulas work **(blind testing)**; whether pH-balance claims are important **(pH scale, acids and bases)**; and the sudsing properties of shampoos **(detergent action)**. It builds scientific inquiry and testing skills by having students form hypotheses and control variables and by challenging them to design testing procedures themselves. *Tests are open-ended: There is no one answer, no desired conclusion.*

Tests encourage cooperative learning. They are designed for groups of four. Students will do some pre-tests at home, but will work together in class to analyze data, solve problems, and develop a scientific evaluation of shampoos. The chart below links tests students will perform with the science skills and concepts those testing activities will help teach.

CURRICULUM SKILLS AND CONCEPTS

Test and Student Databook Page	Highlighted Skills	Science Concepts
Getting Started p. 1	Controlling Variables Blind Testing	Principles of Testing
Soap or Detergent? Pre-Test, p. 2	Comparing, Controlling Variables	Charged Molecules, Hard Water, Detergents
Combing Ease Pre-Test, p. 3	Hypothesizing, Making Observations	Friction, Nature of Hair
Special Formulas Pre-Test, p. 3	Forming Conclusions Controlling Variables	Nature of Hair, Blind Testing
The pH-Balance Test p. 5	Interpreting Data, Measuring pH	pH, Acids and Bases
Sudsing Test p. 6	Controlling Variables, Forming Hypotheses	Detergent Action
Do-You-Like-It? Test p. 7	Controlling Variables, Interpreting Data	Test Design
Interpret Your Test Data p. 8	Ranking, Forming Conclusions	Weighted Scores, Variation

MATERIALS NEEDED
for each small group:

❑ **Test samples:**
2 shampoos (a dry and oily hair formula of the same brand), 3 shampoos (different brands but for the same type of hair).

❑ **For pre-planned tests:**
Liquid soap (*not* a detergent—*Liquid Ivory* hand soap is one of the few available), dishwashing detergent, hard water (dissolve 1 TUMS® in 1 L carbonated water), stirring rod, 2 cups, 2 microscope slides, 2 small single-use bottles for shampoo for each tester, tablespoon, pH paper, beaker, measuring spoon, 15-cm test tube and stopper, timer, ruler, water.

CLASS-TIME REQUIREMENTS:
❑ For 3 pre-tests: 1 class period (plus home-use assignments)
❑ For Tests 1 tand 2: 1 class period
❑ For Tests 3: 1 class period
❑ For data analysis and interpretation: 1 class period

GETTING STARTED

Distribute Student Databooks, one to each small group.

DISCUSS:

1. What are your shampoo preferences? What influenced your preferences? *(Experience? Friends? Hairdressers? Ads?)* What would you like to learn from testing shampoos?

2. What variables could affect how well a shampoo works on your hair? *(Hair type and texture, type of water [hard or soft], shampoo extras like conditioner, hair-styling devices like blow dryers or curling irons, etc.)*

3. When evaluating shampoos, what subjective criteria might vary from tester to tester? *(Definitions of good-looking hair and nice-smelling shampoo.)*

> PEOPLE OFTEN THINK ADVERTISED OR EXPENSIVE BRANDS ARE BEST. HOW COULD THAT AFFECT THEIR JUDGMENTS OF SHAMPOOS? *Ads and price can influence people's impressions of products without their realizing it. When making judgments—especially subjective ones—people can unintentionally favor the popular or pricey item.*

TESTS ALREADY DESIGNED FOR STUDENTS

The following pre-tests and tests describe testing procedures for students to follow. (Some are to be conducted at home while shampooing.) Allow student groups to work independently and solve problems among themselves. Wait until they've completed their testing before discussing or reviewing the tests. The goal is to encourage independent thinking, creative problem-solving, and increased confidence in their scientific abilities.

PRE-TEST 1 SOAP OR DETERGENT?
p. 2

QUESTION: Is it better to wash hair with soap or with detergent?

WHAT STUDENTS WILL DO:
Students will make a soap mixture and a detergent mixture with hard water, then dip a microscope slide in each to see which leaves the most residue. *(Soap does.)* Students will infer which makes a better shampoo. *(Detergent does.)*

MATERIALS FOR EACH GROUP:
Liquid soap and liquid detergent, hard water (made by dissolving a crushed TUMS® tablet in a liter of carbonated water), stirring rod, 2 cups, 2 microscope slides.

OBJECTIVES:
To see how soap and detergent differ in rinsing ability; to become aware of differences between soft and hard water.

CONCEPTS:

Charged molecules: Cleaning agents' molecules have a negatively charged part that's attracted to water. That charge links a molecule to water so it'll rinse out, carrying greasy dirt with it.

Hard water: Hard water contains dissolved minerals, which attract negatively charged molecules. The soap molecules react with the minerals rather than the water and don't rinse out. Instead, they form a greasy precipitate.

Detergents: Minerals aren't as strongly attracted to detergent molecules, as to soap leaving them free to link with water and rinse away. So detergents leave hair cleaner than soap, especially in hard water.

DISCUSS:

1. What did you observe on the microscope slides? *(Soap will leave the most film.)* Why does soap leave the most film? *(Its molecules link with minerals to form a solid, which rinses poorly.)*

2. What variables had to be controlled in this test? *(Size of drops, amount of water, cleaning off the stirring rod, mixing speed and intensity, etc.)*

3. Why do you think we used hard water in this test? *(Hard water contains lots of minerals. Discuss the hard water and detergent concepts.)* What problems could shampooers have if they use hard water (as much of the country does)?

4. Discuss responses to the first balloon.

TO LEAVE HAIR CLEAN, SHAMPOOS SHOULD RINSE AWAY CLEAN. SO WHICH WOULD MAKE A BETTER SHAMPOO—SOAP OR DETERGENT? WHY?
Detergent would make a better shampoo because it rinses away cleaner than soap.

ACTIVITIES:

• **Do shampoos contain detergent or soap?** Develop a test to answer this question. *(Students could repeat this slide-dip test with shampoos and see whether those slides look like the soap or detergent ones.)*

• **Will soap and detergent perform differently if tested in *soft* water?** First discuss responses to the second balloon. What did students hypothesize? Would they like to test their hypotheses? Then repeat the Soap-or-Detergent? procedure, using soft (or distilled) water instead of hard water.

IF YOU REPEATED THIS TEST WITH SOFT WATER (WHICH CONTAINS FEWER MINERALS), HOW MIGHT RESULTS DIFFER? WRITE YOUR HYPOTHESIS, THEN TEST IT.
There would be less of a difference between soap and detergent in soft water. Soap would rinse out well because there are few minerals to interfere.

QUESTION: Why is *dirty* hair easier to comb than *just-washed* hair?

WHAT STUDENTS WILL DO:
The next time they shampoo, students will compare the ease of combing their hair before and after shampooing.

MATERIALS FOR EACH GROUP:
None. (Students will make observations at home, using any shampoo.)

OBJECTIVES:
To understand the nature of hair and what causes it to tangle; to be introduced to friction and lubrication.

CONCEPTS:
Friction and lubricants: Friction is the resistance to motion between two bodies in contact. Lubricants reduce friction.

Nature of hair: Hair shafts, which aren't living, consist of microscopic overlapping scales. After shampooing, the scales stick out, resisting the movement of a comb and producing friction, which makes hair hard to comb. Coatings like oil make the scales lie flat, reducing friction.

DISCUSS:

1. Discuss responses to the balloon.

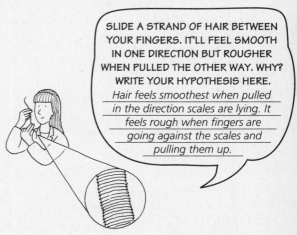

SLIDE A STRAND OF HAIR BETWEEN YOUR FINGERS. IT'LL FEEL SMOOTH IN ONE DIRECTION BUT ROUGHER WHEN PULLED THE OTHER WAY. WHY? WRITE YOUR HYPOTHESIS HERE.
Hair feels smoothest when pulled in the direction scales are lying. It feels rough when fingers are going against the scales and pulling them up.

2. Discuss students' analysis of their results (#4). *(They will infer that there was a coating on their dirty hair that smoothed hair scales, but that shampooing stripped the coating away.)*

SPECIAL FORMULAS, p. 4

QUESTION: Is there a big difference between dry and oily formulas?

WHAT STUDENTS WILL DO:

After a non-tester has coded dry and oily formula shampoos, students will take home small amounts, shampoo half their head with each shampoo, then try to determine which is the dry formula and which is the oily one.

MATERIALS FOR EACH GROUP:

A dry and oily formula of the same brand of shampoo, 2 small bottles per tester, tablespoon.

OBJECTIVES:

To introduce students to blind-testing procedures; to reinforce the importance of controlling variables.

CONCEPTS:

Nature of hair: People's hair differs in numerous ways: in texture, thickness, shape, etc. Chemical treatment (coloring, perming, relaxing, etc.) further changes hair. And different types of hair may react differently to shampoos.

Blind testing: Especially when a test is highly subjective (and judgments could be influenced by preconceptions about the product), it's important that testing be done "blind"— with no knowledge of the product being evaluated.

DISCUSS:

1. Discuss responses to the first balloon. How did you control those variables? What other variables should have been controlled? *(Lathering time, how much you use, how well you rinse, etc.)*

USING A CONDITIONER IS ONE OF MANY <u>VARIABLES</u>. SO IS SHARING YOUR JUDGMENTS WITH OTHER TESTERS BEFORE THE TEST IS OVER. HOW WILL YOU CONTROL THESE VARIABLES? *Either not use conditioner, or use it on both sides. Avoid discussing the test judgments until the test is over since other opinions can bias your judgments.*

2. Were the differences between the two shampoos as big as you expected before the test? Do you think your judgments might have been different if you'd known which was which? Why or why not? *(Explore blind testing.)*

3. Were you surprised with the test results? Could you tell the difference between the oily and dry formulas? Judging from this test, how important are special formulas? *(Discuss responses to the second balloon.)*

HOW BIG A DIFFERENCE IS THERE BETWEEN "DRY" AND "OILY" FORMULAS? USE DATA FROM THIS TEST TO ANSWER. *Answers will depend on the groups' test results. When Consumer Reports had a panel blind-test shampoos, there was no link between the type of hair panelists had and the shampoo-formula they preferred.*

ACTIVITY:

What do the test results mean? Do a statistical hypothesis test. Combine the class's results. How many students correctly identified the formulas? Plot the number of correct and incorrect responses on a bar graph. Then see how that compares with random chance (with just guessing). Have each student flip a coin 10 or 20 times and record the number of times it comes up heads. Plot the number of times heads did and didn't come up on a second bar graph.

Interpretation: If the shampoo-testers really couldn't tell the difference between the formulas, the graph of their correct/incorrect answers will be similar in shape to the coin-flip bar graph. Discuss: If the testers were just guessing, how many are likely to be correct? (50 percent.) How many *more* than that would indicate that they really *could* tell a difference after all?

1. THE pH-BALANCE TEST, p. 5

QUESTIONS: Is each shampoo "pH-balanced"? Is its pH close to 7?

WHAT STUDENTS WILL DO:
After mixing shampoos and water, students will measure the pH of the shampoo solution and give top scores to shampoos in the neutral range (pH between 6 and 8).

MATERIALS FOR EACH GROUP:
3 coded shampoos (1 drop of each), pH paper, beaker, stirring rod, measuring spoon, water.

OBJECTIVES:
To determine the pH of shampoo samples; to reinforce understandings of acids and bases and measuring pH.

> **CONCEPTS:**
>
> **Acids and bases:** In water acids contain more hydrogen ions (+ charges); bases (alkalis) contain more hydroxide ions (- charges).
>
> **pH measurements:** pH is a measure of the hydrogen ion concentration of a solution. The more hydrogen ions, the more acidic it is and the lower its pH.
>
> **pH and hair:** Shampoos' pH should be between 6 and 8.

DISCUSS:

1. What is an acid? What is a base? Would a very acidic or alkaline shampoo be harmful to hair? *(It could break down hair molecules and damage the hair and scalp.)*

2. What variables did you control in this test? *(Amount of shampoo, cleaning the beaker and stirring rod between shampoos, how accurately you read the pH paper.)*

3. Discuss responses to the balloon.

WAS pH A PROBLEM WITH ANY OF THE TEST SHAMPOOS? WRITE YOUR CONCLUSIONS HERE. *Probably not. The vast majority of shampoos have a pH in the neutral range.*

2. SUDSING TEST, p. 6

QUESTION: Which shampoo makes the most suds?

WHAT STUDENTS WILL DO:
Students will add 1 drop of shampoo to 10 mL water, shake, then measure the height of the suds 1 minute later.

MATERIALS FOR EACH GROUP:
3 coded shampoos (a few drops), test tube (at least 15 cm long) and stopper, stirring rod, measuring spoon, timer, ruler, water.

CONCEPTS:
To build observation and measuring skills; to compare different shampoos' sudsing properties.

> **CONCEPTS:**
>
> **Detergent action:** Detergents clean by adhering to dirt particles and linking with water to carry the dirt away.

DISCUSS:

1. Discuss responds to the first balloon.

HOW MANY TIMES YOU SHAKE THE TEST TUBE AND HOW HARD YOU SHAKE IT ARE <u>VARIABLES</u>. HOW CAN YOU CONTROL THEM? *Shake the test tubes the same number of times. Try to do so with the same force.*

2. Discuss responds to the second balloon. How important is sudsing power in a shampoo? *(It isn't a direct measure of its cleaning power, but if people prefer suds, they may use more of a low-sudsing shampoo, which could end up costing more.)*

MIGHT THERE BE A CONNECTION BETWEEN A SHAMPOO'S SUDSING POWER AND HOW MUCH YOU USE WHEN SHAMPOOING? WRITE YOUR HYPOTHESIS AND HOW YOU COULD TEST IT. *If people are used to suds or like suds, they may use more of a low-sudsing shampoo than they would a high-sudsing one. To test measure what's in the bottle before and after shampooing and subtract to determine how much was used.*

A TEST STUDENTS WILL DESIGN THEMSELVES

Testing procedures are not provided for the following test. Each small group must devise its own plan and procedures. The goal is to encourage hands-on, common-sense creativity and problem-solving by students. There are several possible approaches to this test.

3. DO-YOU-LIKE-IT? TEST, p. 7

QUESTION: Which shampoo do people like best?

POSSIBLE PROCEDURES:
Students could evaluate shampoos' aroma, color, and consistency by using either a 1 (poor) to 5 (excellent) scale or by doing paired comparisons (pairing shampoos off, then picking the better of each pair, and counting how many times each shampoo wins). Or students could imitate the Special-Formulas pre-test to conduct a home-use test of the shampoos.

OBJECTIVES:
To understand how to design a controlled test; to devise ways to test and collect data on preferences.

DISCUSS:

1. How could you have done this test? What were the pros and cons of testing methods you did and didn't use? *(Were at-home use-tests too difficult or time-consuming? Would there be too many variables to control, like different types of hair and shampoo preferences?)*

2. How did you decide to do this test? Why? Do you think your results would be repeated if another group followed your test procedure? Why or why not? *(Explore whether students had enough people judge the shampoos and whether those people's preferences are representative of other people's.)*

3. Discuss responses to the balloon. What were your criteria for judging a good shampoo? Have groups compare criteria: Did criteria vary from group to group (or among students in each group)? *(Discuss the importance of researching personal preferences in drawing up criteria for a preference test. Should students conduct a survey?)*

WHAT'S A SCIENTIFIC WAY TO DETERMINE WHICH QUALITIES MAKE A "GOOD" SHAMPOO? *Survey a representative sample (male and female with different types of hair, etc) to determine how a majority feels.*

4. What variables did you control? Which variables weren't controlled? Should they have been? *(This will vary depending on students' test procedures. But a universal variable to control in preference testing is the unintentional bias that can arise from knowing brand names.)*

ACTIVITIES:
- **How are shampoos advertised?** Do advertisers give factual information about their shampoos, or do they try to create appealing images about people who use their shampoos? Analyze magazine ads to determine whether advertised differences among shampoos are real or fantasy.
- **Compare testing methodologies.** Have all groups compare their results. If results and rankings differed, compare methodologies: Can the differences be explained by differences in testing methods (i.e., different controls, different questions asked, different people, different scoring methods)? If so, evaluate and debate which is the better way to test.

DEALING WITH DATA

Students have gathered data and assigned raw scores for the three shampoo tests. Now they have to figure out what it means!

Data alone can't say which shampoo is best. Like all facts, data have to be thought about, evaluated, and interpreted in a useful and meaningful way. If misinterpreted, data can mislead consumers instead of guiding them. While "dealing with data," students will be using basic mathematics skills as well as learning statistics in a hands-on way. They will also be saying "what it all means"— expressing in simple written sentences what their tests revealed about shampoo.

INTERPRET YOUR TEST DATA, p. 8

WHAT STUDENTS WILL DO:
Students will weight test scores and rank the shampoos.

OBJECTIVES:
To think about the data collected and express them in a way that's meaningful to other people.

DISCUSS:

1. Which shampoo test did you think was most important? Why? Do you think scores for that test should count for more when ranking the shampoos? Why or why not? *(This is called "weighting" scores. If tests weren't weighted, shampoos that did well in a less important test but poorly in an important one could be ranked deceptively high, and vice versa.)*

2. Is each group's ranking of the shampoos the same or different? If different, why? *(Were there big differences in test scores? What might have caused the differences? Were the same variables controlled? Were different Importance Factors used?)*

3. Should the information gleaned about hair and shampoos in the pre-tests be used somehow in communicating test findings? If so, how? *(Since there are so many different brands and types of shampoo, and so many different types of hair, perhaps general advice on what shampoo information counts and what doesn't would be helpful to others.)*

EXTRA ACTIVITY: PUT TOGETHER THE CLASS'S TEST DATA

CONCEPTS:

Variation: Data can vary as a result of uncontrolled variables, different testing procedures, and other things. So it's a good idea to compile data from several test groups in order to obtain more reliable results.

Measurement error: Measurements recorded during testing may not be 100 percent accurate.

ACTIVITY:
Post an enlarged copy of the chart on the following page. Have all groups write their scores in the appropriate boxes. (Boxes will have several scores.) Then have the class average the scores, assign Importance Factors to the tests, and compute weighted scores.

DISCUSS:

1. Which do you think is more reliable, the whole class's scores combined or the scores of the individual small groups? Why? *(The more data that are used, the better because it reduces the impact variations will have on the scores. It's like an exam—when there are many questions, each one has less of an impact on the final grade.)*

2. How can we determine which test scores are most reliable (most likely to happen again if the tests were repeated)? Examine the class's raw data on the chart. Which shampoo, if any, has very little variation in its data (small groups' data are similar)? Which has wide variation? Which shampoo's performance could you predict with more confidence? *(The one with less variation in scores.)*

3. Which tests were *most* consistent (subject to the least variation)? *Least* consistent (subject to the most variation)? Explore why.

4. What's the more appropriate way to tally the small groups' raw scores—figure out means or medians? *(Do it both ways and compare.)*

SEND YOUR RATINGS OF SHAMPOOS TO *CONSUMER REPORTS*

The class should fill in this chart and answer all questions about the shampoos. Attach a written summary of the class's conclusions. Then mail to the address below.

WHICH SHAMPOO IS BEST?

"RAW" SCORES

Write the class's combined scores for each test in the boxes below.
Are these ❑ mean scores or ❑ median scores? (Check *one*.)

TEST	A	B	C
1. pH-Balance			
2. Sudsing			
3. Do-You-Like-It?			
TOTALS			

(Raw-Score Totals)

"WEIGHTED" SCORES

1. Assign Importance Factors to the tests. (3=*most* important; 1=*least* important)

2. Multiply the class's combined raw scores by the Importance Factors.

IMPORTANCE FACTOR:	A	B	C
1.			
2.			
3.			
TOTALS			

(Weighted-Score Totals)

(1) **Code**   **Brand**   **Formula**

A _____ _____

B _____ _____

C _____ _____

(2) How many small groups tested the shampoos?_____

(3) Date_____

(4) Person to contact (name and address):

_____

_____

_____

_____

(5) **Mail To:**

**Consumer Reports
Education Division
101 Truman Avenue
Yonkers, New York 10703-1057**

PRENTICE HALL

PRODUCT TESTING ACTIVITIES by Consumer Reports

TESTING SPORTS DRINKS

Testing Sports Drinks has students check out facts behind the myths about sports drinks and in the process learn basic body chemistry. Students will test to see how isotonic the drinks are **(osmosis, salts)**; what their electrolytes are **(salts, ions)**; how much sugar they contain **(calories, energy, and energy reserves)**; and what their most important ingredient is **(water)**. This unit can lead to exploration of kidney and sweat-gland function, homeostasis, dehydration, and the nature and function of salts and sugars.

In the process of testing, students will develop skills of observation, forming hypotheses, controlling variables, analyzing data, and forming conclusions. Rather than judging which sports drink is best, students will compare sports drinks and other drinks (fruit juice and drink) and decide which is the drink of choice during sports activities.

Tests are designed for groups of four. Students will work together to conduct and plan tests, analyze data, solve problems, interpret results, and form conclusions about sports drinks The chart below links tests students will perform with the science skills and concepts those activities help teach.

CURRICULUM SKILLS AND CONCEPTS

Test and Student Databook Page	Highlighted Skills	Science Concepts
Getting Started p. 1	Blind Testing, Defining Problems	Principles of Testing
The Isotonic Test p. 2	Weighing/Measuring, Inferring, Controlling Variables	Cells, Osmosis, Salt Solutions, Blood
Electrolytes in Sports Drinks, p. 3	Data Tabulation, Calculating	Salts, Ions, Atomic Mass
Electrolytes in Other Drinks, p. 4	Data Tabulation, Calculating, Estimating	Electrolyte Strength
How Much Sugar? p. 5	Reading Labels, Ratios	Calories, Sugar Concentrations
Make Your Own Sports Drink, p. 6	Data Analysis, Developing a Product	Concentrations, Sweating, Dehydration
Taste Test p. 7	Designing a Test, Controlling Variables	Sensory Test Design, The Body and Exercise
Cost Analysis p. 8	Calculating Ratios	Weights and Measures
Interpret Your Test Data, p. 8	Forming Conclusions	Data Interpretation

MATERIALS NEEDED for each small group:

❑ **Test samples:**
2 sports drinks (orange flavor), orange juice, orange drink, and their labels.

❑ **For pre-planned tests:**
Water, carrot, 4 300-mL beakers, salt, balance, knife, measuring cup and spoon, aluminum foil, calculator, tissues.

CLASS-TIME REQUIREMENTS:

❑ To do Pre-Test 1: 1 class period to set up; 1 to collect and analyze data
❑ To do Tests 1 through 3: 1 or 2 class periods
❑ To do Test 4: Home assignment
❑ To do Test 5: 1 class period
❑ For data analysis and interpretation: 1 class period

GETTING STARTED

1. Distribute Student Databooks, one to each student group.

DISCUSS:

1. What ideas do people have about sports drinks? *(Discuss responses to the page 1 balloon.)* What ideas might be wrong? What ideas would you like to test? Why? How?

ADVERTISING CREATES IDEAS ABOUT PRODUCTS—IDEAS THAT CAN BE RIGHT OR WRONG. WHAT IDEAS MIGHT PEOPLE HAVE ABOUT THE SPECIAL BENEFITS OF SPORTS DRINKS? LIST THEM HERE.
Mistaken ideas include: They're health drinks, loaded with important nutrients; they make you perform better; people need electrolytes in their drinks. Other ideas: They're a way to replenish lost fluids; they replace energy (calories) and electrolytes (salt).

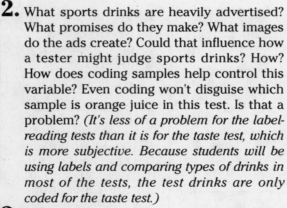

2. What sports drinks are heavily advertised? What promises do they make? What images do the ads create? Could that influence how a tester might judge sports drinks? How? How does coding samples help control this variable? Even coding won't disguise which sample is orange juice in this test. Is that a problem? *(It's less of a problem for the label-reading tests than it is for the taste test, which is more subjective. Because students will be using labels and comparing types of drinks in most of the tests, the test drinks are only coded for the taste test.)*

3. The goal of testing is to come up with reliable results — results that would probably be found again if the tests were repeated. How does controlling variables help you do that? What else should you pay attention to? *(Keep good records, check data, etc.)*

2. Code test samples. Cover brand names and code the sports drinks A and B.

PRE-TEST — THE ISOTONIC TEST, p. 2

QUESTION: How isotonic are sports drinks and other drinks?

WHAT STUDENTS WILL DO:

Students will cut a carrot into four equal pieces, place a carrot slice in an isotonic salt solution and a sports drink, orange juice, and orange drink. The next day, they will weigh the carrots and judge which drink is most isotonic (which carrot's weight loss is closest to that of the carrot that was in the isotonic solution).

MATERIALS FOR EACH GROUP:

250 mL of water, sports drink, orange juice, and orange drink; carrot, knife, 4 300-mL beakers, salt, balance, measuring cup and spoon, aluminum foil, tissues.

OBJECTIVES:

To observe results of osmosis; to understand the meaning of isotonic and osmosis; to be introduced to the concepts of blood cells and plasma.

CONCEPTS:

Osmosis: The passage of water through cell membranes toward the area of greater concentration (of salt, sugar, protein, etc.) to equalize concentrations on both sides of the membrane.

Blood cells and plasma: Fluids in blood cells and plasma are slightly saline (salty). If plasma were diluted, its fluids would pass through the cell membranes into blood cells, increasing their fluid content. If water depletion in the body caused the plasma to become more concentrated, water would pass out of the blood cells.

Body chemistry: The body automatically balances the salt content of blood plasma. It takes needed salt from what you eat and eliminates excess salt through the kidneys.

Isotonic describes a fluid that has similar amounts of dissolved substances (salt, sugar, protein, etc.) as blood.

DISCUSS:

1. Why did the carrots lose weight? (*Explore osmosis and discuss responses to the first balloon.*)

WHY DID THE CARROTS'
WEIGHT CHANGE—WHAT DID THEY
GAIN OR LOSE?
The carrots' total salt and sugar concentration was less than the solutions', so water passed from the carrots into the solutions to equalize both concentrations.

2. What does "isotonic" mean when used to describe sports drinks? (*Having the same salt and sugar concentration as the blood.*) Which carrot's weight loss was closest to that of the carrot that was in the isotonic solution? What does that mean? (*It means that drink is isotonic, too.*)

3. Most of the foods and drinks we take in aren't isotonic. Why isn't that a problem? (*Discuss responses to the second balloon.*)

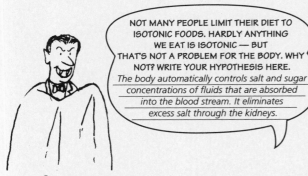

NOT MANY PEOPLE LIMIT THEIR DIET TO ISOTONIC FOODS. HARDLY ANYTHING WE EAT IS ISOTONIC — BUT THAT'S NOT A PROBLEM FOR THE BODY. WHY NOT? WRITE YOUR HYPOTHESIS HERE.
The body automatically controls salt and sugar concentrations of fluids that are absorbed into the blood stream. It eliminates excess salt through the kidneys.

4. What variables had to be controlled in this test? (*The weight of the carrot, the amount of solution, the temperature, etc.*) Why were the beakers covered overnight? (*To prevent evaporation of water, which would have changed the concentrations.*)

ACTIVITY:

Test with "blood" cells. Develop hypotheses: What would happen to blood cells soaked in a salt solution more concentrated than theirs? Less concentrated than theirs? Test hypotheses, using raw fresh meat. Under a microscope, observe the shape of the blood cells when fresh. Then put them in a saltier-than-isotonic solution and in distilled water. A day later, examine them. (*Cells in distilled water will swell; cells in saltier solutions will shrink.*)

1. ELECTROLYTES IN SPORTS DRINKS, p. 3

QUESTION: How much salt is in sports drinks?

WHAT STUDENTS WILL DO:

Sports drinks' electrolytes are mainly sodium and potassium salts. Students will read labels, find mg of sodium and potassium per serving, divide mg of potassium by 2, and add to find the combined electrolyte strength of both salts. (*The mass of a potassium atom is almost twice that of a sodium atom, but they have the same charge.*)

MATERIALS FOR EACH GROUP:

Labels from both test sports drinks.

OBJECTIVES:

To be introduced to the concepts of ionization and atomic mass; to understand what electrolytes are; to perform calculations.

CONCEPTS:

Ions and dissociation: Ions are electrically charged atoms. Ions in salt crystals dissociate from each other when the salt is dissolved (in this instance, a salt dissolves to form ions in solution). Sodium and potassium are positively charged ions; chloride and citrate are negatively charged.

Atomic mass: Atoms and ions of different elements have different sizes and mass. Potassium (at.mass 39) has almost twice the mass of sodium (at.mass 23).

Electrolyte strength: The more ions present in a solution, the greater its ability to conduct electrical current (electrolyte strength). Although each sodium and potassium ion possesses one positive charge, the mass of a potassium ion is almost twice that of a sodium ion. Equal masses of sodium and potassium ions contain nearly half as many potassium ions as sodium ions.

DISCUSS:

1. What do mg of sodium and potassium on sports drinks' labels indicate? (*Electrolyte strength. Both are positively charged ions.*) Why can't you add mg of sodium and potassium *(from the label)* to determine electrolyte strength? (*An ion of potassium has the same electrical charge as sodium but almost twice the mass.*) Why did you divide potassium by 2? (*Because gram for gram, it has about half as many ions as sodium.*)

2. If you were to compare other drinks' electrolyte strength to that of sports drinks, which would be better to use, data for *one* sports drink or the *average* electrolyte strength of two? *(One sports drink might not be representative of all sports drinks. An average of two gives a better indication of "typical." Three would be even better.)*

ACTIVITY:

Count electrolytes in the diet: As a home assignment, have students read food labels and record sodium and potassium per serving. Discuss whether people need more salt in their diets. *(Most Americans take in much more sodium than they need. Excessive sodium has been linked with serious diseases, like high blood pressure.)*

2. ELECTROLYTES IN OTHER DRINKS, p. 4

QUESTION: How do the electrolytes in other drinks compare?

WHAT STUDENTS WILL DO:

After determining the electrolyte strength of orange juice and orange drink (the way they did for sports drinks in Test 1), students will see how these drinks' electrolyte strength compare with that of sports drinks. *(Since orange juice is naturally high in potassium, it will have more electrolytes than sports drinks.)*

MATERIALS FOR EACH GROUP:

Labels from orange juice and orange drink.

OBJECTIVES:

To reinforce understandings of electrolytes and atomic mass; to build estimating skills.

DISCUSS:

1. Which drink has *more* electrolyte strength than the sports drinks? *(Orange juice.)* Does that surprise you?

CONCEPTS:

Table salt (sodium chloride) is about 40 percent sodium and 60 percent chlorine by mass. In solution, a gram (1/4 tsp) of sodium chloride will yield 400 mg sodium ions.

Potassium is an important nutrient (as well as a positively charged ion). Orange juice and bananas are rich sources of potassium.

2. How much table salt would yield the same amount of electrolyte strength as in a sports drink? Discuss student's responses to the balloon. *(About 1/16th of a tsp yields about 100 mg sodium. A serving of most sports drinks has 50 to 150 mg.)*

3. Why don't manufacturers load down sports drinks with electrolytes? Is it possible for a drink to be *too* salty? What would happen? *(Adding too much salt would make body fluids too salty. The body would respond by triggering a response designed to bring in more water to restore the balance — it would make you thirstier! Sea water is about 3.5 percent salt — too concentrated to quench thirst, and fatal if you drink too much.)*

3. HOW MUCH SUGAR?, p. 5

QUESTION: How much sugar is in one serving of a sports drink and other drinks?

WHAT STUDENTS WILL DO:

Students will record carbohydrates per serving (from sports drinks' nutrition labels) and convert that to tsp of sugar per serving. *(Sports drinks have less sugar than juice and orange drink. Too much sugar interferes with absorption of water.)*

MATERIALS FOR EACH GROUP:

Labels from 2 sports drinks, orange juice, and orange drink.

OBJECTIVES:

To understand how the body burns nutrients to produce calories for energy; to convert measurements.

CONCEPTS:

Calories are a measure of energy: One food calorie equals the amount of heat energy needed to raise the temperature of 1 kg of water 1 degree Celsius. Carbohydrates and proteins have 4 calories per g, fat has 9 calories per g.

Sugars are simple carbohydrates, which can be digested and converted to fuel faster than more complex carbohydrates. Glucose is the sugar most readily assimilated by the body. Fructose is sugar found in fruit. Sucrose, the most commonly used sugar, is composed of glucose and fructose. Lactose is milk sugar. Ingredients words ending in -ose are sugars.

DISCUSS:

1. Which drinks had the least sugar per serving? (*Sports drinks and the half-juice-half-water drink are likely to have much less sugar than orange drink or juice.*)

2. How does the sugar content of soft drinks compare to that of sports drinks? (*Discuss responses to the first balloon.*) Why do you think sports drinks have less sugar than most other drinks? (*Too much sugar can slow down the absorption of water and could make strenuous exercisers feel sick.*)

> SOFT DRINKS HAVE 6 TO 8 TSPS OF SUGAR PER 8-OZ. (250 ML) SERVING. HOW DO THEY COMPARE TO SPORTS DRINKS AND OTHER DRINKS?
> *Soft drinks have up to twice as much sugar per serving as sports drinks. Juice and fruit drink also have more sugar than sports drinks.*

3. Do athletes need to continually take in calories to keep from running out of energy? Why or why not? (*Explore how the body stores calories and, except in extreme cases, maintains the right sugar balance in the blood. Discuss the second balloon.*)

> THE BODY AUTOMATICALLY KEEPS THE RIGHT SUGAR LEVEL IN YOUR BLOOD, EVEN WHEN YOU'RE NOT TAKING IN SUGAR. WHERE DO THE BODY'S "ENERGY RESERVES" COME FROM? WRITE YOUR HYPOTHESIS HERE.
> *The body makes sure you don't have too much or too little sugar (available energy) in your blood. If you run low on sugar, it takes stored calories from glycogen in the liver and muscles (and then from fatty deposits). If you take in too many calories, the body stores them in the muscles and liver, and then as fat.*

Testing procedures are not provided for the following two tests. Each small group must devise its own plan and procedures. The goal is to encourage hands-on, common-sense creativity and problem-solving by students. There are several possible answers. *There's no one "right way" to do these tests.*

4. MAKE YOUR OWN SPORTS DRINK, p. 6

QUESTION: What's the best-tasting homemade sports drink?

POSSIBLE PROCEDURES:
Students could dilute juice and add salts and flavorings. Or they could decide they don't need the salt and develop a low-sugar (or no-sugar) drink. Or they may use water.

OBJECTIVES:
To analyze the data gathered about sports drinks and use them to make a sports drink; to do sensory experimentation.

CONCEPT:

Dehydration, hydration: Dehydration is the process of losing water, which can happen during exercise. (As the body burns calories for energy, it gets hotter, so the sweat glands go to work. As sweat evaporates, it cools the skin, controlling body heat.) Dehydration is the condition of having severely depleted body fluids. Hydration (the process of taking in water) should be done before and while exercising, as well as afterward.

DISCUSS:

1. Which is more important, drinking lots of water during exercise or drinking a sports drink? Why? (*Taking in lots of fluids to replace water lost from sweating is the most important reason to drink while exercising. If you don't, your body could lose so much water and salt it wouldn't be able to restore a salt balance, and therefore wouldn't be able to hold water. In that extreme case, an electrolyte-drink could help. Treatments for dehydration from intestinal disorders have formulas similar to a typical sports drink's.*)

BURNING CALORIES RAISES BODY HEAT—BUT SWEATING COOLS THE BODY OFF. THE HARDER YOU EXERCISE, THE MORE YOU SWEAT. WHEN IS THE BEST TIME TO REPLENISH LOST FLUIDS— WHILE YOU'RE EXERCISING OR AFTERWARDS? WRITE YOUR HYPOTHESIS HERE.
It's best for athletes to drink during exercise to avoid dehydration, which is unhealthy and also interferes with performance, since a body low on fluids can't adequately cool itself and tires easily. Athletes often drink quarts of water during strenuous exercise.

2. What should you do when exercising — replenish body fluids as you lose them or replace them when you're dehydrated? Why? *(Discuss responses to the balloon.)*

ACTIVITY:

Package, promote, and sell the home-made sports drink. Have students develop a marketing campaign to "sell" the drink they made. What are its advantages? How does it compare with other beverages students are drinking?

5. TASTE TEST, p. 7

QUESTION: Which "thirst quencher" would you most want to drink while exercising?

POSSIBLE PROCEDURES:

Students might perform taste tests while at rest and during strenuous exercise to determine whether preferences change under differing conditions. The quantity of drink sampled could be varied to determine whether quantity drunk influences choice. Each of these variables would, of course, have to be tested under controlled conditions (each measured separately while the others remained constant). The kind and duration of exercise would be other variables to consider, as would air temperature and humidity, both of which affect the amount and efficiency of perspiration. A simpler test might be providing coded jugs of each drink at a sporting event to see which is drunk the most.

OBJECTIVES:

To understand how to design a controlled test; to reinforce understandings about exercise and maintaining body fluids; to develop sensory testing skills.

DISCUSS:

1. How did you decide to test? Why did you test that way? *(Discuss responses to the first balloon.)*

DO YOU THINK A DRINK THAT TASTES BEST WHEN SIPPED IN A TASTE TEST WOULD ALSO TASTE BEST WHEN GULPED ON A BLAZING HOT BALLFIELD? SHOULD SPORTS DRINKS BE TESTED DIFFERENTLY FROM DRINKS YOU JUST SIP?
Testing drinks under the normal conditions in which they'd be used helps you identify important qualities and characteristics. A sweet drink, for example, might taste best when sipped but might taste sickly sweet when drunk in great quantity while you're active.

2. What variables did you have to control? How did you control each? *(Answers will depend on the test design. But basic variables include the temperature of the drinks, the quantity drunk, the containers they're served in, the sequence they're tried in [since testers may be thirstier at the start], etc. Discuss the second balloon.)*

HOW COLD A DRINK IS MAY AFFECT HOW *GOOD* IT TASTES. HOW WILL YOU CONTROL THIS VARIABLE?
Prepare test drinks in advance, refrigerate them overnight, and serve them all at the same temperature.

6. # COST ANALYSIS,
p. 8

QUESTION: After water, which drink is least expensive?

WHAT STUDENTS WILL DO:
Students will divide container size by 250 mL to find servings per container, then divide price by that amount to determine price per serving.

MATERIALS PER GROUP:
Size and price labels from 2 sports drinks, orange juice, and orange drink; calculator.

OBJECTIVES:
To compare prices on a unit basis and judge value; to build skill at calculations and label reading; to practice working with ratios.

> **CONCEPT:**
> **Unit price:** In order to compare the prices of similar products (which often come in different-sized containers), one has to compare price on a unit basis. Units may be calculated in terms of weight, mass, volume, or "servings."

DISCUSS:

1. Why would it be misleading to simply compare the prices on the drink containers to determine which is least expensive? *(The containers may hold different amounts or the amount needed per serving may differ, as with the half-juice, half-water drink.)*

2. With a product that's likely to be used in great quantities (like a drink for sweating athletes), does price become a more important consideration? Why or why not? How important should price be when you're choosing what to drink while exercising?

DEALING WITH DATA

In most of these tests, the drinks were not given numerical scores. So the data collected must be analyzed and interpreted in a qualitative rather than quantitative way.

Data alone can't say which drink is best. Like all facts, data have to be thought about, evaluated, and interpreted in a useful and meaningful way. If misinterpreted, data can mislead consumers instead of guiding them.

INTERPRET YOUR TEST DATA, p. 8

OBJECTIVES:
To evaluate criteria for sports drinks and to apply the criteria to a set of recommendations; to express a view concerning what the public ought to know about the interrelationships between exercise, perspiration, electrolyte balance, energy consumption, and the drinking of various fluids; to reach conclusions about what to drink during exercise and to express those conclusions in writing.

DISCUSS:

What were your group's conclusions about the best thing to drink while exercising? What data support that conclusion? Was personal judgment involved?

ACTIVITY:

Compile the class's results and send its conclusions to *Consumer Reports*. Much of this testing activity was designed to compare different kinds of drinks and decide which was the best bet for athletes. Use the bar graphs on the following page to help the class put its data together and form conclusions. (Point out to students that the bar graphs are horizontal but work just like the more familiar vertical ones.) Then send the class's conclusions (and any presentation it prepares) to *Consumer Reports*.

By combining small groups' data, the class can decide which test results were the most reliable (which had the least variation in data from group to group).

The class should also decide which of the characteristics tested for are important and which aren't. (*Since replenishing fluids is most important for something drunk while exercising, should taste be the main criterion for judging the drinks? Debate!*)

Have the class prepare a presentation of its findings for the school. Include graphs, tables — whatever is needed to communicate the data.

COMPILE THE CLASS'S DATA ON DRINKS

STEP 1
Bar graph the average electrolyte strength of each drink.

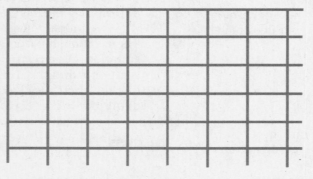

SPORTS DRINK A

SPORTS DRINK B

ORANGE JUICE

ORANGE DRINK

HALF JUICE, HALF WATER

25 50 75 100 125 150 175 mg
(Average electrolyte strength per serving)

STEP 2
Bar graph the average grams of sugar per serving of each drink.

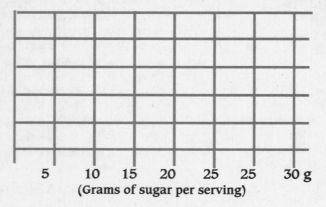

SPORTS DRINK A

SPORTS DRINK B

ORANGE JUICE

ORANGE DRINK

HALF JUICE, HALF WATER

5 10 15 20 25 25 30 g
(Grams of sugar per serving)

STEP 3
Bar graph the average price per serving of each drink.

SPORTS DRINK A

SPORTS DRINK B

ORANGE JUICE

ORANGE DRINK

HALF JUICE, HALF WATER

$.20 .40 .60 .80 1.00 1.10 1.20
(Price per serving)

STEP 4

Rank the drinks in order of taste.

Best-tasting: _____

2nd place: _____

3rd place: _____

4th place: _____

5th place: _____

How did the class's homemade drinks do?
_____

STEP 5

Which drink does the class recommend? Why?

_____
_____
_____
_____
_____
_____

CONSUMER REPORTS wants to see what you've done. Mail your report to: *Consumer Reports* **Education Division 101 Truman Avenue Yonkers, New York 10703-1057**

Name: _____
School: _____
Address: _____
_____

TESTING TOILET PAPER

Testing Toilet Paper helps students discover the science and technology governing the performance of toilet paper: which are thicker (**loft and density**); which are softer (**paper construction**); which disintegrate faster (**degradability**); which are stronger (**gravity, potential and kinetic energy**); and which are more absorbent (**absorption and capillary action**).

Students will also develop basic testing skills: observation, forming hypotheses, controlling variables, recording and analyz- ing data. Testing activities also involve num- ber lines; counting, adding, and averaging; ratio and proportion; units of measurement (time, length, weight, cost); and statistics (variation, sampling).

Tests encourage cooperative learning. They are designed for groups of four. Students work together to conduct and plan tests, analyze data, solve problems, and develop a scientific rating of the test toilet papers. The chart below links each test with the science skills and concepts it helps teach.

CURRICULUM SKILLS AND CONCEPTS

Test and Student Databook Page	Highlighted Skills	Science Concepts
Getting Started p. 1	Controlling Variables, Blind Testing	Principles of Testing
Thickness Test p. 2	Measuring, Making Equipment	Loft, Density, Measurement Error
The Softness Test p. 3	Sensory Observations, Controlling Variables	Paired Comparison Testing, Variation
Flushability Test p. 4	Observation, Timing Experiments	Nature of Paper, Degradability
Wet-Strength Test p. 5	Weighing, Measuring, Controlling Variables	Gravity, Potential and Kinetic Energy
Absorbency Test p. 6	Designing a Test, Controlling Variables	Absorbency, Capillary Action
Cost Analysis p. 7	Critical Thinking, Comparing Data	Geometry, Ratio and Proportion
Interpret Your Test Data, p. 8	Analyzing Data, Forming Conclusions	Weighted Scores, Rating Tables

MATERIALS NEEDED for each small group:

❑ **Test samples:** 4 different brands of toilet paper. Include 1- and 2-ply, store and national brands, all the same color.

❑ **For pre-planned tests:** Paper cups, scissors, small ruler, quarter, marker, cardboard, stapler, glass container (pitcher or bowl), stirrer, timer, facial tissue, water, drinking glass, rubber bands, medicine dropper, lead or steel shot (BB's) or small pebbles, cup, balance.

CLASS-TIME REQUIREMENTS:

❑ To prepare for testing: 1 class period.
❑ For Tests 1 to 4: 1 class period for each test
❑ For Tests 5 and 6: 1 or 2 class periods
❑ For data analysis and interpretation: 1 class period

GETTING STARTED

1. Code test samples.

Students should not know the test samples' brand names until testing is completed. Prepare test samples in advance: Remove packaging and all brand-name identification. Write codes on the inside tube of the toilet papers. Have pens by the test samples so students can code the toilet paper sheets as they take them.

2. Measure outside diameter of each roll before removing any sheets.

Students may need that information for price/volume activities in Test 6.

3. Distribute Student Databooks, one to each student group.

DISCUSS:

1. One thing that will vary in these tests is the toilet papers. But other things (like what you do to them) shouldn't vary. Why not? (*Results wouldn't necessarily be due to the toilet papers. It's best to expose all test samples to the same conditions and procedures.*)

2. Discuss responses to the balloon. How could bias on the part of testers affect test results? How would you control this variable? (*Discuss why toilet papers are coded.*)

> BECAUSE SOME TOILET PAPERS ADVERTISE A LOT, TESTERS MAY THINK THEY'RE SOFTER OR BETTER. TESTER BIAS CAN BE A <u>VARIABLE</u>. HOW COULD YOU CONTROL IT IN THESE TESTS? *Possible tester bias can be controlled by blind testing; by removing all brand-name identification and coding test samples.*

SMITH'S... ONLY THE #1 BEST!

3. The goal of testing is to come up with *reliable* results — results that would probably be gotten again if the tests were repeated. What can help you do that? (*Control variables, collect and record data carefully.*)

4. Some toilet paper tests could be done by one person or by every person in the group. Which do you think is better: Getting lots of data for each test or just one set? Why? (*The more data you collect, the less of an impact variation will have on results.*)

TESTS ALREADY DESIGNED FOR STUDENTS

The first four tests describe the testing procedures students should follow. Allow student groups to work independently and solve problems among themselves. Wait until they've completed their testing before discussing the tests. The goal is to encourage independent thinking, creative problem solving, and increased confidence in their scientific abilities.

1. THICKNESS TEST, p. 2

QUESTION: Which toilet paper is thickest?

MATERIALS FOR EACH GROUP:
4 coded toilet papers (20 sheets of each), large paper cup (at least 180 mL), scissors, small ruler, quarter.

WHAT STUDENTS WILL DO:
After making a thickness-measurer with a paper cup and ruler, students will measure the relative thickness of 20 sheets of each toilet paper, plot thicknesses on a number line, and determine thickness scores.

OBJECTIVES:
To discover ways to measure small differences; to understand measurement error; to discover differences in paper thickness and density.

CONCEPTS:

Measurement error: Measurements recorded during testing may not be precise. (How precisely can one measure with a ruler?) Increasing the number of samples measured and the number of measurements taken reduces the impact slight inaccuracies could have on test results. (In this test, measuring 20 sheets is better than measuring 10; but measuring 40 would be even better, as would measuring each test sample several times rather than once.)

Loft and density: Loft is a consequence of the looseness of the paper fiber at the surface. Magazine paper has a hard surface and low loft; toilet paper has the opposite. Loft is also an indication of density: A looser paper fiber (high loft) will have more air space and thus a lower density.

DISCUSS:

1. Why did you use a quarter on top of the tissues? *(To weigh them down equally and provide a flat surface for the ruler.)* Why did you have to bend over to be at eye level with the cup to read the ruler? *(Because you'd get different readings if you were looking down or up at it. Looking straight at it gives the most accurate reading.)*

2. What variables did this test procedure try to control? *(Whether tissues were lying flat, whether the surface was level, how much pressure was exerted on the tissues, the angle of your eye to the ruler when reading measurements.)* How were they controlled? Are there other ways to control them?

3. Why do you think the test had you measure 20 sheets of each toilet paper instead of just 1 (or 5 or 10)? *(Combining several sheets of one sample can make tiny differences more noticeable and measurable.)* Which do you think gives better (more reliable) data, measuring lots of samples or just a few? Why? *(Explore measurement error.)*

ACTIVITY:

Compare thickness and density of different types of paper. Repeat this Thickness Test on magazine paper, paper towels, and other kinds of paper. Weigh, then compute volume (measure thickness, length and width) and density. Is there a relationship between density and how soft a paper feels? What does that suggest about its fibers? *(Paper that feels softer will usually have lower density because its fibers aren't as tightly woven.)*

2. THE SOFTNESS TEST, p. 3

QUESTION: Which toilet paper is softest?

MATERIALS FOR EACH GROUP:

4 coded toilet papers (3 sheets of each), marker, cardboard (6 16-cm-by-28-cm), stapler.

WHAT STUDENTS WILL DO:

After pairing the test samples into six pairs and stapling them to the pieces of cardboard, students will feel and compare each pair and give a check to the softer one. Testers will add up each toilet paper's checks and use a number line to determine scores.

OBJECTIVES:

To understand the concept of paired comparison testing methods; to control variables; to build skill at following directions and making sensory judgments; to determine differences in paper softness.

CONCEPTS:

Paired comparisons: Pairing off test samples into all possible combinations and systematically choosing the better (e.g., softer, stronger, etc.) one is a valid testing alternative to establishing objective criteria and seeing how test samples measure up. This testing method makes it much easier to do sensory testing (like the "feel" tests here).

DISCUSS:

1. Do you think this procedure of comparing *pairs* of toilet papers is a good way of finding which one is softest? What variables does this testing method control? *(How you define "soft" [standard of reference] and how fairly you apply it.)*

2. Discuss responses to the balloon: How did you control that variable? What other variables did you control?

HOW <u>OTHER</u> TESTERS RATE THE TOILET PAPERS COULD INFLUENCE <u>YOUR</u> JUDGMENTS. HOW CAN YOU CONTROL THIS VARIABLE? *Blindfold each tester and have a partner record his or her judgments; or make a separate scoring sheet for each tester.*

3. Did testers in your group agree or disagree on which one of each pair was softer? If there was a lot of disagreement, what might have caused the variation in testers' judgments? *(Some testers may have more sensitive hands; tissues may be so close in softness that differences are hard to feel; etc.)*

3. FLUSHABILITY TEST, p. 4

QUESTION: How rapidly do the toilet papers disintegrate in water?

MATERIALS FOR EACH GROUP:
4 coded toilet papers (1 sheet of each), glass container (pitcher or bowl, at least 500 mL), stirrer (could be spoon), timer, facial tissue, water, access to a sink.

WHAT STUDENTS WILL DO:
After filling a container with water, students will add a sheet of toilet paper, start the timer, begin to stir, and note how long it takes the toilet paper to disintegrate. (If it hasn't disintegrated after 3 minutes, they stop.)

CONCEPT:
Nature of paper: The ease with which a paper disintegrates in water is related to how it's made: what its fibers are made of, how long they are, how tightly they're woven, etc. Some papers, like toilet paper, are made to disintegrate rapidly; some aren't.

DISCUSS:

1. How did you define disintegration? (What did you look for?) Did all toilet papers disintegrate to the same degree?

2. How could you control the variables identified in the first balloon? Do you think you controlled them adequately in your test? Why or why not?

> THE AMOUNT OF WATER IN THE GLASS, WHETHER YOU CRUMPLED THE PAPER, AND HOW HARD YOU STIR ARE <u>VARIABLES</u>. HOW WILL YOU CONTROL THEM?
> *Measure the amount of water used; crumple them all or use them all flat; count the number and rate of stirs; have the same person do all the stirring.*

---

3. Discuss responses to the second balloon. What was your hypothesis?

> DOES FACIAL TISSUE DISINTEGRATE FAST ENOUGH TO BE USED AS TOILET PAPER? WRITE YOUR HYPOTHESIS HERE.
> *Facial tissue is supposed to stand up to wet sneezes and blowing noses. Disintegrating when wet would cause problems. Most probably don't.*

4. WET-STRENGTH TEST, p. 5

QUESTION: Which toilet paper is strongest when wet?

MATERIALS FOR EACH GROUP:
4 coded toilet papers (1 sheet of each), drinking glass, rubber bands (to fit the glass), medicine dropper, water, BB's (or small pebbles or dry beans), cup, balance.

WHAT STUDENTS WILL DO:
After stretching toilet paper over the mouth of the glass, securing it with a rubber band, and wetting it, students will place BB's on it until it tears. They'll weigh the BB's to see how much weight it took to tear the toilet paper.

OBJECTIVES:
To discover how weighing procedures can be used to test paper strength; to practice controlling variables and working with measurements.

CONCEPTS:
Gravity is a force drawing all objects to the center of the earth. It makes objects accelerate as they fall.

Gravitational potential energy (weight X height) is the potential energy an object has, based on its weight and how far it is from the earth's surface.

Kinetic energy is the energy of an object in motion. The faster the object moves (or the greater its mass), the greater its kinetic energy.

DISCUSS:

1. Which do you think is more important in a toilet paper, wet or dry strength? Why? How could you adapt this procedure to test for dry strength? *(Don't wet the paper.)*

2. Discuss responses to the balloon. Does the height you drop the weights from make a difference? *(See the activity below.)*

THE HEIGHT YOU DROP THE WEIGHTS FROM IS A VARIABLE. WHY?
The greater the height the weights are dropped from, the greater their velocity will be when they reach the toilet tissue, due to the force of gravity.

3. What other variables could affect this test? *(How long the tissue is wet before BB's are poured, how fast the BB's are put on it.)*

4. What measurement errors might have occurred? How accurately can we measure weight? *(Have small groups compare data. Are data the same?)*

5. Is there a relationship between how toilet papers scored in this test and in the Flushability Test (Test 3)? Which do you think is more important?

ACTIVITY:

The falling-force test. Repeat the test procedure using just one toilet paper, but varying the height from which the BB's are dropped.

TESTS STUDENTS WILL DESIGN THEMSELVES

Test procedures are not provided for the following tests. Each small group must devise its own plan and procedures. The goal is to encourage hands-on, common sense creativity and problem-solving. There's no one "right" way to do these tests.

5. ABSORBENCY TEST, p. 6

QUESTION: Which toilet paper absorbs best?

OBJECTIVES:

To understand the concepts of absorbency and capillary action; to learn how to plan a controlled test; to reinforce the importance of controlling variables.

POSSIBLE PROCEDURES:

To find *how much* water the test samples will absorb, students might dip the test sheets into a measured amount of water for a set time, remove them, measure how much water remains, and subtract it from the starting amount. To find *how fast* the test samples absorb water, mark off centimeters on the sheets, then dip one end into water and record how long it takes for water to reach each line.

CONCEPTS:

Absorbency: The tendency to take in or suck up a liquid. The number and spacing of fibers in a toilet paper affect its absorbency. *(More fibers and fibers spaced farther apart absorb more.)*

Capillary action: a phenomenon (resulting from adhesion, cohesion, and surface tension in liquids that are in contact with solids) whereby water molecules "climb" from fiber to fiber. The looser the fibers are, the faster the water will climb.

DISCUSS:

1. Discuss responses to the first balloon. Which did you test for, *how much* water the toilet paper would absorb or *how fast* it would absorb it? Why?

WHICH IS MORE IMPORTANT, HOW MUCH WATER TOILET PAPER CAN ABSORB OR HOW FAST IT ABSORBS WATER? WHICH WILL YOU TEST FOR (OR WILL YOU TEST FOR BOTH)? WHY?
Absorption speed and amount are important but would be measured differently. This balloon is intended to help students define what they're testing for.

2. Describe your test plan: What measurements did you take? What variables did you control? Were any variables not controlled? How did you determine scores?

3. Discuss responses to the second balloon. Do you think there's a relationship between thickness and absorbency? Did the test results support your hypothesis? (*Compare results of this test and the Thickness Test. Graph absorbency against thickness to see if there's a pattern.*)

WHICH TOILET PAPER IS LIKELY TO BE MORE ABSORBENT—A THICKER ONE OR A THINNER ONE? WHY? *A thicker one is likely to be more absorbent because it's likely to have thicker fibers or more spaces between fibers.*

6. COST ANALYSIS, p. 7

QUESTION: Which toilet paper is least costly to use?

MATERIALS FOR EACH GROUP:
Packages from the test samples, data on the diameters of new rolls of toilet paper.

OBJECTIVES:
To use measuring skills to compare apparent vs. actual roll-sizes; to build critical thinking and problem-solving skills; to correlate and analyze the meaning of other test results.

POSSIBLE PROCEDURES:
After recording information from the packages, students might compute cost per sheet and rank samples accordingly. Or they might average several unit costs: cost per sheet; cost per unit of thickness (or weight or volume). Or they might use-test to determine whether people use more of some (thinner, less absorbent) brands than of others, then base cost comparison on those findings.

CONCEPT:
Unit cost: For cost comparisons to be fair, they should be based on a standardized amount or quantity. But efficiency should also be factored in. (A thick paper may require fewer sheets per use.) So unit cost and cost per use aren't always the same. Determining cost per use may involve additional use-testing to determine whether product attributes affect how much is used.

DISCUSS:

1. Discuss responses to the first balloon.

HOW COULD TWO ROLLS OF TOILET PAPER BE THE SAME SIZE (HAVE THE SAME DIAMETER) BUT HAVE A DIFFERENT NUMBER OF SHEETS? *A toilet paper roll that's wound more tightly (or that has thinner sheets) may seem the same size as another (thicker-sheeted) roll but actually have more sheets.*

2. What did you base cost comparisons on? Have small groups compare their cost rankings: Did rankings vary or were they similar? What would be the most realistic basis for comparison? (Try to get a consensus.)

3. Discuss the second balloon. How might someone find out whether people would use fewer sheets if a toilet paper were thicker or more absorbent? (If you use-test, how many people would have to do it for data to be reliable? What variables would have to be controlled?)

IF A TOILET PAPER IS THICKER, MIGHT PEOPLE USE FEWER SHEETS? SHOULD YOU FIGURE COST ON NUMBER OF SHEETS OR ON THICKNESS? WHY? *All the methods cited in this balloon are valid. But basing comparisons on numbers of sheets may not mirror actual use. Basing them on usage, however, could mislead if all people don't use them the same way.*

137.5   25
525   1000
4.5 × 4.4   25 × 3

DEALING WITH DATA

Students have gathered data and assigned raw scores for all six toilet paper tests. Now they have to figure out what it means!

Data alone can't say which toilet paper is best. Like all facts, data have to be thought about, evaluated, and interpreted in a useful and meaningful way. If misinterpreted, data can mislead consumers instead of guiding them. There's no one way to deal with data.

While "dealing with data," students will be using basic mathematics skills as well as learning statistics in a hands-on way. They will also be saying "what it all means" — expressing in simple written sentences what their tests revealed about toilet paper. Data are seen as a means to an end, rather than an end in themselves.

INTERPRET YOUR TEST DATA, p. 8

OBJECTIVES:

To express the data collected so they are meaningful to people with different priorities; to understand methods of communicating test findings.

DISCUSS:

1. Which three tests did you think were most important? Why? Do you think it's fair to base the toilet papers' overall scores on just those three tests? Why or why not? *(This is a method of "weighting"—having the important tests count for more. Otherwise, toilet papers that did well in less important tests but poorly in the important ones could be ranked deceptively high.)*

2. Are small groups' rankings of toilet papers the same or different? If different, why? *(Did they rank tests' importance differently? Were there major differences in scores? What caused the differences? How might they be resolved?)*

3. Discuss how scores for the other three (less important) tests were communicated: What are the pros and cons of using the "blob-symbols" instead of just giving the numerical score?

EXTRA ACTIVITY: PUT TOGETHER THE CLASS'S DATA

CONCEPTS:

Sampling: The samples selected for testing can affect results.

Variation: Data can vary as a result of quality differences within a brand or uncontrolled variables, so it's advisable to repeat tests a number of times.

Measurement error: Measurements recorded during testing may not be 100 percent accurate or precise.

ACTIVITY:

Post an enlarged copy of the chart on the following page. Have all groups write their scores in the appropriate boxes. (Boxes will have several scores.) Then have the class assign Importance Factors to the tests and compute weighted scores.

DISCUSS:

1. Did everyone who tested come up with the same scores for the test samples? Why or why not? Is it possible every sheet of toilet paper A wasn't exactly the same? Can performance vary within a brand? Is it possible measurement errors were made? What kinds?

2. How can we determine which measurements are most reliable (most likely to happen again if the tests were repeated)? What if we performed each test several times instead of once? Should we base toilet paper ratings on the whole class's data? *(The more data that are used, the better, because more data reduce the impact variations will have on the scores. It's like an exam — when there are many questions, each one has less of an impact on the final grade.)*

3. Examine the class's raw data (on the chart). Which toilet paper (if any) has very little variation in its data (small groups' data are similar)? Which has wide variation? Which toilet paper's performance could you predict with more confidence? *(The one with less variation.)*

4. Which tests were *most* consistent (subject to the least variation)? *least* consistent (subject to the most variation)? Explore why.

SEND YOUR RATINGS OF TOILET PAPER TO *CONSUMER REPORTS*

The class should fill in this chart and answer all questions about the toilet papers. Attach a written summary of the class's conclusions. Then mail to the address below.

WHICH TOILET PAPER IS BEST?

"RAW" SCORES

Write the class's combined scores for each test in the boxes below.
Are these ❏ mean scores or ❏ median scores? (Check *one*.)

TEST	A	B	C	D
1. Thickness				
2. Softness				
3. Flushability				
4. Wet-Strength				
5. Absorbency				
TOTALS				

(Raw-Score Totals)

"WEIGHTED" SCORES

Assign Imortance Factors to the tests. (3=*most* important, 1=*least* important)

Multiply the class's combined raw scores by the Importance Factors.

IMPORTANCE FACTOR:	A	B	C	D
1.				
2.				
3.				
4.				
5.				
TOTALS				

(Weighted-Score Totals)

(1) Code   Brand

A _____

B _____

C _____

D _____

(2) How many small groups tested the toilet papers? _____

(3) Date _____

(4) Person to contact (name and address):

_____

_____

_____

_____

(5) Mail To:

Consumer Reports
Education Division
101 Truman Avenue
Yonkers, New York 10703-1057

TESTING YOGURTS

Testing Yogurts helps students discover the science and technology behind yogurt: What makes milk curdle and thicken **(acids, pH)**; how yogurt makes milk thicken **(bacteria, fermentation)**; which yogurts measure up to ideal yogurt taste **(sensory standards, taste and the tongue)**; how yogurts' fat content compare **(protein, fat, nutrition)**; and which one tastes best **(preference testing)**. Collecting, analyzing, and interpreting the data also involve counting and measuring, ratios, percentages, number lines, and basic statistics.

Tests are designed for groups of four. Students work together to conduct and plan tests, analyze data, solve problems, and develop a scientific rating of yogurts. The chart below links the tests students will perform with the science skills and concepts those testing activities help teach.

CURRICULUM SKILLS AND CONCEPTS

Test and Student Databook Page	Highlighted Skills	Science Concepts
Getting Started p. 1	Controlling Variables, Blind Testing	Principles of Testing
What Makes Milk Curdle and Thicken? p. 2	Observation, Comparing, Measuring pH	Acids, pH, Ions and Curdling
The Mystery Ingredient, p. 3	Measuring pH, Hypothesizing	Fermentation, Acids, Bases, Neutralization
The Active-Culture Test, p. 4	Observation, Measuring pH, Hypothesizing	Bacterial Metabolism, Incubation
Sensory Test p. 5	Sensory Observation, Using Continuum Scales	Standards of Reference, Taste and the Tongue
The Protein and Fat Test, p. 6	Percentages, Calculations, Ratios	Fat and Protein, Nutrition
Taste-Preference Test p. 7	Designing a Test, Blind Testing, Controlling Variables	Paired Comparisons
Interpret Your Test Data, p. 8	Critical Thinking, Forming Conclusions, Data Analysis	Weighted Scores, Nutrition

CLASS-TIME REQUIREMENTS:

- ❑ To prepare for testing and to conduct Pre-test 1 and start Pre-Test 2: 1 class period.
- ❑ To complete Pre-Test 2 and start Test 1: 1 class period.
- ❑ To complete Test 1 and do Test 2: 1 class period.
- ❑ To conduct Test 3: 1 class period
- ❑ For data interpretation: 1 class period

MATERIALS NEEDED
for each small group:

- ❑ **Test samples:** 1 plain yogurt with active cultures and 4 strawberry yogurts, including whole-milk, low-fat, and non-fat types (one 6- or 8-ounce container of each). Make sure some claim to have live cultures. All yogurts should have similar freshness dates and be refrigerated after purchase.

- ❑ **For pre-planned tests:** Milk, vinegar, lemon juice, tea, chocolate syrup, pH paper, paper cups, graduated cylinder, teaspoons, large beaker, baking soda, yogurt-maker with 4 cups, strawberry jam, sugar cubes, water, ruler, paper towels, paper plates, plastic spoons, tablespoons, marker, yogurt containers, calculator.

GETTING STARTED

1. Code test samples.

Yogurts should be stored in covered containers coded A through D for students to scoop from (and each should have its own serving spoon). Preparations should be done by someone who will not be doing these tests. Save the containers for Test 3. (And be sure to keep all test yogurts refrigerated.)

CAUTION: Before testing, ask if any students have an allergy to milk or milk products. If so, they shouldn't do any of the tasting in this test. They can help prepare and blind-code the yogurts and conduct the non-tasting tests. (If students have a very strong allergy to milk, they shouldn't do this test at all.)

2. Distribute Student Databooks, one to each group.

DISCUSS:

1. What do you like and dislike about yogurt? Do you think there's a difference among various types of yogurt (lowfat, etc.)? Among various brands? Which of these variables should we limit? Why? *(Discuss responses to the balloon on page 1.)*

THE TYPE OF YOGURT (LIKE NON-FAT OR FROZEN) AND FLAVOR (LIKE STRAWBERRY OR VANILLA) ARE <u>VARIABLES</u>. SO IS THE YOGURT BRAND. WHICH OF THESE VARIABLES WOULD YOU LIKE TO TEST FOR? HOW WOULD YOU CONTROL THE OTHER TWO VARIABLES?
If students want to compare brands, they'd keep the flavor and type of yogurt the same. If they want to test for type, they'd keep the flavor and brand the same. (The tests students will do control just one of these variables—flavor. All test yogurts will be strawberry.)

3. The goal of testing is to come up with reliable results (results that would probably be found again if the test were repeated) and valid results (results that reflect actual differences among the products). How does controlling variables help you do that? What else should you pay attention to? *(Collect data carefully and keep good records.)*

TESTS ALREADY DESIGNED FOR STUDENTS

The two pre-tests and the first three tests describe the testing procedures to follow. Allow student groups to work independently and solve problems among themselves. Wait until they've completed their testing before discussing or reviewing the tests. The goal is to encourage independent thinking, creative problem-solving, and increased confidence in their scientific abilities.

PRE-TEST 1 — WHAT MAKES MILK CURDLE AND THICKEN? p. 2

QUESTION: What characteristic is shared by liquids that make milk curdle and thicken?

MATERIALS FOR EACH GROUP:

Milk (40 mL), vinegar, lemon juice, tea, and diluted chocolate syrup (10 mL each), pH paper, 4 paper cups, graduated cylinder, 4 spoons.

WHAT STUDENTS WILL DO:

After using pH paper to measure the acidity of four solutions (vinegar, lemon juice, tea, and chocolate), students will add milk, observe which mixtures curdle, and infer that the characteristic shared by those that curdled is acidity (pH under 5).

OBJECTIVES:

To gain skill at measuring pH; to infer the correlation between acidity and curdling; to express observations in writing.

CONCEPTS:

Acids and pH: Acids are compounds that easily give up a hydrogen ion (+ charge). pH measures a solution's hydrogen-ion concentration: the pH of acids ranges from 0 (strong acid) to 7 (neutral).

Ions and curdling: Casein, a protein in milk, has the form of a spherical micelle. Casein micelles are covered with negatively charged amino acids so they repel each other and stay suspended in the milk. When acid is added, it neutralizes the negative charges and allows micelles to stick together, coagulate, and become insoluble.

DISCUSS:

1. What relationship did you find between a mixture's pH and whether lumps formed? *(Acidic milk mixtures will curdle [form lumps]; non-acidic milk mixtures won't.)*

2. What are acids? *(Substances with available positively charged hydrogen ions.)* What must they be reacting with? *(Bases [amino acids, proteins], which have an affinity for hydrogen ions.)* What's the result of this reaction? *(Things that were suspended in milk [milk proteins] are clumping together and becoming a solid.)* Once students understand acid-base reactions, explain the concept of ions and curdling.

PRE-TEST 2 — THE MYSTERY INGREDIENT, p. 3

QUESTIONS: Can a yogurt *with active cultures* make milk thicken? How?

WHAT STUDENTS WILL DO:

Students will prepare two yogurt-milk mixtures, add a base (baking soda) to one, leave both in a yogurt-maker overnight, then observe which got thicker. *(The base will neutralize the acid, keeping that mixture from thickening. The other [non-neutralized] mixture will thicken, indicating that an acid is making the milk thicken.)*

MATERIALS FOR EACH GROUP:

Plain yogurt with active cultures, 100 mL *pre-heated* milk, large beaker, baking soda, 2 teaspoons, graduated cylinder, pH paper, yogurt-maker (2 cups and heating unit). **The milk should be heated to 75°C and cooled to 40°C (or lower) before class starts. (The milk can be prepared several hours before it's used.)**

OBJECTIVES:

To build skill at measuring, hypothesizing, controlling variables, and taking pH measurements; to understand fermentation, acids and bases, and neutralization.

CONCEPTS:

Fermentation: In the yogurt-making process, a bacterial culture "digests" the lactose in milk, breaking it down into lactic acid, carbon dioxide, and water. When the lactic acid reaches sufficient levels to reduce the pH to about 4.5, the milk protein (casein) coagulates into curds, thickening the milk into yogurt.

Acids, bases, and neutralization: Acids are compounds that yield positively charged hydrogen ions in solution. Bases react with the hydrogen ions in solution. When an acid and base react, the pH of the solution settles somewhere between the pH values of the acid and base. In this pre-test, the baking soda neutralizes the lactic acid from the culture and prevents the milk from curdling.

DISCUSS:

1. Which yogurt-milk mixture got thicker overnight? *(The one without the baking soda [base].)* What probably caused it to thicken? *(Acid.)*

2. If neither mixture thickened, what might have happened? *(What if the yogurt cultures weren't active? What if the milk hadn't been pre-heated? Discuss responses to the first balloon.)*

> BACTERIA AND ENZYMES IN MILK CAN INTERFERE WITH THE BACTERIA IN YOGURT. WHY DO YOU THINK IT'S IMPORTANT TO USE PRE-HEATED MILK IN THIS TEST? *Heating deactivates the bacteria and enzymes that could interfere with yogurt's bacteria. If not done, the yogurt's culture might not digest the lactose and produce the acid that thickens milk.*

3. There's no "acid" in yogurt's list of ingredients. Could it be the active culture that adds acid to thicken the milk? How? *(Explore fermentation and the yogurt-making process.)*

4. Discuss responses to the second balloon. The same active cultures were in the baking soda mixture. Why didn't that mixture thicken? *(The base neutralized the acid, so it couldn't thicken the milk.)*

> IF ACID IS THICKENING THE MILK, WHAT WOULD HAPPEN IF YOU ADDED A BASE (LIKE BAKING SODA) TO THE MIXTURE? WRITE YOUR HYPOTHESIS HERE. *It would neutralize the mixture. Adding a base would use up the positively charged ions so they wouldn't be available to react with the amino acids and make the casein stick together.*

1. THE ACTIVE-CULTURE TEST, p. 4

QUESTIONS: Which yogurt has the most live bacteria? (Which turns milk the thickest?)

WHAT STUDENTS WILL DO:
After mixing 4 test yogurts in pre-heated milk, students will measure the mixtures' pH, set the mixtures in a yogurt-maker, then compare how thick they are the following day. *(The thicker the mixture, the more active bacteria the yogurt had.)*

MATERIALS FOR EACH GROUP:
4 coded strawberry yogurts (5 mL each), 200 mL pre-heated milk, pH paper, yogurt-maker (4 cups and heating unit), graduated cylinder, spoon. **The milk should be heated to 75°C and cooled to 40°C before class starts. (The milk can be heated several hours before it's used.)**

OBJECTIVE:
To understand fermentation and pH.

CONCEPTS:
Incubation is the process of maintaining conditions favorable to growth and development; with active cultures, such conditions involve maintaining heat levels favorable for bacterial growth.

Bacterial metabolism: Since bacteria digesting lactose form the acid that thickens milk, the more live bacteria in the culture the more acid they'll produce and the thicker the milk is likely to get.

DISCUSS:

1. Discuss responses to the balloon. What was your hypothesis? Do the data from this test support your hypothesis?

WHAT IS THE RELATIONSHIP BETWEEN A YOGURT-MIXTURE'S pH AND THE NUMBER OF ACTIVE BACTERIA IN IT? WRITE YOUR HYPOTHESIS HERE.
The more active bacteria in a mixture, the more lactose they'll digest and the more lactic acid they'll produce, which will lower the pH. So the lower the pH, the more active bacteria the mixture probably has.

2. Why were the test mixtures kept warm overnight? *(Explore incubation. If left at room temperature, other bacteria will interfere with the growth of yogurt cultures.)* What happens to the active culture when yogurts are kept refrigerated? *(The cold makes them less active but doesn't kill them.)*

3. Discuss responses to the Data Analysis question. *(The lower a mixture's ending pH, the thicker it should be.)*

4. Why do you think people who are allergic to lactose, the sugar in milk, are usually able to eat yogurt? *(The lactose has been broken down by bacteria.)*

ACTIVITY:
Culture-claims on labels: Check out what yogurt labels say about active cultures. Did yogurts that claim to have active cultures perform better than ones that didn't make that claim? Using test data, decide how meaningful those culture-claims are.

2. SENSORY TEST, p. 5

QUESTION: Which yogurt comes closest to ideal yogurt taste?

WHAT STUDENTS WILL DO:
Students will use references (sugar, etc.) to define sensory extremes and judge where each yogurt falls between those extremes on sweetness, flavor, and sourness scales. Scores depend on how close a yogurt comes to the *middle* of the scales.

MATERIALS FOR EACH GROUP:
4 coded strawberry yogurts (about 250 mL of each), strawberry jam, sugar cubes, water, 100 mL plain yogurt, ruler, milk (about 600 mL), paper towels, paper cups and plates and plastic spoons (2 per tester), 6 serving tablespoons, marker.

OBJECTIVES:
To understand the role standards of reference play in sensory testing; to develop skill at making sensory observations.

CONCEPTS:
Standards of reference define sweetness or sourness relative to a specific thing. References give descriptive words a measurable meaning so the data testers collect will be comparable.

(continued)

> **Tastes and the tongue:** There are four basic types of tastes (sweet, sour, salty, and bitter). Taste buds that detect these tastes are in certain locations on the tongue: sweet at the tip; bitter at the back; salty and sour on the sides. When looking for these particular tastes, it helps to know where to focus your attention.

DISCUSS:

1. Could a yogurt get a high score in this sensory test even if you *disliked* its taste? *(Yes: There's a difference between testing for ideal sensory qualities [as done here] and preference testing.)*

2. Did the strawberry jam and sugar help you better define the tastes you were judging? Why or why not? *(The reference standards in this test are the extremes — they don't represent what the yogurt taste should be. Instead, they define the two extremes a yogurt should fall between. References that define actual ideal tastes would be easier to use.)*

ACTIVITIES:

- **Re-test, using an "ideal" yogurt as the reference standard.** Select a lowfat strawberry yogurt with active cultures and about 40 grams of carbohydrates per 8-oz serving and establish that as the "ideal" taste. (Make sure it's fresh.) Then repeat the test, using this yogurt to define ideal sweetness, sourness, etc. Change the scoring scale to run from 1 to 5, with 5 being the ideal yogurt's qualities.

- **"Map" the tongue.** Work in pairs. Use cotton swabs to apply sugar, salt, and lemon solutions to the tip, back, and sides of the tongue. Where is each taste the strongest? Have your partner record your observations. Then reverse roles and record your partner's observations. In the end, see if you could correctly locate most of your taste buds. Discuss how the tongue is an instrument for making scientific observations.

- **Find correlations.** Was there a correlation between the yogurts' pH (measured in Test 1) and their sourness in this test? Was there a correlation between the yogurts' sweetness and sourness in this test? Graph scores to help with comparisons. *(Contrary to what many people believe, sweet and sour are not opposites. A food can be both sweet and sour, or neither.)*

3. THE PROTEIN AND FAT TEST, p. 6

QUESTIONS: Which yogurt has the *least* fat? The *most* protein?

WHAT STUDENTS WILL DO:

Using nutrition labels, students will calculate the percent of calories each yogurt gets from protein and from fat and determine scores accordingly. (The higher the protein percent and the lower the fat percent, the higher the scores.)

MATERIALS FOR EACH GROUP:

4 coded yogurt containers, plain lowfat yogurt container (coded P), calculator.

OBJECTIVES:

To build awareness of the fat and protein content of food; to practice calculating percents.

> **CONCEPTS:**
>
> **Fats** are nutrients that supply more than twice the energy (calories) of proteins and carbohydrates. They also play a role in cushioning organs and insulating the body. But taking in too many calories in the form of fat is linked with heart disease and some forms of cancer, as well as obesity.
>
> **Proteins** are nutrients that play an essential role in the growth and repair of body tissues.

DISCUSS:

1. How big a difference did you find in the yogurts' fat content? What do you think accounts for that? *(Yogurts' fat content is related to the type of milk they're made from — whole, lowfat, or skim [nonfat].)* Did any yogurt get more than 30 percent of its calories from fat? *(The whole milk yogurt probably did.)* Does this mean you shouldn't eat it? *(You can balance out the fat by eating lower-fat foods at other meals.)*

2. Compare the yogurts' fat scores with their scores in the Sensory Test (page 5). Is there a link between a yogurt's fat content and its taste? Which would you consider more important in a yogurt, taste or nutrition? Why?

3. Why did you multiply the grams of fat by 9 but grams of protein by 4? *(Per gram, fat has more than twice the calories of proteins or carbohydrates.)* What are the pros and cons of including fat in your diet? *(See the concept of fat.)*

WHICH HAS MORE PROTEIN PER SERVING, FLAVORED OR PLAIN YOGURT? WHAT MIGHT TAKE THE PLACE OF PROTEIN IN FLAVORED YOGURTS? WRITE YOUR HYPOTHESIS HERE. *The plain yogurt will have more protein (and more calories from protein) because none of its protein is displaced by sugar and flavoring, as happens with the flavored yogurts.*

4. Which had more calories from protein, the flavored yogurts or the plain one? What might account for that? (*Discuss responses to the balloon.*)

A TEST STUDENTS WILL DESIGN THEMSELVES

Testing procedures are not provided for the following test. Each small group must devise its own plan and procedure. The goal is to encourage hands-on, common sense creativity and problem-solving by students. There's no one "right" way to do this test.

4. TASTE-PREFER-ENCE TEST, p. 7

QUESTION: Which yogurt do most people prefer?

POSSIBLE PROCEDURE:
Students could taste each yogurt and give it a score from 1 (yuck) to 5 (yum). Or they could pair-off the test yogurts (making sure every yogurt is paired once with every other yogurt), pick the better tasting of each pair, then pair-off the winners and repeat the procedure until they've identified one yogurt as the best tasting.

OBJECTIVES:
To understand how to design a test; to reinforce the importance of controlling variables.

CONCEPTS:

Preference testing attempts to identify personal preferences for a product in order to predict which brand-model others will like. It differs from sensory or intensity testing, which compares products to reference standards, independent of testers' likes and dislikes.

Paired-comparison testing is a method of identifying the best product by the process of elimination — products are paired off and the better one of each pair selected, then winners are paired off and compared until you arrive at one winner. This testing method is particularly appropriate for preference testing where it's hard to identify ideal characteristics or standards ahead of time.

DISCUSS:

1. How did you conduct this test? Why? (*Discuss responses to the balloons.*)

SOMETIMES IT'S EASIER TO TELL WHAT YOU LIKE BEST BY THE PROCESS OF ELIMINATION—BY COMPARING TWO AND PICKING THE BETTER ONE, THEN COMPARING WINNERS.

GEE, I'D RATHER TRY THEM ALL AT ONCE AND PICK THE WINNER. WHICH WAY WOULD YOU RATHER TEST? *Perhaps taste each one and give it a score. Perhaps do paired comparisons and find the winner by the process of elimination. What's important is the reasoning behind what students choose to do.*

2. What variables did you control? How? (*Answers will depend on how students tested, but may include temperature of the yogurts, sequence they're tested in, whether taste of previous yogurt has been cleaned from the mouth before tasting another, etc.*)

3. Have small groups compare their test results: Are the different groups' rank orders the same? If not, why?

DEALING WITH DATA

Students have gathered data and assigned raw scores for all the yogurt tests. Now they have to figure out what it all means!

Data alone can't say which yogurt is best. Like all facts, data have to be thought about, evaluated, and interpreted in a useful and meaningful way. There's no one right way to deal with data.

INTERPRET YOUR TEST DATA, p. 8

WHAT STUDENTS WILL DO:

After deciding how important each test was, students will multiply test scores by their Importance Factors to determine weighted scores, then rank the yogurts in order of quality.

OBJECTIVES:

To become aware of different ways to interpret and express data; to understand weighted scores; and to form conclusions.

CONCEPT:

Weighted scores: Some tests measure characteristics that are more important than those measured by other tests. How yogurts scored in the important tests should count for more — have a greater impact on the yogurts' overall ranking.

DISCUSS:

1. What are the most important qualities for a yogurt to have? Why? Which tests do you think were most important? Why?

2. Did one yogurt do best in all the important tests or were different yogurts better at different things? *(Yogurts that scored high in the taste tests might have lower protein and fat test scores because reducing fat can affect taste and texture, and adding sugar can replace some of the protein.)* Which would be more important to you, a yogurt's taste or its nutritional profile? Why?

3. What are the pros and cons of weighting scores? Did weighting the scores change the yogurts' ranking order? *(Have each group interpret its data with and without weighted scores. Which ranking is more meaningful? Why?)*

EXTRA ACTIVITY: PUT TOGETHER THE CLASS'S TEST DATA

CONCEPTS:

Variation: Data can vary as a result of uncontrolled variables and of using people as measuring instruments (for sensory and preference tests).

Measurement error: Measurements taken during testing can be subject to variation due to differences in testing among groups (like how "thickness" was defined or how sensory standards were defined). A reliable measurement is closely repeatable from one test run to another.

ACTIVITY:

Make an enlarged copy of the chart on the following page. Have all groups write their raw scores in the appropriate boxes. (Each box will have as many numbers as there are groups.) Then have the class average the scores, assign Importance Factors to the tests, determine weighted scores, and decide the overall ranking of the yogurts.

DISCUSS:

1. Did everyone who tested the yogurts come up with the same raw scores? Why not? Is it possible measurement errors were made? Is it possible variables were controlled differently (or not controlled at all)?

2. How can we determine which measurements are most reliable (most likely to happen again if the test were repeated)? What if we performed each test several times instead of just once? What if we based the yogurts' ratings on the class's combined scores, instead of on just one group's scores?

3. Examine the class's raw scores (on the chart). Which yogurt (if any) has very little variation in its individual test scores? Which yogurt's performance could you predict with more confidence? *(The one with the least variation in scores.)*

4. What's the best way to tally the groups' raw scores — calculate mean or median scores? *(Try both. Do scores differ? Do rankings differ? Which scoring method is more appropriate?)*

SEND YOUR RATINGS OF YOGURTS TO *CONSUMER REPORTS*

The class should fill in this chart and answer all questions about the yogurts and their data. Attach a written summary of the class's conclusions. Then mail to the address below.

WHICH YOGURTS ARE BEST?

"RAW" SCORES

Write the class's combined scores for each test in the boxes below.
Are these ❑ mean scores or ❑ median scores? (Check *one*.)

TEST	A	B	C	D
1. Active-Culture				
2. Sensory				
3. Protein				
4. Fat				
5. Taste-Preference				
TOTALS				

(Raw-Score Totals)

"WEIGHTED" SCORES

1. Assign Importance Factors to the tests. (3-*most* important; 1-*least* important)

2. Multiply the class's combined raw scores by the Importance Factors.

IMPORTANCE FACTOR:	A	B	C	D
1.				
2.				
3.				
4.				
5.				
TOTALS				

(Weighted-Score Totals)

(1) **Code**   **Brand Name**   **Type** (lowfat, non-fat, whole milk)

A _____ _____
B _____ _____
C _____ _____
D _____ _____

(2) How many small groups tested the yogurts?_____

(3) Date_____

(4) Person to contact (name and address):

_____
_____
_____
_____

(5) **Mail To:**

**Consumer Reports
Education Division
101 Truman Avenue
Yonkers, New York 10703-1057**

SCIENCE CONCEPT INDEX

Concept	Product Testing Activity	Unit
Abrasion	Paper Towels	13
Absorbency	Jeans	9
	Toilet Paper	17
Acids, bases	Antacids	1
	Shampoos	15
	Yogurts	18
Adhesion	Bandages	2
	Glues	8
	Nail Enamel	11
Atomic mass	Sports Drinks	16
Bacteria	Yogurts	18
Blood	Sports Drinks	16
Buffers	Antacids	1
Calories	Popcorn	14
	Sports Drinks	16
Carbohydrates	Cereals	5
	Sports Drinks	16
Capillary action	Paper Towels	13
	Toilet Paper	17
Carbonation	Bottled Water	3
Clothing construction	Jeans	9
Chemical reactions	Orange Juice	12
Concentrations	Sports Drinks	16
Conduction	Disposable Cups	6
Crystals	Bottled Water	3
Degradability	Disposable Cups	6
	Orange Juice	12
	Toilet Paper	17
Density	Popcorn	14
	Toilet Paper	17
Detergents	Shampoos	15
Digestion	Antacids	1

Concept	Product Testing Activity	Unit
Elasticity	Bubble Gum	4
Electrolytes	Sports Drinks	16
Electrostatic attraction	Food Wraps	7
Energy (potential and kinetic)	Toilet Paper	17
Equivalence point	Antacids	1
Evaporation	Bandages	2
	Food Wraps	7
	Glues	8
	Jeans	9
	Lip Balms	10
	Nail Enamel	11
	Paper Towels	13
Experimental controls	Food Wraps	7
	Lip Balms	10
Exponential decay curve	Bubble Gum	4
Fabric	Jeans	9
Fermentation	Yogurts	18
Flavor intensity	Bubble Gum	3
	Cereals	5
Friction	Shampoos	15
Gas Solubility	Bottled Water	3
Glossiness	Nail Enamel	11
Gravity	Toilet Paper	17
Hair	Bandages	2
	Shampoos	15
Healing	Bandages	2
Heat	Disposable Cups	6
	Lip Balms	10
Insulation	Disposable Cups	6
Ions	Sports Drinks	16
	Yogurts	18

Concept	Product Testing Activity	Unit
Light	Food Wraps	7
Loft	Toilet Paper	17
Molds	Food Wraps	7
Molecular action	Food Wraps	7
Neutralization	Antacids	1
	Yogurts	18
Nutrition	Cereals	5
	Popcorn	14
	Yogurts	18
Opacity	Nail Enamel	11
Osmosis	Sports Drinks	16
Oxidation	Food Wraps	7
	Jeans	9
Oxygen permeability	Bandages	2
	Food Wraps	7
Paired comparisons	Bandages	2
	Bottled Water	3
	Food Wraps	7
	Orange Juice	12
	Toilet Paper	17
	Yogurts	18
Paper	Paper Towels	13
	Toilet Paper	17
pH	Antacids	1
	Shampoos	15
	Yogurts	18
Phase changes	Popcorn	14
Pigments	Nail Enamel	11
Polymers	Bubble Gum	4
	Food Wraps	7
	Nail Enamel	11
Polarization	Food Wraps	7
Porosity	Cereals	5
	Glues	8
	Paper Towels	13
Predicting	Popcorn	14
Preference testing	Bubble Gum	4
	Orange Juice	12
	Sports Drinks	16
Ratios	Bubble Gum	4
	Popcorn	14
	Toilet Paper	17

Concept	Product Testing Activity	Unit
Reaction rates	Antacids	1
Reference standards	Lip Balms	10
	Orange Juice	12
	Yogurts	18
Representative samples	Disposable Cups	6
	Jeans	9
Sensory system	Cereals	5
	Orange Juice	12
Skin	Bandages	2
	Lip Balms	10
Solids	Bottled Water	3
	Glues	8
Solubility	Bubble Gum	4
	Cereals	5
	Lip Balms	10
	Shampoos	15
Solvents	Glues	8
	Nail Enamel	11
Taste	Bottled Water	3
	Orange Juice	12
	Sports Drinks	16
	Yogurts	18
Temperature	Glues	8
	Lip Balms	10
Tensile strength	Bandages	2
	Food Wraps	7
Titration	Antacids	1
	Orange Juice	12
Vapor permeability	Bandages	2
	Food Wraps	7
	Jeans	9
Variation	Paper Towels	13
	Popcorn	14
	Toilet Paper	17
Viscosity	Nail Enamel	11
Vitamins	Orange Juice	12
Volume	Cereals	5
	Popcorn	14
Water	Bottled Water	3
Water repellence	Lip Balms	10

Variation, sampling, weighted scores, measurement error, and other statistics concepts are in the data interpretation sections of most of the activities.